Dennis Altman is a Professorial Fellow in Human Security at La Trobe University, Melbourne, and was Visiting Professor of Australian Studies at Harvard. He has written eleven books exploring sexuality and politics, and their inter-relationship in Australia, the United States, and now globally. These include *The Homosexualization of America*, *AIDS and the New Puritanism*, *Rehearsals for Change*, *The Comfort of Men* (a novel), and his memoir *Defying Gravity*. His book *Global Sex* (Chicago University Press) has been translated into five languages. Most recently he published *Gore Vidal's America* (Polity) and *51st State?* (Scribe). In 2008, Altman was appointed a Member of the Order of Australia.

THE END

OF THE

HOMOSEXUAL?

DENNIS ALTMAN

UQP

First published 2013 by University of Queensland Press
PO Box 6042, St Lucia, Queensland 4067 Australia

www.uqp.com.au
uqp@uqp.uq.edu.au

Cover design by Design by Committee
Typeset in Janson Text 11/15pt by Post Pre-press Group, Brisbane
Printed in Australia by McPherson's Printing Group

Cataloguing-in-Publication Data entry is available from the National Library of Australia
http://catalogue.nla.gov.au/

ISBN (pbk) 978 0 7022 4981 5
ISBN (pdf) 978 0 7022 5165 8
ISBN (epub) 978 0 7022 5166 5
ISBN (kindle) 978 0 7022 5167 2

University of Queensland Press uses papers that are natural, renewable and recyclable products
made from wood grown in sustainable forests. The logging and manufacturing processes
conform to the environmental regulations of the country of origin.

In memory of Anthony Smith (1959–2012),
who died before he could read the final draft.

CONTENTS

INTRODUCTION

In 1975 I was invited by a student group to speak about homosexuality at the Townsville campus of James Cook University. The local paper reported my talk, which led to hostile questions being asked in the state parliament, where I was referred to as 'a bare-footed practising homosexual', and an attack upon me by Premier Joh Bjelke-Petersen. Thirty-five years later I was invited by the vice-chancellor of Central Queensland University to Rockhampton to give a similar talk, chaired by federal Liberal MP Warren Entsch. This time the local paper editorialised its support for the event, and I was a guest on both local radio stations.

My invitation to central Queensland followed a Morgan poll that claimed the area was the most homophobic in Australia, with far greater numbers willing to term homosexuality 'immoral' than was the case in inner-urban areas. (While that survey suggested the least homophobic areas of Australia were the two territories and Western Australia, other data disagreed, although rural areas, particularly in Queensland and Tasmania, do seem considerably more homophobic than inner cities.) Interestingly, the local gay and lesbian folk I met in Rockhampton seemed less convinced that this was the case, and were well aware of the distinctions between how people might answer hypothetical questions and how they might actually behave.

Flying north from Brisbane, I was tempted to believe I was entering a different country; the men in the departure lounge – one with a T-shirt proclaiming 'Jesus Saves', others with surfer gear and heavy tats – would not have been a common sight back at Tullamarine. But walking around Rockhampton, with its slightly stuffy and old-fashioned downtown area, reinforced my sense that Australia is a remarkably homogenous country, and that apparently different attitudes between regions are more likely to reflect economic status and demography, not some particular essential difference between state cultures.

This was in fact my fourth visit to provincial Queensland to address gay issues. After my first foray to Townsville, I flew to Cairns in 1988 to speak at the public meeting that led to the formation of the Queensland Association for Gay Law Reform. By then, the National Party government was disintegrating under allegations of corruption; within two years of the founding of QAGLR, the incoming Labor government would decriminalise homosexual activity.[1] The Cairns meeting was chaired by the local state Labor MP, and was notable for a speech by local identity Ted Kelk, who spoke of the 'cold anger' he had experienced whilst hiding his identity until he could retire from his job as a high-school principal. And at the end of 1993 I first visited Rockhampton for a conference at the university entitled 'Voices of a Margin', which brought together speakers from all the predictable indicators of disadvantage.[2]

Seventeen years later, Rockhampton appeared to have changed little. However, *The Boy From Oz* was playing at the town's theatre – an interesting reminder that Australia's two most successful musicals (the other being *Priscilla, Queen of the Desert*) are, as they used to say, as camp as a row of tents. What had changed was the assumption of a kind of normality around homosexuality, so that the vice-chancellor could joke publicly about his wife's attraction to the men pictured in a Queensland gay calendar. It was inconceivable that a vice-chancellor would have felt sufficiently relaxed about sexuality to make such comments twenty years earlier. Of course, prejudice and hostility remain: a week after I was in Rockhampton, the visiting American author Armistead Maupin encountered blatant homophobia in a restaurant in Alice Springs, when a barman told him the toilets were 'reserved for real men'. Tourism Central Australia was quick to apologise, and the Melbourne *Age* followed up with an apologetic editorial.[3]

Anyone over fifty in Australia has lived through extraordinary changes in how we imagine the basic rules of sex and gender. We remember the first time we saw women bank tellers, heard a woman's voice announce that she was our pilot for a flight, watched the first woman read the news on television. A majority of women are now in the paid workforce; in 1966 they made up twenty-nine per cent. When I was growing up in Hobart it was vaguely shocking to hear of an unmarried heterosexual couple living together, and women in hats and gloves rode together in the back of the trams (now long since disappeared). As I look back, it seems to me that some of the unmarried female teachers at my school were almost certainly lesbians, although even they would have been shocked had the word been uttered.

In 1955 Princess Margaret had been forced to repudiate marrying a divorced man. Since then, three of Queen Elizabeth II's four children have divorced, and the current heir to the throne is married to a woman with whom he obviously had an affair during his previous marriage. Most of my female schoolmates who went to university were on teachers' scholarships, and would be expected to resign from the department if they married, which not infrequently happened because of unplanned pregnancies. Abortions were illegal but were often performed under appalling conditions; the occasional girl was known to have suddenly made a trip 'to Melbourne' in search of one.

Homosexuals were invisible, at best referred to in guilty jokes that I generally failed to understand. Barry Humphries wrote of this period that 'Pooftahs were happily confined to the small hermetic world of ballet and window dressing',[4] but this was a snide half-truth. (Not surprisingly, Humphries did not appear to think lesbians were even worth a snide reference.) In the same way, our cities were overwhelmingly racially homogenous: an overt white supremacy was dominant, reinforced through the notorious White Australia Policy and through the legal inequality of Aborigines, and deep prejudice existed against the few non-Caucasians living in Australia. When I was growing up I recall several Chinese-Australian families, but they were regarded as alien and exotic, even though some had been in the country for a century – far longer than the families of many of my classmates, who treated them with contempt.

During the 1970s, when Australia saw the first public affirmations by gay men and women, homosexuality was regarded with deep suspicion – as a vice, as a crime or, at best, as an illness. Sexual behaviour between men was illegal in all states, and very few women or men publicly acknowledged their homosexuality. Even if the anti-sodomy laws were rarely applied, police harassment and entrapment, and fear of disclosure to families and employers, maintained a low-level reign of terror sufficient for most homosexuals to spend considerable effort managing constant subterfuge and evasion. The current world, in which there are openly gay politicians, judges and even the occasional sports star, was literally inconceivable. We used to worry about being bashed for walking hand-in-hand. Young queers now worry about wedding planning, even though the threat of violence is still real, and in some areas possibly increasing.

The last decade, in particular, has seen extraordinary progress towards the normalisation of homosexuality across the western world.* Legal protection exists in most jurisdictions against discrimination based upon 'sexual orientation', and same-sex partnerships are increasingly acknowledged by civil (if not religious) institutions. Openly homosexual politicians are increasingly evident, and a significant 'pink vote' is now courted during elections. No mainstream television series seems to be without its gay and lesbian characters, and there is a

---

* A disclaimer: While I am uncomfortable with the term 'western world', I use it here not in its Cold War sense but to include those countries in Western Europe, North America and Australasia that share a common affluence, a set of liberal–democratic principles, and a strong rhetorical commitment to civil liberties, even if these are often flaunted in practice.

well-established targeting of a gay/lesbian market in travel, real estate and consumer advertising. In 2012 the high-rating television station Channel Nine resuscitated the reality show *Big Brother*; the winner was openly gay and proposed to his partner on live television.

Those of us old enough to remember the period in which a large-scale gay movement began have lived through a revolution, and it is difficult for us to make sense of it. Change occurs at a number of levels simultaneously, and is often contradictory and uneven. Looking back over four decades, one can trace major shifts in the discourse, representation and regulation of homosexuality – all of which terms are open to multiple meanings. Nor does change occur without cost. Many activists find that, as they age, they feel a nostalgia for a remembered past, which seems increasingly preferable to the present. Gore Vidal, of whom I have written elsewhere, wrote a novel that identifies the 'golden age' as the decade following World War II, but in effect he is writing about his youth, which is where most of us locate that period.

The changing Australian attitudes reflect a much larger global story, where new images of the self and possibilities for activism circulate increasingly rapidly. The American influence has been particularly significant, and through its media the US has shaped how most of us imagine the world. Americans have been role models and reference points for changing images of sex and gender from Marilyn Monroe and James Dean through to the characters of *Glee* and *Sex in the City*. Our generation lived through a major shift in emphasis from British attitudes and culture to an increasing embrace of that of the United States, a change that paralleled the steady increase of non-British immigration to Australia.[5] At the same time, the realities of globalisation, in all its diverse meanings, mean that even local stories have to be told through an awareness of the wider world.

Of course, for me it is difficult to disentangle what has changed in the larger world from the realities of my own ageing. As soon as one relies upon personal observation, one has to recognise the extent to which these observations are distorted as well as enhanced by the personal. A friend wrote several years ago on Facebook:

I'll be in New York this weekend, and it turns out to be the Black Party. That used to get me as excited as when I was a little boy about to open presents on Christmas Eve. Now the person who could get excited about either seems impossibly remote, barely half-remembered, from another lifetime.

Another friend, browsing recently through a gay bookshop, remarked that *The Joy of Gay Sex* seemed to have been replaced by *The Joy of Cooking*, although it is worth noting that *The Joy of Gay Sex*, originally published in 1977, has been reissued and revised several times by writers drawn from my generation.

For much of my adult life I have travelled frequently to the United States, and my sense of gay community and identity has been shaped as much by that experience as by the much longer periods in which I have lived in Australia. The dogged anti-Communist crusader of the 1960s and 1970s Frank Knopfelmacher once called me an agent of US cultural imperialism. In a sense, he was right: my time in the States influenced me enormously. At the time that people like Knopfelmacher were defending America's war in Vietnam, opponents of that war like me were drawing equally on the United States for intellectual and cultural inspiration. The growth of gay assertion in most western countries owes a great deal to the States, and this impact continues through popular culture and increasing travel. One of the major gay discos in Sydney during the 1970s had a large mural of San Francisco, as if to symbolise the freedom that awaited us at the end of the rainbow.

I became a gay activist by accident, largely as a result of living in New York in 1971, when the gay liberation movement was starting. Inspired by the new movement – and determined to become 'a writer' – I developed an outline for a book on gay liberation. After a number of futile attempts to find a publisher, I met Harris Dienstfrey, whose small publishing house, long since vanished, was prepared to take a gamble, and *Homosexual: Oppression and Liberation* found a home. Thanks to a lukewarm review in *Time* magazine, and a more enthusiastic one by Martin Duberman in *The New York Times*, the book survived its first publication by an obscure publisher to become a mass-market paperback and it was subsequently translated into several languages.

In Australia, Richard Walsh, then managing Angus & Robertson, acquired the book and published it in 1972. *Homosexual* has a continuing life: in 2011 I went to Japan to give several lectures to mark its publication there, and in early 2012 a two-day conference in Melbourne commemorated its fortieth anniversary.[6] What struck me most at the conference was how the experiences I had lived through were increasingly being seen as historical events to be researched by a growing number of lesbian and gay activists. The last chapter of *Homosexual* had been entitled 'The End of the Homosexual?', hence the title for this book.

To make sense of change requires us to focus on a number of arenas simultaneously. As change occurs, it creates new possibilities but it can also reinforce old patterns – which may be why so many young people today regard 'hippies' with distaste. In a familiar cycle, yesterday's radicalism becomes tomorrow's nostalgia. So it is with sexuality. The changes over the past forty years have not replaced one mode of being homosexual as much as they have added new ones. The world of hustlers, drag queens and self-denial described in John Rechy's 1965 novel *City of Night* can still be found, alongside well-dressed professional women and men at gay business fundraisers. The simultaneous existence of old-fashioned 'queens' and edgy transsexual 'queers' illustrates Raymond Williams' discussion of 'residual and emergent cultures',[7] whereby new forms don't necessarily displace as much as they complement existing modes. Drawing on the Italian Antonio Gramsci to develop a cultural reading of Marxism, Williams stressed that while certain cultural forms are dominant, they coexist with varieties of 'experiences, meanings and values' that grow out of previous social formations, while others develop either as alternatives to or in active opposition to what is taken for granted by most people.

It is not hard to sit in a clearly gay urban space and see both the past and the future of gay life; what was once shocking is now taken for granted. A casual passer-by on Santa Monica Boulevard in West Hollywood, for example, can watch go-go dancers clad in the most revealing of briefs, while young pierced and tattooed queers walk by, largely disinterested. Rather like individuals, all cultures have complex and multiple identities, and change often means the incorporation rather than the replacement of old forms. During my most recent visits to that strip – one of the few remaining clearly gay zones in the United States – I saw three generations of queer life, from an elegant lesbian couple walking their matching dogs, to young guys, uneasily still in their teens, half-cruising for money and opportunity. 'Ghettoes' function as sites for both nostalgia and initiation, and if places like West Hollywood, the Castro and Chelsea have traditionally functioned as spaces to which young queers come from rural and small-town America, they are now increasingly playing this role internationally.

Major changes in the understanding of homosexuality reflect larger social and cultural shifts. One example: it is likely that the invention and spread of the internet has changed patterns of sexual behaviour as widely as did the contraceptive pill forty years ago. In both cases the changes were neither foreseen nor intended, and in both cases the impact of new technologies was partly dependent on political and ideological forces. My own real discovery of the 'gay world' – a term popularised by a 1968 book[8] – came in the mid-1960s in New York City, and my story straddles a number of countries, above all the United States, where I have lived for about eight years of my life at various points. There are many ways of making sense of this story, and this book does so by drawing heavily on my own experiences of the past four decades, and on the very considerable secondary literature that is now available. Writing this book is as much an exploration of the traps and uncertainties of memory as it is of recorded social and political history.

Memory has suddenly become a major topic in queer circles: in 2012 thousands of people signed up to websites for 'lost gay' Sydney,

Melbourne, Auckland and so on, while in Brussels a special colloquium was organised to remember the 'homosexual militancy' of the 1950s. In some ways, these moves grew out of a number of celebrations of the fortieth anniversary of the Stonewall Riots in 2009. A raid in June 1969 on the Stonewall Inn, a well-known homosexual bar in Greenwich Village, New York, provoked a number of patrons and passers-by to fight back against the police, triggering several nights of riots that have since been mythologised as the founding event of the contemporary gay movement.[9] Much has been made of the coincidence that the riots took place on the eve of Judy Garland's funeral, and Garland's character in *The Wizard of Oz* probably gave rise to the euphemism 'friends of Dorothy' to describe homosexual men. In 1988 Edmund White declared Stonewall to be 'the turning point of our lives';[10] certainly the years between 1969 and 1972 represented a major tipping point in homosexual awareness and assertion across the western world.

Books from the early period of the gay movement are now being reissued, and 'vintage' (that is, pre-AIDS) pornography is now widely dispersed through the internet, and in some cases has become collectable. Even so, there are still very few ways in which young people discovering their homosexuality have the means to learn much of the history of their sexuality, and of the ways in which homosexuals have been regarded historically.

Maybe there is something about forty years, which marks the coming to adulthood of a third generation since Stonewall; whatever the reason, I find myself talking increasingly with far younger people, for whom my memories help make sense of their history. Intergenerational friendships have their own particular challenges, involving as they do implicit assumptions about motives and hierarchy; older men, in particular, are assumed to want sex, while younger women and men are usually thought to be cultivating their elders for financial or career advancement. One of the greatest pleasures in writing this book has been the discovery that we learn from each other, and often in ways that seem counter-intuitive. (I recognise this is a somewhat more optimistic view of intergenerational friendships than that of the Australian sociologist Peter Robinson, as reported a few years ago in his study of how male gay worlds were changing.[11])

Maybe, too, there is a desire amongst younger queers to find an equivalent to the family-tree version of history that is so strong in ethnic communities. This is expressed beautifully in performance artist Tim Miller's account of his own sexual ancestry:

> ... in my history of tongues, I had sex with David Roman, who had sex with Allen Ginsberg, who had sex with Neal Cassidy. Who had sex with Gavin Arthur, who had sex with Edward Carpenter, who had sex with Walt Whitman: Daddy of our American tongue.[12]

There is something revealing about the very title of the anthology from which this quote comes – *Who's Yer Daddy* – which recalls Judy Chicago's *Dinner Party*, an art installation of the 1970s which assumed a table set for thirty-nine historical and mythical women, and which for a time was a cult work among many lesbians.

As we age, there is an inevitable move towards both nostalgia for the past and uncertainty about the present, and I realise I was already experiencing this when I wrote my only novel, *The Comfort of Men*, back in 1993. That book ends as the narrator sits in a café on Oxford Street, Sydney's most famous gay strip, watching a passing young man who reminds him of his earlier self, and reflects:

> I am touched by feelings of surprising tenderness for his apparent fragility. Young men of his generation rarely strike me in this way; usually I am irritated by their assurance and their sleekness, their sense that all history began when they had their first orgasm. But they have inherited the world we built, and they in turn are continuing to change and develop the world in which we shall grow old.[13]

PART ONE

HOMOSEXUALITY BEFORE THE GAY MOVEMENT

In the 1930s and 1940s ... these monstrous practices, denounced by biblical and traditional common laws alike, were considered not only social but also political crimes against community standards, crimes that had to be obliterated whenever detected. People who had fallen so low as to engage in them must either be cured for their own good, forcibly if necessary, or be put away for the protection of society.

Harry Hay, founder of the Mattachine Society ('Birth of a Consciousness', *Harvard Gay & Lesbian Review*, Winter 1995)

WHAT HAS CHANGED? WHAT REMAINS THE SAME?

Homosexuality has long been a touchstone for anxieties and conflict around sexuality. It is not surprising that Freud began his seminal *Three Essays on Sexuality* by discussing 'inversion', which he saw as part of the human condition: 'Psychoanalytic research ... has found that all human beings are capable of making a homosexual object-choice, and have in fact made one in their unconscious.'[1] Freud was, of course, writing of a particular time and place, but his observations about the fluidity of human sexuality are borne out by considerable anthropological and historical evidence. It is unfortunate that Freud's openness to sexual realities has been overlaid by the prejudices of psychoanalysts who came after him, so that he is often associated with judgmental views of homosexuality that are far removed from his own.

Freud's theories have been badly misunderstood, but they were matched by empirical evidence. The post-World War II panics around homosexuality that spread across most of the English-speaking world were in part triggered by the most provocative finding of Kinsey's 1948 study of male sexuality: a claim that thirty-seven per cent of American men had experienced homosexual activity leading to orgasm. The figure was almost certainly exaggerated, as was the later claim that homosexuals constituted ten per cent of the population, but the myth of the 'ten per cent' still shows up in some popular journalism.[2] What was important about this, and about Kinsey's subsequent study of female sexuality, was that it revealed that a large number of people had experienced either homosexual activity or attraction without adopting an identity based upon it.

Homosexuality, but particularly male homosexuality, has troubled western societies for a very long time, as is clear from the long history of legal and religious sanctions against the 'unmentionable crime'. Today it appears that the focus of anxiety has shifted from Anglo-American societies to many parts of the non-western world, where nationalist and religious mobilisation against homosexuality – which is often defined as a western colonial import – is common. Ironically, earlier 'western' views of sexuality stressed the exotic and oriental nature of homosexuality, which was depicted as a vice particularly common in the tropics. As Rudi Bleys has argued, rising hostility to homosexuality as a sign of unwanted western influence is seen under a number of apparently different conditions:

> The repression of homosexuality in post-colonial discourse on ethnic, cultural and/or national identity, moreover, can be noticed at many levels from some forms of popular music to official policies defining male-to-male sexuality as 'alien' to one's own culture, and it has gained particular agency in the wake of decolonization (most countries), modernization (Japan, Central Asian countries, Iraq), communism (China, Cuba, Mozambique), or fundamentalism (Iran).[3]

Perhaps the clearest example is the extent to which laws against sodomy, imposed by the British Empire in the name of morality, remain in most of its former colonies, although they have long been repudiated in the imperial centre. When nationalist leaders invoke tradition, culture and religion as grounds for not accepting homosexuality, they are often drawing on nineteenth-century colonial laws, bolstered by missionary activity.

Over the past decade there has been a marked increase in hostility and persecution directed at homosexuals in many former British colonies, particularly in Africa but also in the Caribbean and Malaysia, fuelled both by religious fervour – as often Christian as Muslim – and by a desire to define homosexuality as a sign of western imperialist decadence. Examples such as the framing of Malaysia's deputy prime minister, Anwar Ibrahim, for sodomy in 1999 (and again ten years later), the quite extraordinary vitriol directed at gay organising in a number of African countries, and the homophobic hatred expressed in much of Jamaican reggae all suggest the troubling salience of homosexuality in contemporary politics.[4] Attempts to include sexuality within the commitment to human rights expressed by the Commonwealth have so far been unsuccessful.

The Case of Australia

The shifts in attitudes toward homosexuality are among the most dramatic of all changes in Australian mores over the past four decades, but they were shaped by larger social and cultural changes that are reflected in our now very different attitudes towards race, gender and national identity. Australia today is a very different country to the one in which homosexual activism first emerged, and the story of our changing views about sexuality is part of a larger story about how Australia itself has changed.

There is a particular Australian story of growing acceptance of homosexuality, one to which the actions of individual activists, and of other political and cultural developments, is central. A number of factors came together in Australia to make rapid shifts in attitudes to homosexuality possible. In many ways, the invention of a new style of gay/lesbian community and identity was as much a product of the changes Donald Horne identified in his book *The Time of Hope* as of overseas influences or local activism. Horne wrote of the period between 1966 and 1972 as being a period when 'some of the established common sense was being upset'[5] and new ideas and mores were challenging basic assumptions about society. Horne ends *The Time of Hope* by asking what had changed.

Almost thirty years later, Raewyn Connell – herself a participant in the radical politics of the period, and Australia's best known sociologist of gender – addressed the same question as she reflected on the 'new left' of the 1960s. Like Horne, she sees the period as one in which large numbers of new ideas and possibilities emerged; she describes the new left as 'a collective midwife … a kind of social and cultural catalyst – not a world historical force in its own right but something that helped larger and slower processes along'.[6]

For me, the crucial element of the era Horne called 'the time of hope' and Connell 'a startling assertion of vivid life' was the sense of reimagining the world that was expressed through a plethora of social and cultural movements, ranging from 'black power' groups to new forms of theatre and music. This might be the place to acknowledge that both 'community' and 'identity' are slippery concepts, and even though I use them consistently, it is with an awareness that they can be simultaneously liberatory and restrictive, setting arbitrary restraints on how an individual might perceive her or his life.

It is common to dismiss the sixties as inconsequential in Australian life, no more than a faint echo of overseas events. For some, the real shift came in the supplanting of Britain as the most significant cultural influence within Australia, in favour of the United States. Julie Stephens, for example, has argued that the best way to understand the impact of the decade is to view it through the American experience.[7] But as Horne asserted, there were specific Australian resonances to the general cultural upheavals of the period, and these were reflected in the ways in which Australia moved from a rigidly exclusionary immigration policy to accepting immigrants from across the world – and, in time, to an official adoption of multiculturalism.

Of course, the flowering of Australian theatre and film that we associate with this period was not necessarily particularly supportive of homosexuality. In fact, there was an ocker aggression to much of the cultural effusion of the time, as in the 1972 film *The Adventures of Barry McKenzie*, which I saw at the time as deeply, even frighteningly, homophobic.[8] The ostensibly counter-cultural worlds of our inner cities often echoed dominant attitudes towards sex and gender, in which lesbians remained invisible and homosexual men were conflated with drag queens. Indeed, the popularity of drag shows in the 1960s paved the way for two of Australia's most famous theatrical productions: the long career of Dame Edna Everage and the film *Priscilla, Queen of the Desert*. While other countries have similar traditions, in few has drag been so central a part of theatrical life; I was amused when the San Francisco author Aaron Shurin began his discussion of drag in San Francisco by noting that 'the boys from Down Under perfected the art of drag names'.[9]

The strength of much of gay and lesbian history is that it tells history from the bottom up, drawing on the experiences of those involved. Its weakness is that it often fails to recognise the extent to which these particular voices are in turn shaped by larger social and cultural changes, both within the country and from beyond. Sexual cultures are increasingly shaped by global forces, and, because of our shared language, Australians are open to British and particularly to American influence. The emergence of women's liberation groups in Australia from 1969 onwards owed a great deal to American writers and to journals such as *Off Our Backs*, which, as Anne Summers has written, 'introduced us to a repertoire of new concepts and ideas', even though Australian feminism would quickly develop its own particularities.[10] In a globalising world we often conflate our own experiences with broader influences, so that disentangling them becomes problematic.

Two images come to mind. The first is of a Melbourne bookshop, where a group of lesbians sat cheering a repetitive loop of the film clip in which the American comedian Ellen DeGeneres 'came out' publicly on *The Oprah Winfrey Show* in 1997. The other is being with a group of young Filipino gay men – their term – as they talked about their lives; I came to realise they were describing them through frames taken from American television and novels. How we imagine and manage our identities is often the product of imported images that we blend with local circumstances to produce versions that feel authentic to us.

But the changes of the past few decades are not merely products of new cultural influences. More accurately, these influences reflect larger shifts in the very nature of western societies, and the growth of what was once called 'post-industrial society', meaning a society in which the emphasis is increasingly on white-collar work, as distinct from manufacturing or primary industries, and on consumption rather than production. In such societies there has been a marked increase in higher education, in women entering and remaining in the workforce, and in personal consumerism, all of which have opened up more space for people to break away from the limited conventional ways in which they can organise their personal and emotional lives. The huge shifts in overall attitudes to sexuality, whereby sex has become commodified and sexual pleasure recognised as an end in itself, have created an environment within which homosexuality has been able to develop as an alternative form of identity and behaviour.

The very creation of the homosexual person – now most commonly known as 'lesbian' or 'gay' – is itself only possible within certain sorts of socioeconomic conditions, which allow enough space for people to reject traditional assumptions about the organisation of sex and gender. We tend to forget how recent such identities are, bound up as they are with the development of capitalist consumer society. As John D'Emilio has argued:

> In divesting the household of its economic independence and fostering the separation of sexuality from procreation, capitalism has created conditions that allowed some men and women to organize a personal life around their erotic attraction to their own sex. It has made possible the formation of urban communities of

lesbians and gay men and, more recently, of a politics based on sexual identity.[11]

Histories of urban homosexual communities in major western cities have shown how gay or lesbian subcultures have long coexisted with large groups of people who experienced same-sex behaviour or desire without necessarily adopting these as a basis for identity.[12] This remains common in most parts of the world, where family and economic pressures mean that many homosexuals marry someone of the opposite sex and have homosexual relationships and/or sexual encounters on the side.

For those of us old enough to remember the 1960s, or earlier, the changes in being homosexual are enormous. From a time when almost everyone accepted the need to hide their sexual preferences, often even to enter into sham marriages, we now live in a world in which homosexuality is largely taken for granted as a part of life – so much so that 'coming out' publicly often feels redundant.

It may seem as if we have achieved a huge amount, and on balance we have. But while overt hostility is much more muted – except amongst certain people fuelled by religious belief or bigotry – a less overt dismissal of homosexuality as totally valid remains pervasive. One of my colleagues, a woman of deep liberal principles, was initially deeply disturbed when she discovered her thirty-year-old son was gay. And I still read reviews in progressive journals in which the homosexuality of key authors is elided or passed over in what Christopher Isherwood once called 'annihilation by blandness'. More worryingly, it remains a major struggle to persuade people in international development agencies, most of whom see themselves as progressive and empathetic, to take seriously even gross abuses against people because of their sexuality.

Unlike other forms of identity, such as those founded in gender, race or religion, one's sexuality is formed in opposition to rather than as an extension of one's family life, so that to recognise one's homosexuality, to act upon it and then to disclose it are all markers that separate rather than reinforce familial ties. Of course, there are exceptions – there are families who embrace their homosexual children – and there are many people who experience similar breaks in rejecting religion, or indeed adopting new religious beliefs. But for the great majority of homosexuals 'coming out' is a complex and often difficult path, which explains the centrality of the theme in queer film and literature. It's a story with many variations, from a father coming out to his son (as in the film *Beginners*) to a woman discovering her attraction to another just after her wedding (as in *Imagine Me and You*).

In Andrew Haigh's prize-winning film *Weekend* (2011), coming out to parents, friends and co-workers is a constant motif. The New Zealand novelist Witi Ihimaera wrote in his remarkable novel *Nights in the Gardens of Spain*:

> When it comes to the crunch, coming out is the greatest of all confessions. Nothing is more difficult to acknowledge. When we become ourselves we reach right back to the time when we were conceived out of our parents' passion. We murder their lives. There can never be any forgiveness.[13]

The writer Robert Dessaix once remarked that the traditional novel is inherently heterosexual – it is 'unconsciously based on ... the generation of meaning through heterosexual coupling and reproduction'[14] – but he failed to note that the equivalent in homosexual writing is the search for identity outside the conventional family. Without understanding the importance of coming out, it is impossible to grasp how events like Sydney's Mardi Gras or gay festivities in towns like Daylesford and Coffs Harbour are still, in some ways, deeply political.

It's hard to recall the cruelty with which homosexuality was routinely treated in the west until just a few decades ago. Imprisonment and 'aversion therapy' (using electrodes) was commonplace enough to scare many men into deep secrecy, while lesbians, though less likely to be imprisoned or punished, were scorned and marginalised. Less than half a century ago a character in a novel by Ruth Rendell (writing as Barbara Vine) set in working-class London could reflect that: 'It would be preferable to have syphilis or be certified as mad than to admit his homosexuality.'[15]

The psychic costs of hiding or denying one's sexual desires were considerable; while many people managed to live fulfilling lives in semi-concealment, others experienced lifelong guilt, anxiety and fear of exposure. Graeme Blundell's biography of Graham Kennedy, probably the best known television personality in Australia for several decades, only hints at the loneliness and self-censorship that was required for him to hide what was generally suspected, and what he was forced to disguise through increasingly unconvincing heterosexual performances, including a rumoured engagement with singer Lana Cantrell.[16] Even today there are many young homosexuals who drop out of school or become estranged from their families because they cannot reconcile their sexuality with other parts of their lives.

There is a growing literature that tries to convey the changes that have occurred over two generations, from a time when homosexuality was literally an imprisonable offence to today, when it is increasingly accepted, at least in the west, as a normal part of the human spectrum. When I was growing up homosexuality was hidden, and homosexuals – then referred to, if at all, as 'poofs' and 'dykes' – lived double lives as regimented as those of spies in a le Carré novel. Perhaps the best depiction of the shifts comes in Alan Hollinghurst's first novel, *The Swimming Pool Library*, which gradually reveals the secrets of an ageing lord, who has moved between his secret homosexual life and 'circles where good manners, lofty savoir-faire and plain callousness conspired to avoid any recognition that homosexuality even existed'.[17]

The changes in Australia seem particularly striking because the conventional view was that Australia was particularly hostile to expressions of homosexuality, despite evidence for its existence from the origins of white settlement[18] – and indeed, but amid a very different cultural setting, within Indigenous Aboriginal cultures. The legacy of the convict system and British prudery created a country in which an emphasis on 'mateship' meant a particularly strong sense of the differences between women and men, and the corresponding 'natural' rules of sexual attraction. The anthropologist Robert Brain, writing some years after the emergence of gay liberation, claimed that Australians 'regard homosexuality with an out and out dread';[19] the historian Geoffrey Bolton writes of 'a very strong tradition of cultural prejudice dating from Australia's convict origins'[20] but does not explain the nature of the connection. One of the most striking passages in what is arguably the first great Australian novel, Marcus Clarke's *For the Term of His Natural Life* (1872), describes the flogging to death of a young convict charged with sodomy.

Even so, the importance of policing the boundaries of male bonding, which were the consequence of considerable separation between men and women during early settlement, seems to me more significant. Indeed, the historian Russell Ward, writing in the 1950s, saw within mateship a possible 'sublimated homosexual relationship',[21] and there were clear examples of such relationships throughout the nineteenth century.[22] Even so-called Bohemians, such as the artist Norman Lindsay, were shocked by homosexuality,[23] and as late as 1965 the poet and critic Kenneth Slessor, an enthusiastic member of the then National Literature Board of Review, could write:

> I regard homosexuality … as an anti-social disease which must be recognised … and accurately described. But I would maintain that society is justified in resorting to censorship if this anti-social practice is presented by the arts in such a way as to make it appear desirable, attractive or condoned.[24]

It is hard to imagine any comparable literary figure in other western societies making such a claim in the mid-1960s, although it helps explain why books such as James Baldwin's *Another Country*, along with resolutely heterosexual novels such as *Portnoy's Complaint*, were still banned in Australia at the time.

In the same way, Australia lagged behind Britain and Canada in decriminalising homosexuality, even though the 1957 Wolfenden Report in Britain, and the subsequent legal changes ten years later for 'consenting adults in private', were reported in Australia. It appeared, however, that Australian wowserism trumped the cultural cringe. Little wonder that many Australian homosexuals felt the need to expatriate themselves, including such figures as the lesbian artist Agnes Noyes Goodsir (1864–1939), who was part of the legendary Parisian art world of the 1920s, and, somewhat later, Robert Helpmann, Donald Friend and Jeffrey Smart. Two of our best homosexual writers – Patrick White and Sumner Locke Elliott – left Australia, and while White returned (of which more later), Elliott remained in New York until his death. In fact, he only 'came out' through his last novel, *Fairyland* (1990), which contains a scathing account of the prejudices and fears faced by the 'poofters' he left behind when he fled to the United States shortly after the end of World War II. Both Friend's diaries and Smart's memoirs – entitled *Not Quite Straight* – speak openly of their sex lives.

The former Greens leader Bob Brown has spoken of how he sought aversion therapy to 'cure' his homosexuality in the 1970s, and as late as 1989 a man was held without bail in Roma, Queensland, on charges of homosexual behaviour (bail being refused on the grounds that he was likely to reoffend).[25] Three years later a Victorian jury released a twenty-three-year-old man who had killed a much older man with a kitchen knife, and then set fire to his flat, because of alleged sexual advances.

Homosexuals of older generations grew up with a strong sense of self-doubt, sometimes self-loathing, which often caused considerable psychological damage that was carefully disguised or sublimated into other areas of life. Not an inconsiderable number of people went into Catholic orders as a way of escaping the realities of their sexual feelings. Because of the strong stigma against homosexuality, many men and women grew up believing they were unique and spent years trying to understand why they could not respond to what society upheld as 'natural'.

If today's messages about our sexuality are more sophisticated – there is now, after all, powerful opposition to branding homosexuality as a sin, an illness or even a deviance – these negative attitudes persist nonetheless. The push for same-sex marriage is, at least in part, a search to resolve those taboos, and to persuade ourselves, as much as others, that there is no moral or ethical distinction between sexual preferences. Perhaps I might be guilty of the reverse motive: namely, resisting marriage out of some outmoded desire to stress the particularity of homosexuality, much as some older men thought decriminalisation would remove the thrills of being illicit.

Contemporary society is both solidifying sexual identities and breaking them down. On the one hand, there are now the almost obligatory homosexual characters in television shows, especially those coming from the American channel HBO: *Six Feet Under*, *Modern Family*, *The United States of Tara* and *Desperate Housewives* all have overt gay or lesbian characters. A few years ago, the show *Queer Eye for the Straight Guy* was hugely successful on the premise that there was a clear divide between two tribes; any sense that the 'straight guy' might be attracted to his gay role models was scrupulously avoided. Proving that imitation can be even tackier than the original, this program inspired several television reality programs called *Playing It Straight*, in which heterosexual women were asked to pick the sexuality of good-looking young men, thus reinforcing the idea that no sexual ambivalence was possible. In more recent television programs, however, there is an increasing number of fixed homosexual identities as well as suggestions that these can be fluid, and that homosexual desire can cut across traditional definitions.

Oddly, Australian television has lagged behind that of both Britain and the United States, despite the early success of *Number 96*, which introduced an openly gay man to a mass television audience in the early 1970s. A few years later came *Prisoner*, set in a women's prison, in which there were considerable lesbian references, although without such a clean-cut role model as Joe Hasham of *Number 96*. Not until the 2010s did shows like *Neighbours* and *Home and Away* incorporate regular homosexual characters into their scripts, apparently after viewer demands.

Since the 1990s Australians have been far more influenced by the emergence of openly homosexual characters on American and sometimes British television, even if gay characters in series such as *Melrose Place* and *Will and Grace* were rarely, if ever, allowed to display their sexuality on-screen. A 1994 episode of *Roseanne* that showed a genuinely sexy kiss between two women caused a stir that today seems slightly absurd;[26] by 2001, the American remake of the British series *Queer as Folk* was screening on free-to-air television, with graphic scenes of male-to-male – and occasionally lesbian – sex. In *Friends* there was a lesbian wedding as early as 1996, but no homosexual sex.

Popular culture remains caught between normalising and exoticising homosexuality, presenting it as both a separate and distinct culture and as part of everyday life. In the throwaway evening newspaper *mX*, distributed on Melbourne and Sydney public transport, there have been several sets of letters about 'straight-boy crushes', while the term 'bromance' has entered the vernacular to acknowledge the possibility of very close emotional, if not sexual, bonds between men. In one sense, then, we may indeed be approaching 'the end of the homosexual', which some gay liberationists saw as the ultimate goal of the movement forty years ago.

Theories and Terminologies

In the last chapter of *Homosexual: Oppression and Liberation* I predicted that increasing acceptance of sexual diversity would mean a disappearance of identities based upon sexual 'orientation'. This forecast failed to recognise both the persistence of identity politics and, equally importantly, the growing globalisation of sexual politics. Nor could it have anticipated the AIDS epidemic, which has both decimated and reinvigorated homosexual 'communities' across the world. But in its rather utopian view of a greater acceptance of sexual diversity it was accurate.

What today might one mean by 'the end of the homosexual'? It could, after all, be taken literally to mean that homosexual identity and behaviour vanish, which is presumably the goal of at least some fundamentalists who regard homosexuality as an unambiguous mark of sin. Equally, it could be interpreted narrowly to mean the end of a certain sort of homosexual stereotype, either as victim (as in the 1961 Dirk Bogarde film of that name) or as a figure of fun and ridicule (as in the 1970s British television comedy *Are You Being Served?*), with men always depicted as very effeminate and women as heavily butch (as in the 1968 film *The Killing of Sister George*). Given the current vogue for openly gay/lesbian characters, we might easily forget how recent such characters are in popular culture; until the end of the 1960s they were usually coded, such as the mannish women who appear frequently in Agatha Christie's novels, or the foppish men played by Edward Everett Horton in 1930s films.[27] Vito Russo's book *The Celluloid Closet* lovingly uncovered large numbers of examples of such stereotypes, and they were common in Australian theatre and stand-up comedy.

More realistically, the phrase might mean the end of seeing homosexuality as a primary marker of identity, so that sexual preference comes to be regarded as largely irrelevant, and thus not the basis for either community or identity. This comes closest to what I imagined forty years ago, although my original views were born of a Freudian utopianism that expected some ongoing polymorphous perversity in which we would all become undifferentiated sexual beings. This was a not uncommon view in the late 1960s, and can be found in some of the writings of Norman O Brown, and, above all, in Gore Vidal's novel *Myra Breckinridge*, which I have argued elsewhere should be regarded as the founding text of queer theory.[28] In what became both a bestseller and the basis for a truly dreadful movie, a woman who is, in fact, a homosexual man revenges her/himself on a heterosexual male stud with the aim of symbolically reversing the sex/gender order.

I need to acknowledge a particular relationship with *Myra*. In 1971 a zealous Sydney Airport customs official seized my copy of the book, which became the basis for a Council of Civil Liberties trial aimed at

Australia's draconian censorship laws of the time. Customs won the case – Judge Levine concluded that there were passages in the book 'introduced for the sake of dirtiness, and from the sure knowledge that notoriety earned by dirtiness will command for the book a ready sale' – but the laws were soon abolished. Defending Vidal in court led to my long acquaintanceship with him, although it was limited by my position in the literary pantheon. After all, as Vidal once observed, 'in the world of stars no one is a stranger'. I was invited to stay at his villa at Ravello, but not, sadly, at the same time as either Princess Margaret or Mick Jagger.

Gay liberationists looked towards the elimination of rigid gender and sexual roles, which, as Jill Johnston argued, 'must inevitably mean the collapse of the heterosexual institution with its role playing dualities which are defined as domination of one sex over another'.[29] The psychiatrist Charlotte Wolff went even further: 'I am convinced that the atom bomb will destroy us all if we do not in time achieve an alternative, that is, a bisexual society', she wrote.[30] Few of us took the slogan 'Make Love, Not War' quite so literally.

At the same time, my first book also charted the development of new gay affirmation, and the creation of new spaces, whether lesbian feminist collectives, such as Amazon Acres in northern New South Wales, or the now forgotten fantasy of 'gaying' the underpopulated Alpine County, in northern California. Over the past four decades it has become apparent that greater acceptance does not necessarily mean a declining sense of identity. Indeed, in some ways the two seem to be interrelated, which is a conundrum worth exploring.

A note on terminology: 'gay' was originally recuperated by radicals in the early 1970s to describe both women and men, and, when we remembered, transsexuals. It quickly turned into a term applied only to men, and from an adjective – 'gay power', 'gay liberation' – to a noun: 'gays and lesbians'. In the 1980s other terms were added: bisexual, transgendered, intersexual, queer – the latter seeking to become a new portmanteau word – which also quickly became yet another marker of identity. In this book I alternate between using 'homosexual' and 'queer', taking both as generic terms that cover both women and men, and I recognise that we are often talking of both sexual attraction and self-presentation. It is important to remember that *homo* in the case of 'homosexual' means 'same' rather than 'male'; while many people dislike the word because of its rather clinical sound, others have reclaimed it. While I was writing this book, for instance, large posters appeared around inner Melbourne advertising a party for 'homosexuals and those who love them'.

The debates over terminology hide a larger question: namely, whether we are talking of a discrete minority, defined by sexual practice (and, in some cases, by gender non-conformity), or of a more general fluidity of sex and gender that rejects clear divisions between 'gay' and 'straight'. Some still continue to conflate the fluidity of sexuality with that of gender, so that sexual attraction to one's own sex merges with a desire to repudiate the biological characteristics of gender, in an almost perverse return to older concepts that homosexuality was born of a rejection of one's 'natural' biological sex.

Feminist and gay theorists insisted upon distinct categories of sex and gender, as in Gayle Rubin's seminal 1975 essay 'The Traffic in Women', in which she argued that the 'sex-gender system' is 'the set of arrangements by which a society transforms biological sexuality into products of human activity'.[31] This distinction has become both accepted and contested, and theorists such as Judith Butler and Donna Haraway have questioned some of the assumptions about what is biologically 'given' and what is socially determined;[32] even Rubin herself has modified some of her original positions.[33] Indeed, Butler uses drag to demonstrate her argument that gender is essentially performative, and largely learnt; she has written of her own discovery, as a 'bar dyke', that some men could perform a femininity she didn't want for herself far better than she could.[34] The ongoing attraction of 'drag' for both lesbians and gay men suggests that there are links between gender non-conformity and homosexual desires, even if many homosexuals feel uncomfortable in acknowledging them.

One of the problems of confusing sexuality and gender is that it assumes that all 'tomboys' or 'sissies' are inevitably homosexual, which is particularly confusing for those who break the mould, as illustrated by the character of the football coach in *Glee*, an extremely butch woman who likes men. As a character in David Stevens' play *The Sum of Us* (1990), later filmed, put it:

> I don't want to live in a world that begins and ends with being gay.
> I like having all sorts of people around. I like it at work or the footy
> when the other blokes rage me about what I am ... And I don't
> want to live in a world without women ...[35]

It used to be assumed that there was a clear division between essentialists (who argued for inborn characteristics and desires) and constructionists (who saw sexuality and gender as shaped largely by social and historical forces). I thought those terms were now confined to sociology courses, but early in 2013 I met a young performance artist in Los Angeles who declared himself to be 'an essentialist' and saw an unbroken line of 'forefathers' stretching back to ancient China and Persia.

I used to think that sexuality was far more fluid than gender, but as Kath Weston has pointed out: 'In an era of gene splicing, cyborgs, plastic surgery, mutant ecologies and transgender politics, biology now appears more mobile.' She goes on to argue that this also means that: 'Social constuctivism, which had symbolized the investment in change of scholars and activists alike, could prove more difficult to subject to conscious intervention than biology.'[36] At the same time, there is a greater recognition that a minority of people are genuinely intersexed – that is, born with a mix of physical and chromosomal characteristics that fall outside the conventional binary definitions of 'male' and 'female'. Thus, we are moving into a world in which sexual desires may be more impervious to change than physical markers of gender.

At the risk of overgeneralisation, it is probably true that homosexuality is almost always linked to some form of repudiation of the dominant gender order, even though many people who reject that order may not experience homosexual feelings. It is no longer true that homosexuals think of themselves as a 'third sex', as did the German theorist Karl Heinrich Ulrichs in the nineteenth century, but the sense of being somehow gender deviant persists, often in new forms, such as the growing number of 'butch' lesbians who are identifying themselves as 'trans-men'. In general usage there is extraordinary confusion; as I write this, the local 'gay and lesbian' newspaper has a story headed: 'Study looks at impacts of being gay in school', which assumes that 'compulsory heterosexuality' and assumptions about 'masculine' and 'feminine' are the same.[37] But even those homosexuals who present themselves as conventionally 'feminine' or 'masculine' are likely to feel at times some ambivalence about the restrictions of the gender order, and to see their sexuality as in some ways linked to a repudiation of what society expects of 'a man' and 'a woman'.

Sexuality encompasses desire, behaviour and identity, which do not always match. Indeed, many people who experience homosexual feelings, and often homosexual behaviour, are likely to strongly deny any sense of identity, and may indeed express overt hostility to other homosexuals. It was recognition of this that led to the coining of the term 'men who have sex with men' – or MSMs – in the 1980s, because of the need to reach such men for HIV prevention.[38] A decade later the American media started referring to 'the down low', an expression used to describe African American men who were behaviourally bisexual but refused any homosexual identity. I have always been uncomfortable with this usage, as it seemed to suggest this was a particular characteristic of the black community when it in fact describes a largely universal phenomenon.[39] The only truth behind the expression appears to be evidence that African American men are more likely to be behaviourally bisexual than other Americans, which may be related to class and complex social pressures,[40] while increasing numbers of African American women are publicly identifying as bisexual.

There is ongoing discomfort with the term 'MSM' – which, it is claimed, 'strips gay communities of visibility and relevance'[41] – but it has increasingly come to be used as another form of identity even though it was invented precisely to acknowledge that many men who seek homosexual sex also deny any form of homosexual identity. Indeed, the term 'LGBT' ('lesbian, gay, bisexual and transgender') – or sometimes 'LGBTI' (adding 'intersex') – has lost its connection to the specific meanings of its composite words; one US government official told me he liked the term because it avoided any mention of sex. The ultimate example of the compromise between political correctness and common sense may be the phrase I came across in an American community paper: 'male LGBT'.

There has been more resistance to this term in Australia. In 1993 the Sydney community was bitterly divided over a move within the Gay and Lesbian Rights Lobby to include a 'bisexual and transgender agenda', which was rejected, and the Lobby has retained the name 'gay and lesbian'. (Its Victorian equivalent, however, proclaims that it 'works for and with the whole gay, lesbian, bisexual, transgender, intersex and queer community'.) Indeed, it is now very difficult to have an honest discussion about what commonalities and differences might exist amongst the various groups that constitute the 'alphabet soup'.

Terminology is a minefield of sensitivities and political correctness: an 'adults-only panto' called *TrAnnie*, written and performed by gay men, and programmed for the Sydney Opera House in 2012, drew fury from trans activists, who complained bitterly about the use of the term in a story about a trans paedophile; they succeeded in having the show's name changed to *Trashley*. The very term 'transgender', which came into popular usage in the 1990s, is enormously charged, and is used to cover a range of different gender and sexual subjectivities.[42]

My original hypothesis of 'the end of the homosexual' grew out of a radical reading of sexuality that saw human sexuality as fluid and malleable, rather as queer theory would twenty years later. This view runs up against a re-emerging tendency to define homosexuality as an essential characteristic: one either is or is not homosexual, and this division should be recognised as a basis for identity.

While this has not historically been the case for most societies, in the contemporary western world a certain binary essentialism has helped create a powerful group identity based on the ethnic group model.[43] The demand to fix and name identities is precisely the reason why terminology becomes so important: both homosexuals and the larger society have a need for a clear-cut taxonomy, in which sexual minorities can be seen as distinct and therefore as deserving of rights. In pragmatic terms, what Jeffrey Weeks once called 'a necessary fiction' has become the basis for 'LGBT' politics.[44] While I was writing this book, a colleague received a request from a senior state health officer for 'an estimate of the size of the Gay, Lesbian and bi-sexual population in NSW', as if the terms were completely unproblematic.

More recently, there has been considerable debate about the supposed biological basis for homosexuality, which reinforces the idea of fixed sexual identities that are inborn. In a sense, this is a contemporary scientific riff on the older idea that homosexuals were people caught between two sexes, a view that comes through in the writings of several generations of authors, including that of Virginia Woolf and Patrick White.

White explicitly saw the homosexual as 'part woman and part man', and he claimed that this ambivalence gave the person special insights into human nature. This theme underlies his novel *The Twyburn Affair*. As he wrote in *Flaws in the Glass*: 'Ambivalence has given me insights into human nature, denied, I believe, to those who are unequivocally male or female – or Professor Leonie Kramer.'[45] (Kramer was a pioneering critic of Australian literature but was unsympathetic to White; she and I clashed in the early 1970s when she complained that I was invited to lecture to medical students at the University of New South Wales.) White was generally unsympathetic to the gay movement, seeing sexuality as a 'ludicrous' basis for a political cause.[46]

In the 1990s there was a flood of research claiming to establish the existence of a 'gay gene', drawing on behavioural genetics, neuroendocrinology and psychological theories of sociobiology.[47] So far no conclusive evidence exists, despite very considerable effort to discover it, and even a biologist as eminent as Richard Dawkins has argued that such a gene exists, though he was unable to demonstrate it. Indeed, we have moved remarkably slowly since Kenneth Walker wrote, over seventy years ago, that: 'There still exists the fundamental difficulty of deciding whether the condition is congenital or acquired. The truth ... is probably that it is both.'[48]

The language of the 1940s grates, but no more so than some current pretensions of scientific research. There have even been claims that one can detect sexual orientation by appearance: in one study 'participants viewed facial photographs of men and women and then categorized each face as gay or straight 60% of the time'.[49] One researcher has claimed that sexual orientation is based upon 'brain hemisphere domination', but admits he is seeking a biological explanation for political purposes.[50] Even though such researchers usually acknowledge that the level of certainty they provide is insufficient for everyday life, the assumption that people divide naturally into 'gay' and 'straight' is deeply troubling, given what we know about the ways in which sexual behaviour, fantasies and identities can vary across a lifetime. As Jeffrey Weeks has consistently argued, biology provides 'a set of potentialities, which are transformed and given meaning only in social relationships'.[51]

Mainstream advocates of gay and lesbian rights in the United States often use biological arguments to counter the claims of moral conservatives that sexual behaviour is a choice that can be controlled; many homosexuals like to claim that they are 'born this way', and that choice does not come into it. (The pop icon Lady Gaga even adopted the phrase in a 2011 hit song.) The enthusiasm for a genetic explanation is particularly strange; were such a gene discovered, there would presumably be arguments about how it might be instantly modified. Indeed, the former Chief Rabbi of Britain, Lord Jakobovits, has made exactly this claim.[52] In 2012 California banned 'reparative therapy' for minors, in part because evidence suggests that most people are very unlikely to change their basic sexual orientation.

It is easy to understand why the assertion of a biological cause is attractive to many homosexuals, who can post on the website 'Born

This Way' 'snapshots that capture them, innocently, showing the beginnings of their innate LGBT selves. It's nature, not nurture!' The snapshots in question show little tomboys, or boys dressing in their mother's clothes, returning to a basic confusion between sex and gender that reinforces the most simplistic assumptions about homosexuality. A Freudian reading might retort that those who become heterosexual will repress memories that might suggest otherwise.

Any questioning of this simplistic nonsense (as I regard it) is met by outrage, as television star Cynthia Nixon (of *Sex and the City*) discovered when she talked openly of her lesbianism as 'a choice' and was then pressured by gay movement leaders to recant the term.[53] Although there is no more conclusive evidence for the 'gay gene' than there was when Dean Hamer first postulated its existence in 1993, it has become an article of faith amongst many people, and has entered into pop culture in surprising ways.[54] (Hamer suggested a gene associated with a marker on the X chromosome as influencing homosexuality in males.[55] He subsequently suggested a genetic basis for religious belief, which seems even more dubious.)

This view of sexuality runs counter to the theories and discoveries of both Freud and Kinsey, whose belief in sexual fluidity is also reflected in popular culture, as in the ironic 'gay-o-meter', which appears to have adopted Kinsey's scale for sexual attraction to the modern world of celebrity. It ranks people according to their likelihood of being attracted to someone of the same gender, with ultimate 'gayness' being described as 'Simmonsgay'; I assume this is referring to physical fitness guru Richard Simmons, who is not publicly out, and it is clearly to be read with some irony. On this scale Tom Cruise rates as a 4 and Nicole Kidman as a 6; since these 'judgments' are based on small numbers of responses from fans, they are of course meaningless, except as an antidote to the idea that there is a simple inborn binary of heterosexuality or homosexuality.

Teresa de Lauretis accounted for the complexities of sexuality well when she wrote: 'Sexual identities are neither innate nor *simply* acquired, but dynamically (re)structured by forms of fantasy both private and public, conscious and unconscious, which are culturally available and historically specific.'[56] But even amongst activists, the more radical view of human sexuality as open-ended and fluid has given way to misleading assumptions about biological determinism, which are contradicted by large amounts of evidence that human sexuality is moulded by a variety of factors and is amenable to changes of various sorts.

Instead of seeing 'bisexuality' as a description of human potential, it has become another form of identity, even though it could more easily be seen as a denial of sexual identities altogether. One still finds people who claim that 'bisexuals' are 'really' homosexual but are unwilling to admit it, which was a common line amongst earlier generations of activists. I rather like the novelist John Irving's account of his own sexuality:

> It turned out that I liked girls, but the memory of my attractions to the 'wrong' people never left me. The *impulse* to bisexuality was very strong; my earliest sexual experiences – more importantly, my earliest sexual *imaginings* – taught me that sexual desire is mutable.[57]

'Bisexuality' is a tricky term. It has been used to describe having the characteristics of both genders as well as being attracted to both women and men, but it was only with the onset of political correctness that it came to describe a particular social identity. At times this verges on the absurd, as in advertisements for a 'gay and bisexual men's bathhouse'; since the venue is intended for men who want to meet other men for sex, a bisexual man would presumably be interested only to the extent he was keen to act upon his 'gay' desires. I am equally puzzled by an advertisement for a 'bi massage' offered by a single man in one Sydney newspaper, but I assume it is intended to reassure potential customers that a naked massage from an attractive man does not necessarily make one homosexual.

Talk of 'the end of the homosexual' used to be a predominantly radical script, one that assumed categories and identities would vanish in some post-counter-cultural world of liberated sexuality. It is echoed in the term 'post-gay', which was fashionable a decade or so ago and described the new fluidity and acceptance of sexual diversity. Yet the story of the past forty years is not simply one of linear progress towards acceptance, nor of successive generations simply experiencing their homosexuality in very different ways. This sort of progress is what the psychoanalyst Bertram Cohler had in mind when he wrote of today's 'gay lifestyles' as 'one of several possible sexual lifeways' and speculated that 'the search for self-acceptance and respect from the community' would become less necessary.[58] Cohler suggested that:

> It is inevitable that life writing by gay men in future generations will show little of the subversive character of life stories written in earlier generations. These life stories may consider homosexuality as just one aspect of a life story in which marriage, work and parenthood become more significant than the experience of same-sex desire.

Yet old patterns persist and repeat themselves – also a psychoanalytic trope – and there is no indication that anxieties about sexual desires and identities are disappearing. Homosexual teenagers are still far more likely to commit suicide than others,[59] and drug and/or alcohol abuse remains high among lesbians and gay men, open or not. The image Cohler conjures up may apply to small educated enclaves in liberal America; it would certainly apply to the rather romantic depiction of the male couple in the television series *Brothers & Sisters* (2006–2011) – of the five siblings, it was Kevin, the gay one, whose relationship was the most conventional. For most young people, however, coming to terms with their homosexuality is more complex than this suggests, and homophobia remains real.

Hatred and Acceptance

Back in 2005 the psychologist Ritch Savin-Williams wrote: 'My lifetime professional dream – that homosexuality will be eliminated as a defining characteristic of adolescents, a way of cutting and isolating, of separating and discriminating – is within reach.'[60] Savin-Williams does not discuss the brutal murder in 1998 of Matthew Shepard, which for many stands as a reminder of the stark reality of continuing homophobia. More recently, there have been reports of several US college students committing suicide after being harassed because of their homosexuality, while bullying of 'fags' and 'dykes' in schools remains widespread and vicious. Australian research suggests that a high level of bullying and abuse continues in schools, and indeed may be growing as general awareness and visibility of gender and sexual difference increases.[61]

So far, I have used the term 'homophobia' to encompass hostility towards and denial of homosexuality, which was the psychologist George Weinberg's intention when he coined the word to describe: 'the dread of being in close quarters with homosexuals – and, in the case of homosexuals themselves, self-loathing'.[62] Not all discrimination against people based on their sexuality necessarily results from this dread, and 'self-loathing' is a term that is too easily deployed to describe anyone who might infringe communal norms. Not declaring one's sexuality publicly is often termed self-loathing, for example, but it might result from a perfectly sensible desire to protect one's safety – or, indeed, not to be pigeon-holed.

While 'homophobia' is the term most commonly used to cover the discrimination, denial and persecution of people because of their homosexuality, the word is probably less useful for analysis than 'heteronormativity', which focuses on the structures and beliefs that maintain assumptions that heterosexual relations are *normal* and that homosexuality is *deviant*.[63] Think, for example, of a version of the Cinderella story in which she is rescued by a princess, not a prince, and consider how that challenges so many of the assumptions with which we grow up. In everyday life, heteronormativity is acted out through the ways in which almost all popular culture, from fairy stories to grand opera, assume that all relations of sex and love are inevitably heterosexual, with homosexuals playing at best supportive or slightly comical figures to one side. This is why the occasional television advertisement that suggests couples can be same-sex is so important, in that it challenges the taken-for-granted images with which we all grow up.

There is also an important distinction to be drawn between *homophobia*, with its emphasis on individual pathology, and *heteronormativity*, which emphasises systematic discrimination – or which, as Tom Boellstorff put it, 'operates at the level of generalized belief and social sanction, rather than on an emotive plane'.[64] Writing in 2004 of Indonesia, Boellstorff argued that, during the past decade, a particular form of *political homophobia* had developed, which involved a new violence directed against 'gay men' (and less often lesbians) who were seen as threatening a particularly masculinist nationalism. By this, he means that a certain sort of heterosexual masculinity, often reinforced by religious precepts, becomes something to be upheld and enforced by the state as part of a certain ethos of national identity and resistance to what is seen as the decadence of western societies, which are both admired and scorned. Similar views have been expressed by the current President of Egypt, Mohamed Morsi, who studied in the United States and has expressed both his admiration for American technical savvy and his dislike for American sexual permissiveness.

These views may seem predictable in Islamic countries – in the case of Indonesia, fundamentalist Islam is in the minority but politically influential – but similar attitudes are widely expressed in parts of the world influenced by Christianity, whether it be the Russian Orthodox Church or the variety of Protestant evangelical churches in much of Africa, the Caribbean and Papua New Guinea. Homosexuality has caused huge rifts within the Anglican Church, with American Episcopalians allowing openly homosexual ministers and many African congregations seeing this as completely unacceptable. The Church of England, following its own tradition of pleasing no one by trying to please all, has decreed that gay clergy are acceptable as bishops, provided they remain celibate.

In some ways, the current political homophobia seems to echo that of the Cold War, when anti-Communist zealots in the United States linked the threat of Soviet influence to that of homosexuality – which is ironic, given the persecution of homosexuals within the Soviet Union itself. It was even more ironic that men such as J Edgar Hoover, who almost certainly was homosexual, perpetuated this link and sought to remove known homosexuals from government service. There were echoes of this in Australia: in 1951, as Garry Wotherspoon has written, a number of church leaders 'linked the danger from outside (the Communist threat) with the danger from inside (moral decay)' and sought to unite 'behind a common banner (the restoration of moral order) which would protect Australia from external and internal enemies'.[65]

Boellstorff's analysis helps explain what is often seen as rising homophobia in many parts of the 'developing' world, and links concerns around changing sexual and gender norms to larger sociopolitical factors. Homophobia might be explained as expressing individual psychological needs, which leads to it being understood as an individual psychological flaw that should be corrected – a mirror image of the homophobe's view of homosexuality – but it might also be used to explain state actions and scapegoating.[66]

The progressive discourse of much contemporary writing about homosexuality fails to recognise the extent to which those of us whose identity is bound up with our sexuality still struggle against internalised heterosexual norms. Martin Duberman, writing as someone whose homosexual identity predates gay liberation, observed: 'The shame caused by stigmatization has made a significant contribution to certain formative aspects of gay culture.'[67] It is tempting to ascribe this feeling of shame as the experience of an older generation, symbolised by the reluctance of people such as Somerset Maugham, Susan Sontag or even Stephen Sondheim to deal directly with homosexuality in their writings. But such attitudes persist among far younger people, as is clear from the enormous popularity of the 'coming out' story in gay films and novels, and the language of 'fag-bashing' that is so common amongst teenagers.

Musing on his gay identity, the writer Daniel Mendelsohn – who was nine at the time of the Stonewall protests – writes of gay bars in ways that are reminiscent of thirty years ago:

> Betraying their origins in shame and concealment, most gay
> bars are still narrow and small, spaces hidden away from the
> street ... Walking from these hidden entrances to the bar itself
> always seems like running a gauntlet of sorts.[68]

If Mendelsohn is right, most homosexuals still carry the sense of inferiority that 'gay pride' aimed to obliterate. The writer Frank Browning pointed out as long ago as 1998 that 'pride itself has no necessary political meaning'; he linked it to American concepts of individualism and self-esteem.[69] There is now a considerable theoretical literature on homosexual shame and abjection, and recently there have been attempts to recuperate 'shame' amongst some queer radicals.[70] As Rupert Smith puts it in his fictitious blog of a contemporary young gay man, there is an 'air of illegality that we all seem to crave'.[71]

Equally, there is a specific sort of 'glass ceiling' encountered by homosexuals. There has been some limited discussion of this term in relation to homosexuals in employment and sport, but I am thinking here of the broader sort of pressures that mean we are overlooked because society still assumes a heterosexual model of behaviour and relationships. I regularly receive fundraising invitations addressed to 'Mr and Mrs Altman', as if any other marital status were unimaginable. Part of my aim in writing this book is to tease out the contradictions that still persist around homosexuality.

Changing Spaces

Over the past thirty years, an increasing number of inner-urban areas have seen the rise of visible gay and, to a lesser extent, lesbian communities, with certain areas clearly marked by the sheer number of same-sex couples and the range of businesses catering to them.

This is true not only in the United States but also in cities such as Sydney, Toronto (which masqueraded as Pittsburgh for the American version of *Queer as Folk*), Manchester (home of the original version of that series), Berlin, Paris, Madrid, Amsterdam and Mexico City; the phenomenon is largely confined to western cities, however, and it is more obvious in the case of men than women. Alice Springs is sometimes referred to as the lesbian capital of Australia – like Northampton, Massachusetts, and Santa Fe, New Mexico, in the United States – while there is believed to be a lesbian concentration in a few inner areas of Melbourne and Sydney, such as Northcote and Leichhardt. There is some discussion of just why the Alice has become a lesbian centre in Eleanor Hogan's recent book on the town, even though her discussion reeks of heteronormativity:

> ... it seemed that an eighties trucking dyke aesthetic had taken hold of the population. The town was full of people with ruggedly chopped home haircuts wearing shirts, singlets, Adventurewear shorts and Blundstone boots ... at a glance it was difficult to tell apart a tradie returning from a maintenance job or a lesbian coming home from a social justice mission to an Aboriginal mob out bush ... My explanation for this particular 'desert change' is that extremes of distance created a situation similar to that experienced within prison and other isolated, sex-segregated populations, where straight women sometimes become lesbians, temporarily or otherwise, in response to the lack of available men.[72]

As gay and lesbian businesses have become more visible, some of the features of an older gay culture have disappeared, in particular some of the spaces traditionally used by homosexual men for sexual encounters. All cities have their spaces, whether acknowledged or not, that serve as locations for commercial or casual hook-ups, but the increasing visibility and commercialisation of gay life means – ironically – that many of these areas have declined in importance in cities undergoing major gentrification. The classic example is the remaking of

Manhattan's west side, and the destruction of the old piers alongside the West Village; indeed, much of what is looked back on now as 'the golden age' of New York gay life, with its sex bars and clubs in areas like the Meat Market, was possible only because the city was going through a period of economic decline.

In the same way, various sites known for cruising in the inner cities have largely been displaced by new urban developments. The old warehouses along Melbourne's docks, once the home of wild dance parties, have disappeared in the urban renewal that has produced the sanitised streets of Docklands, while the famous 'Wall' in Sydney's Darlinghurst is no longer a meeting place for free or paying hook-ups. Public toilets, often known as 'beats', were infamous sites both for sexual encounters and for police entrapment, although they are far less significant in an era of sex-on-premises venues and the internet. Wynyard Station in Sydney and the bus interchange at Brisbane's North Quay were long known as places where men met for sex.[73] Most seaside cities have sections of beach that are known as meeting-places for sex, though they too are declining under the pressure of development and surveillance. Casual cruising in streets and shopping malls now typifies cities in developing countries, where there are fewer commercial or private spaces available for homosexuals to meet. A friend of mine tells of touring Tehran, and her guide pointing to the park, full of shadowy men, while commenting ironically that 'Iran has no homosexuals'.

At least in rich countries, the growth of commercial space, including (for men) sex-on-premises venues, has made street cruising less common, and large-scale commercial dance parties have, to some extent, replaced private parties. Women, for whom public cruising has rarely been a practical option, are often linked through complex social networks that may originate in sporting or social clubs. In this century gay men, in particular, increasingly make use of modern electronic communications: websites such as Gaydar, Scruff and Grindr, for instance, allow for instant hook-ups with other men seeking sex in the vicinity. Of course, the development of new options supplements older ones, rather than necessarily replacing them, and some men will go to dance parties and then go home to meet men through their iPhones.

But most homosexuals, even those who are openly so, do not live in inner cities, nor do they spend most of their time interacting with other homosexuals. The so-called 'gay ghettoes' remain places of exoticism in a sea of people who live out homosexual lives much like those of most other people. Wayne Brekhus has addressed this reality in his colourfully titled book *Peacocks, Chameleons, Centaurs*,[74] which stresses the suburban identity of many American gay and lesbian people, as well as their difference from the stereotypical figures of, say, *Will and Grace* or *The L Word*. A quick examination of entries on gay/lesbian dating websites bears out the same observation for Australia.

What is most interesting about Brekhus's book is that he points out that *suburban* can be as much of a social identity as *homosexual* – a point both obvious and striking, as more homosexuals seek long-term relationships and, often, children. Think, for example, what this might mean for social policies around health or ageing, given that the dominant aim of activists is to provide LGBT-specific services rather than to argue for the opening up of existing ones to a range of people. For some radicals, this means a certain sort of recuperation into mainstream society, where 'respectable' homosexuals are seen as deserving of full rights, even as others remain marginalised despite their real needs.[75]

Yet cities remain zones of freedom for sexual and other minorities. As Julie Abraham has written in the afterword to her book *Metropolitan Lovers*:

> Homosexuals have struggled to escape their status as horrors only to find themselves amongst the most desirable ... The cities in which gays now serve as signs of authentic urbanity may remain distinct places. But the experience of social difference these cities offer will be safely limited.[76]

If the growing acceptance of homosexuality also reduces the importance of specific geographical spaces in which lesbian or gay identities can be divulged, we have to beware of simple assumptions about 'open' versus 'closeted' homosexuals. Most people live their lives juggling various identities, which take on differing importance depending on the circumstances. There are openly lesbian couples in rural areas and closeted gay men in inner Sydney.

New possibilities do not so much replace old mores as they add to them. Think of 'drag', the idea of dressing as someone of the opposite sex. Cross-dressing has been a staple of entertainment for centuries – Shakespeare's heroines were all played by men dressed as women, and 'trouser roles' are common in opera. The latter have sometimes produced interesting homoerotic overtones, as in Donizetti's *Lucrezia Borgia*, in which a soprano, singing a male role, expresses her love for the leading male character. But cross-dressing has also been closely associated with homosexual subcultures, and it persists in popular culture; examples are *La Cage aux Folles* or *Priscilla, Queen of the Desert*, films that were reborn as Broadway musicals. Beneath this association lies the idea that homosexuality only makes sense if it is seen as a failure to become appropriately 'masculine' or 'feminine'.

It used to be assumed that the desire of men to dress as women (cross-dressing among women was always both more ubiquitous and less remarked upon) was a product of narrowly prescribed gender and sexual codes. When Christine Jorgensen underwent a widely publicised operation in 1951 to remove her male genitalia, the matter was presented as 'relieving the distress of a troubled homosexual'.[77]

Of course, the great majority of drag queens had no desire to 'be' women: drag was something they adopted in particular times and places. Drag shows used to be central to much of the entertainment in homosexual venues; during the euphoria of gay liberation, 'radical drag' – men dressed as women but in beards, or women wearing men's clothes but in full make-up – posed as a subversive act. Nonetheless, it was largely assumed that drag would disappear as a central part of gay life as the idea that homosexuality was an expression of one's failure to meet gender expectations partly collapsed.

But this has not happened: drag remains iconic in gay life, and every gay pride event features drag queens – and, increasingly, drag kings, who for the past decade have come together at the annual International Drag King Community Extravaganza in the United States. Indeed, it has been claimed that the 'Imperial Court System', which organises drag balls across the United States, is second only to the Metropolitan Community Church as the world's largest gay organisation.[78] This might suggest the deep conservatism of so much of homosexual life – or, indeed, the central role of San Francisco in the gay imagination, given that the founder of the Courts was one of that city's first gay activists, Jose Sarria. Since 2000 there has been a visible 'drag king' scene in Australia, with semi-regular gatherings at certain pubs, especially in Melbourne.[79]

Not all gay men – and certainly not all lesbians – welcome the continuation of drag. Writing of the Sydney Gay and Lesbian Mardi Gras, one commentator complained of 'the lazy marketing strategy of putting a few blokes in frocks up front as shorthand for "gay" … Drag is a historical relic of the days when we had to be always hidden, or in disguise.'[80] But clearly for many homosexuals there is a link between expressing their sexual desire for the same sex while at the same time masquerading, parodying and celebrating the other. For others, there is a deep discomfort provoked by any signs of transgender, which reminds them of the common assumption that being homosexual is to have some of the characteristics of the opposite gender, which many homosexuals, both women and men, vigorously deny. Drag, as employed by both women and men, can be simultaneously misogynist and subversive, it can both uphold and subvert gender roles, and it can be an expression of transgender desires while also reinforcing homosexual fantasies.

Meanwhile, new expressions and identities have emerged along with a major shift in the discourses of 'transgender'. No longer does the term necessarily conjure up images of being trapped in the wrong body; rather, there is an increasing demand to see gender as a continuum, from which different identities and body shapes can be created. A few even describe themselves as 'ungendered', using the pronoun 'per' (from 'person'). For some, trans is the most radical expression of sexual radicalism, although there are feminists who still argue that, even after surgical reassignment, no man can become a 'real woman', and would debar transgendered women from feminist gatherings.

The American term 'dude' is now increasingly being used internationally to describe 'masculine identified gender queers, female to male transsexuals, transmasculine folk and female to male transgendered people'.[81] At the same time, some transsexuals still speak of their experience in the most essentialist of terms, as is true of Australian author Josephine Emery, whose account of her transition from man to woman suggests a deep belief in gender stereotypes and an unease with homosexuality that would be echoed by many of those most hostile to someone in her situation.[82]

Fascination with the fluidity of gender seems to be growing, even if gender nonconformity and homosexuality often collide (and elide), as is clear from several recent and remarkable Australian novels, Kim Westwood's *The Courier's New Bicycle* and Steve Holden's *Somebody to Love*. In Holden's novel a transsexual mortician hides from contempt in the north-west Tasmanian town of Burnie; in a dystopian future, Westwood's hero worries that: 'Those who present androgynously as I do are a walking, talking question mark for the community to feel perturbed about.'[83]

Back in 1970, few people used the word 'gay' – and if they did, it was an adjective rather than a noun (a place was 'gay', not a person). In the space of two generations we have created essentially a new sort of ethnicity, one based not on inheritance but on shared sexuality. Like other ethnic groups, those who are perceived as part of this group – and, whatever their sexual desires, all butch women and effeminate men are likely to be so labelled – will probably encounter hostility, persecution and sometimes violence, despite very real changes in cultural attitudes over the past few decades. While data is inevitably patchy, several recent surveys suggest that up to a third of gay men and lesbians have encountered violence, most often in public.[84]

While there have been huge changes in the perception of, understanding of and support for homosexuals, most of us retain a certain wariness, knowing that one can never be sure when one might face a verbal or indeed a physical attack because of one's perceived sexuality.

THE WORLD THAT MADE GAY LIBERATION

Like many others of my generation, it took me a long time to come to terms with my homosexual feelings. I had several unknowing crushes while an undergraduate at the University of Tasmania in the early 1960s, and when I was perhaps nineteen I discovered a small patch of beach, a long walk from our house, where men played furtively with each other. I think my biggest shock was to encounter a fellow student there, who seemed more at ease than me with the tiny underworld of 'gay Hobart'.

I also found, through the sort of serendipitous sense that so many men have in their early sexual lives, a men's gym and sauna in Melbourne, the nearest metropolis, where again some amount of furtive sex play went on. But I resisted any sense of myself as homosexual, which then seemed to commit one to a life of deceit and exclusion, although I do remember reading the Penguin edition of D J West's *Homosexuality* – first published in hardback in 1955 – and wondering whether ... But this was a time of silence about such matters; I well remember the blushes and embarrassment of my history lecturer as he tried to explain the supposed homosexuality of several English kings.[1]

Looking back, West's book is an excellent mirror of popular attitudes at the time. 'Given a simple choice,' he wrote, 'no one in his right mind would opt for the life of a sexual deviant, to be an object of ridicule and contempt, denied the fulfilments of ordinary family life, and cut off from the mainstream of human interests.' The last section of the book is entitled 'Prevention by Tolerance', and the book ends with a warning: 'No doctor should advise a young person to rest content with a homosexual orientation without first giving a grave warning about the frustration and tragedy that so often attend this mode of life.'[2]

West's attitudes were similar to those expressed in Marijane Meaker's book on lesbianism, *We Walk Alone*, first published under a pseudonym in 1955. As someone who was herself lesbian, Meaker stated: 'The lesbian is the little girl who couldn't grow up. Whether she is a perpetual tomboy ... or whether she is a charming and very "feminine" adult child, she is an immature and abnormal woman. Her world is self-centred and centred on her other selves.'[3] Self-flagellation was a common characteristic of homosexuals in that period.

My real initiation into 'the life' came when I went as a naive twenty-one-year-old graduate student to study at Cornell in the mid-1960s. I became friendly with a fellow student from Florida, whom I realised only later was also homosexual, but who gave me a copy of John Rechy's *City of Night*, which had become a sensation for its graphic depiction of the gay underworld as seen by a hustler working his way across Times Square, Hollywood Boulevard and the French Quarter of New Orleans. Rechy's book broke a number of taboos, not least that of discussing the relationship between sex and money, which often gay men remain reluctant to discuss. I suspect that while some straight men might boast of using prostitutes, many more gay men will never admit to paying for sex. Perhaps to do so is to admit that, even in a world which is rich in possibilities for instant sexual hook-ups, one is just not desirable enough to score; that is, to admit to paying might be to admit to failure. Since casual sex has now become far more acceptable among young heterosexuals, it would be interesting to know if similar assumptions are developing.

Rechy's book alerted me to the homosexual undertones of the YMCA, captured a decade later in the famous Village People song, and also, perhaps, to the use of red lights as a sign of sexual availability. The graduate dorm at Cornell stood atop a steep street that wound down to the town centre of Ithaca, and walking down from Cascadilla Hall one evening I saw a red globe burning in a back window of the local Y. Fuelled by lust, anxiety, trepidation and some amount of chutzpah, I found the room; its occupant was indeed homosexual and eager. I remember little about him, though he was, as Tennessee Williams might have put it, kind.

During my time at Cornell, I stayed several times in YMCAs in New York City, then renowned for their open cruising, which went on all night between communal showers and open bedrooms.[4] By following an apparently intent young man across the Village, I also discovered one of the institutions of the homosexual world of New York, the St Marks Baths, which was then transitioning from its existence as a communal baths for the men of the lower East Side to a centre for openly gay sex. The first times I went there, I saw young and attractive men flaunting themselves in the basement pool and prowling the corridors of the first floor, while old Jewish men from the neighbourhood lay in the steam rooms on the ground floor, apparently oblivious to or unconcerned by the activities going on around them.

Several generations of homosexual men have come to terms with their sexuality through bathhouses, which provided spaces in which to meet and to consummate – and, sometimes, to initiate – relationships. Gore Vidal has written of meeting his life partner, Howard Austen, at the most frequented bathhouse of 1950s New York, the Everard, and I was later to meet several partners at baths in Sydney and Paris. Indeed, there is a history to be written of the gay bathhouses of the world, from the end of the nineteenth century, when Paris and Vienna had several famous venues – the Kaiserbrudl in Vienna, which was reputedly frequented by the Emperor's brother, still remains open, a baroque maze of many levels – to the sumptuous saunas such as Bangkok's Babylon or the day sauna in Amsterdam.

Back at Cornell, I was unsure how to find other homosexual men: there were rumours that they hung out in the music room in the ironically named Willard Straight Hall, though I never found them. I remember telling my best friend about my New York City adventures, and he was appropriately shocked – and concerned for my future life. Thus, I learned in those days how to stay silent, and how to be deliberately vague about the attractions of New York.

This knowledge stayed with me when, young and homesick, I dropped out of graduate school with a masters degree and returned to Australia to take up a lectureship in politics at Monash University in Melbourne. I only stayed there for two years before moving to Sydney, which was where men of my generation went to be gay. By some irony that I cannot resist mentioning, I arrived in Sydney in the same week as Justice Michael Kirby met his lifetime partner, Johan van Vloten.[5]

By the time I arrived in Sydney in 1969, the sixties had come to Australia. Australia's involvement in the Vietnam War, which had been opposed by the Labor Party from the outset, was dividing the country, with a growing anti-war and anti-conscription campaign. As universities became the sites for anti-war protests, the Returned Servicemen's League called for the expulsion of all protesting students. The federal election the following year suggested that the long period of conservative rule was declining, as Gough Whitlam won a huge swing to Labor and established himself as prime minister in waiting. The small numbers of activists who saw themselves as the pioneers of a new Australian identity were overwhelmingly male and Anglo-Irish; the next forty years would see real growth in diversity as the intellectual and political elites slowly opened up to include women and newer immigrant groups.

Two American theatrical works came to Australia at the end of the 1960s and had a huge impact on the changing cultural and social mores. Symbolically, the sixties were imported to Australia as a rock musical, *Hair*, set in the United States, which opened in Sydney amid huge controversy in 1969. But for me the musical – which seems to appear as a motif in every book I have ever written – also symbolised a new openness about homosexuality. The same year, Mart Crowley's play *Boys in the Band*, which dealt with homosexuality in a way rarely seen before on stage, also came to Australia. Its Melbourne production led to charges against three of the actors for their 'obscenity' on stage. The charges, which ultimately were upheld by the Supreme Court of Victoria, made no mention of the homosexual theme of the play, although a review in the Melbourne *Sun* concluded: 'I feel this play, while part of a pendulum swing in morals, also indicates a permanent shift in attitudes.'[6]

Crowley's play was an important milestone, as it lifted some of the stigma against discussing homosexuality in public. It was also the occasion for my first ever comment on the issue: I wrote a short rejoinder to a very hostile review in *Pol Magazine*, which I was not brave enough to sign.[7] Only recently, I discovered that a production of the play in Mexico had also been important in the early days of that country's gay movement.[8]

Sydney at the turn of the decade had gay bars, saunas and meeting places that echoed in some ways the glimpses I had already seen in New York. Already Oxford Street in the inner east was beginning to see a concentration of gay bars, discos, gyms and clothing stores, rather as would happen in parts of other large western cities, and it was not accidental that the 1978 protest march that led to the Mardi Gras parade took place there.[9] For the next decade Oxford Street remained the centre of Sydney's gay life, the most visible sign of the new assertion, or, as Neal Drinnan put it, 'pornography going somewhere to happen'.[10]

One of the lazy pleasures of academic life in those days was the right to sabbatical leave without a clear project or commitment. Thus, in August 1970 I went to New York, with the vague intention of becoming involved in some sort of political activity. My first act was to enrol in the congressional campaign of Bella Abzug, a leading anti-war campaigner, in lower Manhattan, and for some reason I only dimly remember I was sent to take delivery of a small truck from Brooklyn – the only time in my life I have been rash enough to drive in New York City. I also faced the immediate problem of housing, and through an advertisement in the *Village Voice* I ended up sharing an apartment with a painter called Adolph Garcia in the

East Village. Adolph lived in a sprawling seven-room apartment on Second Avenue, decorated with his paintings of feet – naked, half-shod, elaborately pedicured – which had become a meeting place for the new gay newspaper *Come Out*. Without any effort on my part, I was suddenly involved in one of the collectives that made up the larger gay movement in New York.

The Stonewall riots the previous summer had spawned a new and energetic gay activism, which became all-consuming for those of us caught up in the movement. (In fact, several activist groups already existed at the time of Stonewall, and one of the early American activists, Frank Kameny, originated the slogan 'Gay is Good' a year before Stonewall.) The first gay pride march in New York took place in June 1970 to commemorate Stonewall, and the last weekend of June remains the time for gay and lesbian celebrations in many parts of the world. As we shall see, in Australia it was soon abandoned in favour of summer events, though the name Stonewall lives on in a bar on Oxford Street, Sydney.

The radical gay movement grew out of the whole set of attacks on conventional ideas that constituted the rethinking of politics that was one of the marks of 'the sixties'. In the United States the anti-war, civil rights and feminist movements were all essential to the development of gay liberation, but so too was the more generalised attack on conventional mores and assumptions represented by what Theodore Roszak termed the 'counter culture'. His book was one of three or four – along with Kate Millet's *Sexual Politics* and Herbert Marcuse's *One-Dimensional Man* – that had a lasting impact on how I saw the new world that seemed to be emerging.

Similar changes were happening elsewhere; modern gay liberation was not born alone at the Stonewall Inn, as current mythology (and several films) encourages us to believe. There were simultaneous developments of a new sexual radicalism in California, while the 1968 student movements in Paris and Italy saw the emergence of radical homosexual groups, which drew on the heady mix of radical Freudianism, Marxism and anarchism that characterised that period.

But they were short-lived and failed to have the impact that the new gay activism had in the United States.

Perhaps the most fundamental idea that infused gay liberation was the feminist slogan 'the personal is political'. Feminists married the anthropological to the conventional political-science definition of power, stressing that 'the political' was an element of both public and private life, and that it was most important where it was least apparent, as in the division of domestic chores. The idea that our sexuality was not something to be hidden and denied but rather could become the basis of political and social assertion was the dramatic breakthrough of gay liberation, one that, in time, would be adopted by a far wider range of homosexuals than those who were initially attracted to the leftist rhetoric of the early movement. Ironically, the politicisation of homosexuality has equally been the product of the right-wing, usually religious, groups that fought bitterly against all forms of acceptance, often furthering very nasty homophobia in the process.

As a specific movement, gay liberation lasted only a few years, to be supplanted by more assimilationist and pragmatic campaigns for equality. But as a set of ideas, which contained within them a series of still unresolved questions – relations between women and men; assimilation or difference; whether gay life allowed for different forms of relationships and sexual freedoms to the presumed heterosexual norm – it remained significant. The very term 'liberation' pointed to the inspiration of radical anti-colonial and anti-racist movements, while the term 'gay pride' was derived from African American assertion that difference could be a mark of achievement, not something to be overcome. The British playwright Alexi Kaye Campbell has used the term 'the pride' to conjure up the differences between gay life in the 1950s and the present.

I had gone to New York in search of a book to write, and it was the new movement that gave me my subject. In some ways, it would in fact set the path for the rest of my intellectual life. That book grew directly out of my immersion in the new gay liberation culture of New York, and may have had its specific genesis in a campaign against *Harper's*

Magazine organised by the Gay Activists Alliance. Then editor Midge Dector, who later became a prominent neoconservative, and wrote an embarrassingly panegyric biography of Donald Rumsfeld, had published an article by the critic Joseph Epstein titled 'Homo/Hetero: The Struggle for Sexual Identity'. In it Epstein wrote: 'I do think homosexuality an anathema, and hence homosexuals cursed ... If I had the power to do so, I would wish homosexuality off the face of this earth.' When the GAA's request to publish a rejoinder met with no response, the group organised a sit-in, and some of us submitted our own pieces to *Harper's*, to no avail.[11] Out of this incident I resolved to write a book about the new gay affirmation, and began trudging around New York City in search of a possible publisher.

In his article Epstein had written:

> *They are different from the rest of us* ... Cursed without clear cause, afflicted without apparent cure, they are an affront to our rationality, living evidence of our despair of ever finding a sensible, an explainable, design to our world.

Leaving aside the Old Testament language, it was clear that Epstein was drawing on a view of sexuality that was as far from mine as was possible. As someone who had read enough Freud to recognise that he had extraordinary insights into the social control of sexuality (alongside what struck me as the less plausible specifics that underlie psychoanalysis as therapy), I was attracted to the radical readings of sexuality that were taken up by now largely forgotten theorists such as Wilhelm Reich and Norman O Brown, and more contemporary figures such as Herbert Marcuse and Paul Goodman. From my very amateurish readings of these writers, and from my involvement in the extraordinary emerging networks of gay activism, I developed a sense, rather than a clear theory, of gay assertion, which acknowledged the fluidity of sexual desire, and a sense that both repression, in the Freudian sense, and oppression, with a more political meaning, were collapsing in the crucible of social, cultural and political change of the time.

While he is now almost totally forgotten, Marcuse, who had fled Hitler's Germany for the United States, was very important in helping a small number of us reconcile our leftist sympathies with an understanding of sexuality derived from a radical reading of Freud. Indeed, in his book *Eros and Civilisation* Marcuse explicitly saw the homosexual as a potential revolutionary. At the time, this seemed a very exciting concept – although when I reread an interview I gave in 1974, I see that I was already then questioning the extent to which this was a somewhat romantic fantasy.[12] But being influenced to read Freud, I discovered in his work an eloquent plea for acceptance both of human variety and of human weakness.

One of the small tragedies of the Americanisation of psychoanalysis is how Freud has been distorted to create a popular myth of homosexuality as the immature product of inappropriate parenting. As psychoanalysis was redefined as a totally medical profession, it shaded into the dominant prejudices of the psychiatric profession, who increasingly saw their role as one of 'normalising' homosexuals, sometimes through brutal methods such as aversion therapy and even lobotomies. Indeed, Freud's heirs bore out his own warning that they should 'disregard the dissimilarities, whether inborn or acquired, in the sexual constitutions of human beings; it cuts off a fair number of them from sexual enjoyment, and so becomes the source of serious injustice'.[13]

It is not surprising, therefore, that one of the key targets of gay liberation was psychiatry, and some of the earliest gay liberation demonstrations were directed at doctors who supported aversion therapy to 'cure' homosexuality. One of the defenders of such therapies, Neil McConaghy, was an early target of Sydney gay liberation. In 1974 the American Psychiatric Association voted to delete reference to homosexuality as a 'psychiatric disorder', and it was followed by other professional organisations.[14]

Homosexual: Oppression and Liberation drew heavily on literature rather than on social science; there was in fact very little meaningful research on sexuality of the sort that has now become common. One of the extraordinary features of the time was that it seemed possible to read every significant book dealing with homosexuality, and women and men of my generation sought out novels with possible gay themes or characters with extraordinary diligence, which was much harder in Australia than in most countries because of our rigid censorship laws. Now there are entire bookshops devoted to gay writing, and it no longer seems possible or even interesting to read everything, but for older generations it was one of the few ways of finding affirmation. When I wrote my first book I relied less upon academic literature and more on the handful of novels – Baldwin's *Another Country* and *Giovanni's Room*; Isherwood's *A Single Man*, even Radclyffe Hall's *Well of Loneliness* – that had helped me shape the possibility of creating a life based on asserting my sexuality.

Already there existed a specific genre of lesbian crime fiction and several lesbians, such as Patricia Highsmith and Mary Renault, had already published bestselling books with obvious male homosexual themes, which had a huge gay following.* I had not yet read Highsmith's lesbian novel, *The Price of Salt*, which she published in 1952 under a *nom de plume* with the small feminist Naiad Press, even though it had sold almost a million copies in paperback. For others, it was film that encouraged the imagination of other sexual possibilities; both women and men speak of the importance of women such as Marlene Dietrich and Greta Garbo as alternative models to those presented by suburban Australia, even if the messages were coded in ways that we didn't fully understand. As far back as the 1930s, women heard of the lesbian bars of Paris, which played the role of an imaginary gay Mecca – rather as San Francisco would become in the 1970s.

The excitement of the times is caught vividly in a short reflection by one of the key women in the New York Gay Liberation Front, Martha Shelley, who in August 2012 wrote the following to me:

---

* The American writer Daniel Mendelsohn has written a deeply moving account of the ways in which Renault influenced him, and of his long correspondence with her, even though they were several generations and continents apart; see Daniel Mendelsohn, 'The American Boy', *The New Yorker*, 7 January 2013, pp 49-61.

This is what I remember of the meeting during which we came up with the name 'Gay Liberation Front.' It was a hot afternoon and we were drinking beer in one of the Mattachine offices. I don't recollect coming up with the name, just that I shouted, 'That's it, that's it, we're the Gay Liberation Front!' and pounded my hand on the table. Then I noticed that my palm was bleeding, because I'd been slamming it down on a pop top. So I was at least two sheets to the wind.

Dick Leitsch heard us shouting, and he came in, pretty upset. He accused us of starting another organization right there on his turf and trying to draw away membership from his. I said, 'We're not starting a new organization. That's just the name of the march committee.' But I knew even then that I was lying through my teeth. The gay movement was taking off in a radical new direction, and there was nothing he could do about it.

The other things I remember – and these are so much more important – are that we danced our asses off, we got laid, most of us got over internalized self-hate, and we changed the world.[15]

I remember long meetings at the Alternate University in an old building on 14th Street, which had been established to provide 'revolutionary education'; its 1970 Fall prospectus demanded: 'We must combat elitism, sexism, racism and liberalism – and fear.' Amidst the revolutionary fervour and rhetoric, there was a regular gay night, an opportunity for venting (then known as 'consciousness raising'), cruising and general socialising outside the bars.[16]

All social movements need these moments of total commitment, when people spend long periods of time bonding, squabbling, planning, egging each other on to imagine new possibilities and new activities. I was to see this again over the years, first in the emergence of gay liberation in Sydney, and then, twenty years later, in the passions of the ACT UP movement, when AIDS for a time regenerated a gay activism that both looked back to the early 1970s but was also confronting the realities of a generation that was dying without, it seemed, much concern from anyone in authority.

I started writing the book in New York, but it was also shaped by several visits I made to California – especially one at the very end of 1970, when my then boyfriend came from Australia and we spent a few days over the new year holiday in San Francisco. We stayed in an old hotel in the Tenderloin, a part of downtown San Francisco that was then very run-down, despite its proximity to the smarter shops and the grand civic offices of the city. For us, the attraction was its proximity to Polk Street, then the centre of gay life in the city. One of the gay bars in the area, Compton's, had seen a riot back in 1966, when police had attempted to arrest a drag queen, and at that time young men cruised up and down Polk, looking for love, comfort or at least some spare cash.

On New Year's Eve we ate at the Mint, a restaurant on Market Street that has now morphed into a karaoke bar, then we went to a bar called, I think, the Fantasy for a drag show, and ended up at a new year's dance hosted by SIR, the Society for Individual Rights. SIR was one of a small number of early American homosexual rights groups that would be swept aside in the euphoria of gay liberation, but for two young men from Australia the very idea of a gay organisation hosting a large party was extraordinary. The first time I had seen men dancing together was less than a year past, at the Stonewall Inn in New York, just a few months before the riots that would make the inn a symbol of the new gay liberation movement.

It was not surprising that San Francisco came for a time to seem the 'gay capital' of the world, despite the fact that Los Angeles was actually a more significant site of early homosexual politics, and arguably has a larger and more complex gay and lesbian world.[17] As the historian John D'Emilio reminds us, San Francisco flourished as a port during World War II, and many men and women who found it a safe place to explore their sexuality in the midst of wartime returned afterwards to settle. This, after all, was the city that housed the beat poets of the 1950s and the hippies of the 1960s, a city that, from its nineteenth-century origins, seemed more open than most to people who lived outside the mainstream. By the 1970s the city could claim to be the 'gay Mecca', not just for Americans but also for travellers from across the world; Armistead Maupin's *Tales of the City*, which began as a series in a San Francisco newspaper, cultivated this image.

While the American 'homophile' movement began in Los Angeles, the first significant lesbian organisation, the Daughters of Bilitis, was founded in San Francisco, which has a fifty-year history of lesbian activism, varying in the extent of its interconnection with the gay male world. Some forms of lesbian separatism thrived in the Bay Area, but lesbians would be equally crucial in developing early communal responses to the AIDS epidemic in the 1980s. California remains the US political jurisdiction in which gay money and power is most significant. Perhaps it is no accident that so many powerful contemporary female politicians from California – such as House Democratic leader Nancy Pelosi and Senators Barbara Boxer and Dianne Feinstein – all had very close links to the gay movement in their early careers.

The idea of San Francisco as gay capital of the United States – and, by extension, of the rest of the world – was legitimised by two major studies, Manuel Castells' *The Power of Identity*, published in 1997, and Richard Florida's *The Rise of the Creative Class*, which had a far wider reach, in 2002. Florida grabbed considerable attention because of his claim that tolerance and diversity were essential to urban vigour, and that the presence of a large and visible gay and lesbian population was one of the best measures of such vigour. Using a particular interpretation of census data (since sexual preference and behaviour is not yet counted in any national census), he demonstrated correlations that seemed to establish 'the concentration of gays as a predictor of high tech industry' and claimed that San Francisco led the country in both.[18] No wonder gay bars across the world named themselves after the Castro, or, as in the case of one in Bogotá in the 1980s, Las Calles de San Francisco. For men and women of a certain generation, going to San Francisco almost became part of one's gay initiation, and even today young queers across the world talk of visiting the Castro and Valencia Street.

The Castro is now regularly included on bus tours of San Francisco for tourists, and it remains the centre of a certain sort of male gay culture, which was captured in cinematic form in Gus Van Sant's 2008 film *Milk*. That film recreated images of the Castro from the late 1970s, when the gay movement seemed to be at its high point, and when the election of Harvey Milk to the San Francisco City Council signalled the emergence of homosexuals as a political force within American domestic politics.

Harvey Milk was assassinated in 1978, but thirty years later, when I was back again in San Francisco, the Castro was remarkably recognisable from the images of his time. True, his photo shop was gone, as were some of the other shops and restaurants of the period, but the same mix of small businesses, cafés, bars and street life remained, anchored by the ornate art-deco towers of the Castro Cinema, one of the few movie theatres to still have a playable organ. If you sit in one of the older establishments that line the street – the Norse Cove, say, whose name recalls the Scandinavian settlers of the area, or the Twin Peaks, the first gay bar in the city with plate-glass windows so patrons were visible to those passing by – you will see many men and some women who might have lived there during the days of Harvey Milk. You will also see much younger people dressed in styles similar to those that seemed ubiquitous in the 1970s: denim, checked shirts, boots and facial hair (for men), while women's hair is often shorter than men's.

Of course, some things have changed. There is at least one bar that attracts a self-consciously 'queer' crowd, and on Market Street several of the pivotal institutions of the area, including a large sauna and massage parlour, and the pioneering Walt Whitman bookstore opposite, have disappeared. Moustaches have largely vanished – facial hair is now more designed and trimmed – and many more bodies are tattooed and pierced.

Bodies themselves have changed, too, after decades of gym culture,[19] though it is increasingly difficult to differentiate between 'gay' and 'straight' body fashion. The impact of AIDS meant that the famous San Francisco bathhouses were closed down, after bitter debates about their contribution to unsafe sex, but other sex venues have sprung up, and street cruising seems largely to have yielded to online sex sites. Indeed, one can see men sitting in crowded cafés and bars busy on internet chat sites, quite oblivious to the possibility of cruising in their immediate physical space. The bodies remain disproportionately white: rising prices have meant that the Castro has not reflected the demographic changes of the past forty years in California, although Asian men are certainly present in greater numbers. As is too often the case, however, the most likely place to encounter black or Hispanic men is in service jobs rather than as customers.

The once thriving lesbian world around Valencia Street seems to have diminished, but since 1993 there has been an annual San Francisco Dyke March, which attracts tens of thousands of women each summer. San Francisco is also striking for the number of organisations that include both women and men, whether it be marching bands, sporting clubs or the well-established LGBT history group.

As I was caught up in the melodramas of gay liberation life in San Francisco and New York in the early 1970s, changes were happening back in Australia that were to make possible some quite new ways of living for those who were homosexual. I was already in New York when John Ware and Christabel Poll launched the Campaign Against Moral Persecution (CAMP) and started the first major homosexual rights group in the country.* The name was, of course, a deliberate reference to how we then termed ourselves, in a world that a writer for the 'progressive' magazine *The Nation* had described, after his daring foray into two Sydney 'camp cabarets', as 'enchanted caverns for a humdrum group of camp men and women seared by the leering intolerance of weekday society'.[20] That remarkable Australian dancer and writer Noel Tovey recalls that 'camp meant out of the closet, outrageous, funny and often sad'.[21]

Very quickly, groups sprang up in all the capital cities of mainland Australia. By the time I came back from New York, in the early part of 1971, there was a thriving movement into which I could throw myself.

---

* There had been several short-lived precursors, including a Melbourne-based chapter of the Daughters of Bilitis.

PART TWO

TRIUMPH – AND TRAGEDY

It starts in 1962, long before Stonewall, when no gay person, no matter how intelligent, was self-accepting. And it ends at the close of the 1980s when gays, partly because of the battle against AIDS, had come to have a lot of self-respect in the sense of being agents in the world.

Edmund White, speaking of his novel *Jack Holmes* in an interview with Michael Erhadt (*Gay & Lesbian Review*, Jan–Feb 2012, p. 32)

THE 1970s: NEW AFFIRMATIONS

I was back in Sydney for what was possibly Australia's first 'gay demonstration', when a small group of us descended in October 1971 on the headquarters of the Liberal Party in Sydney to protest against the possible preselection of a conservative morals crusader for a safe federal seat. The excitement of the demonstration, which included a number of heterosexual supporters as well as some people 'coming out' for the first time, marked a new stage in homosexual affirmation, and would lead, seven years later, to the famous events that saw mass arrests at the inaugural Mardi Gras.

The following year, an Adelaide University lecturer, George Duncan, was drowned at a cruising spot on the Torrens River, most likely by police officers.[1] That murder, which received considerable media coverage, was crucial in hastening the beginnings of a serious push to decriminalise homosexual behaviour; at the time, the historian Jill Roe wrote: 'Not since the 1830s enquiry into the effects of transportation on convicted persons has there been such smouldering concern about homosexuality.'[2] The year after Duncan's death, former Liberal prime minister John Gorton and Labor minister Moss Cass

65

introduced a successful resolution supporting decriminalisation in the House of Representatives, which in turn helped bring about law reform in the Australian Capital Territory.

The first serious move to decriminalise male homosexuality came at roughly the same time in South Australia, when a Liberal backbencher, Murray Hill, introduced a private member's bill, which was supported by the Labor Party.* By contemporary standards, the bill was very restrictive, and it became more so when the state's upper house limited it in order to make consent a defence against conviction in cases involving sexual acts in private between two men over 21 years of age. By the end of that year, though, homosexual acts were, if not exactly legal, then not exactly illegal either. In 1975, after several years of cross-party discussion, South Australia became the first Australian jurisdiction to enact homosexual law reform.[3] It is an interesting reflection on Australian disinterest in its own history that so dramatic an incident as the Duncan drowning seems to have been largely forgotten. It inspired nothing more creative than a radio documentary and – in almost a parody of the Australian fashion for remembrance – a small memorial plaque.

South Australia was followed by Victoria in 1980, but decriminalisation was a slow process in others states, and New South Wales saw a long, drawn-out struggle because of the strength of conservative Catholics within the Labor Party. Quiet and persistent lobbying was important in changing the law in Victoria, but in New South Wales opposition to decriminalisation helped to mobilise increasing numbers of people who were angered by the resistance of both major political parties. It was not until 1984 that Premier Neville Wran, after some years of procrastination, successfully introduced a private member's bill that passed both houses.

Until the public battles around decriminalisation in Tasmania, which came at the end of the 1980s, this was the most heated political

---

* Hill's son Robert, who would himself become a senior Liberal cabinet minister and Australia's Ambassador to the United Nations, spoke at a public meeting in Adelaide in 2012 of his role in helping his father draft that bill.

battle for gay rights in Australia. It also led to ongoing suspicion of the Labor Party amongst a number of gay activists, and contributed to the ability of Clover Moore to win election to the New South Wales Parliament as an independent in 1988. She remained a member for over twenty years, adding the role of Lord Mayor of Sydney in 2004. In 2012, after legislation disqualified her from holding both positions, she was replaced as the Member for Sydney by the openly gay marriage advocate Alex Greenwich.

This early period of gay and lesbian history has been well chronicled, originally by Denise Thompson in *Flaws in the Social Fabric*, then by Graham Willett in *Living Out Loud* and Robert Reynolds in *From Camp to Queer*.[4] My own role during this period was always deeply ambivalent, and certainly lacked the commitment of activists such as Lex Watson and Sue Wills, who were colleagues of mine at Sydney University and, for a time, the co-presidents of CAMP. In part, this was due to my own deep ambivalence about being in Australia at all, which led me to have extended periods out of the country.

The University of Sydney played an extraordinarily central role in the development of the gay and lesbian movement in Australia. In addition to Lex and Sue, it was also home to the historian Garry Wotherspoon and the (now dead) playwright Nick Enright, one of the very first people to come out publicly. It's little wonder that Tony Abbott, who started his political career at Sydney, appeared to be so obsessed by the threat we all posed to him, though it was only when I read David Marr's *Quarterly Essay* on Abbott in 2012 that I realised he was a student there while I was teaching in the Department of Government, and that he had been actively campaigning for leadership in student politics on an anti-gay platform.[5]

I was spoilt by the early attention given to *Homosexual*. For a brief time I became a public figure, and made a series of visits to other cities to help launch new gay and lesbian movements. Even the soon-to-be prime minister, Gough Whitlam, wrote to me after the publication of the book, expressing his hope that:

> A change of government ... will have a profoundly liberating effect on the whole community, and that, in such an atmosphere, the community will shake itself free of a great deal of the preoccupations and hang-ups which have led to so much persecution.

There was certainly a new mood among some of the Whitlam ministry, elected late in 1972, although this was hardly sufficient to explain why one former Labor member, the Queensland conservative Senator Albert Field, claimed that the Whitlam government 'was more interested in looking after homosexuals than jobs'.[6]

The Whitlam era was the period in which the gay and lesbian movement established itself in Australia. Shortly after the foundation of CAMP and the first street demonstration came the first clearly 'camp' magazine, *William & John*, which questioned a society that 'cheers when two men beat each other senseless in the boxing ring but would blush and become sickened at the sight of two men embracing each other in genuine love and affection'. This insight would become the trope of several films in succeeding decades – think of *Fight Club* and *Brokeback Mountain*. Already taboos on homosexuality were breaking down in the media; those who are old enough to have gone to the movies in 1971 will remember the gasp in the audience when Murray Head and Peter Finch kissed in the film *Sunday Bloody Sunday*.

As gay movements emerged across the western world, they took inspiration both from the local conditions and from the American example. Thus, some of us objected to what we saw as the bourgeois and legalistic aims of CAMP and established small gay liberation groups in Sydney, Melbourne and Adelaide, heavily influenced by images from the United States. By 1972, when Germaine Greer toured Australia to celebrate the publication of *The Female Eunuch*, we were able to involve her in a 'gay liberation' forum at Sydney University despite her own somewhat ambivalent attitudes towards homosexuality; this event is sometimes seen as the official birth of radical gay liberation in Australia.[7]

All successful social movements create their own social worlds, and that of gay liberation was intense – sometimes bordering on hysterical – and, above all, sexual. Some of its members, especially the women and those men most influenced by it, scorned the commercial world and the 'objectification' of bodies that it encouraged, but most of us were happy to objectify and be objectified in return. Nonetheless, there was an ambivalence in our attitudes to the emerging commercial gay and lesbian worlds, and some resistance to what we foresaw as homosexuality being recuperated and tamed by 'the market'. In some ways, these fears have proved justified, even if the commercial world has opened up space for many more people than did the political movement.

Gay liberationists prided ourselves on our support for the reborn women's movement, and some of the central figures of the early movement were women. We drew inspiration from the anti-war protests, student unrest and the new feminism, claiming to be part of a wider movement for radical social transformation. It is too easy to forget the utopian claims of second-wave feminism, which challenged not only the dominant assumptions about gender but also those of hierarchy and authority, and the accepted notions of the limits of human nature itself. When feminists decided to boycott the 1973 Sydney May Day celebrations in protest at a 'Miss May Day' contest, Sydney Gay Liberation supported them in a statement that began: '"Sexual revolution" is itself part of a total movement to change society at its roots ...'[8] At an anti-war rally at Sydney University in 1970, the poet Kate Jennings – later to become an established (and conventionally married) writer – declared: '... you'll say I'm a manhating, bra-burning lesbian member of the castration penis-envy brigade, which I am.'[9]

But at the same time there was a celebratory side to gay liberation. No other movement so encapsulated the famous saying attributed to Emma Goldman that 'if I can't dance, I don't want to be part of your revolution'. The founding myth of the Australian movement – the 1978 parade in Sydney that led to police arrests and then the formation of Mardi Gras – revolved around people coming together to celebrate rather than to organise politically, even though it grew out of a political march.

Gay liberation also rested on the idea that homosexuality was a primary – indeed, perhaps an exclusive – identity; this was a myth that would become increasingly problematic for those both in Australia and in the United States who felt uncomfortable with the dominant leftist, white, male character of the movement. The rhetoric seesawed uneasily between seeking affirmation and integration; as the American writer Vito Russo once observed, we wanted home movies for ourselves that also captured mainstream audiences.

It is commonplace to note that many lesbians felt competing links to the women's movement, while homosexuals with strong religious or racial identities were often uncomfortable with the assumptions of radical gay identity and the movement's hostility to conventional morality. It is less often acknowledged that a *majority* of the men and women who were developing a sense of homosexual identity were very wary of the new radicalism, and only gradually were drawn into political activism. Part of the story of the past forty years is the ebb and flow of activism, and the ways in which certain moments brought large numbers of homosexuals into at least short-term political engagement.

While the idea of 'the homosexual' had existed for over a century – the term was first coined in 1869 – the contemporary models of gay and lesbian community and identity were basically imagined and institutionalised during the 1970s, and since then have become powerful in the global imaginary. This is not to deny the reality of major shifts, within both homosexual worlds and the larger social environment – most particularly, the significant steps towards greater acceptance. Despite all the changes that have occurred, however, we are still in a world that is marked by the paradigm shifts that began forty years ago.

Gay liberation only involved a tiny number of homosexuals in cities across the western world, with occasional outriders beyond, as in Mexico and Argentina, about which I would not learn for many years. In some parts of the non-English-speaking world the idea of dissolving sexual identities, and opposition to the binary categories of sex and gender, were asserted through embryonic gay movements long before the birth of 'queer theory'. The Catalan Gay Liberation Front (FAGC) adopted 'the strategic aim of dissolving the categories "homosexual/heterosexual"', while the early Mexican gay movement rejected the idea of 'gay cops or a gay ghetto like San Francisco'.[10] But commercial pressures and American influence were too strong, and gradually both a gay movement and a commercial gay world emerged in these places, superficially at least with strong American influence.

The rise of gay and lesbian movements in the 1970s both captured and took advantage of a whole set of new perceptions and openness around homosexuality, much as a huge wave can carry a surfer triumphantly to shore. With the media feeling able to report gay activism, as it rarely had in earlier times, large numbers of people suddenly had a whole set of new possibilities, out of which new communities could be forged. Activism generated a new self-confidence, which was sometimes displayed with more bravado than the activists truly felt, which in turn increased the space for social acceptance.

Increasingly, people felt able to assert their homosexuality openly. After that first gay demonstration in Sydney back in 1971, three people rushed to come out to their parents. In 1976 Bob Brown, then beginning his career as an environmentalist in Tasmania, came out through a long feature story in the Launceston *Examiner*, the first person who would have a successful political future in Australia to do so. (Brown entered state parliament in 1983, but in the previous year's state election campaign his homosexuality had consistently been used to smear him.[11])

'Coming out' was seen by many of us as the best weapon against homophobia, a perfect example of the claim that the personal is political. The idea of coming out still remains powerful within the gay movement – in fact, the term lives on in the name of a bar in Rome. Frank Moorhouse has claimed it is the first known example of 'a strategic abandonment of privacy as a way of confronting and disarming a stigma'.[12] For a period during the 1990s there was a major debate about 'outing' people who both hid their homosexuality and used their positions to further discrimination and stigma, which seemed true of a number of American right-wing politicians. The rise of outing was possibly connected with the anger against such celebrities as Liberace, Rock Hudson and Rudolf Nureyev, who failed to disclose their sexuality even when they were dying of AIDS.

Despite the ebullience of the early movement, however, real barriers remained, and most homosexuals still carried a deeply internalised sense of inadequacy. Family, church and career remained the three pillars that maintained deception as the slowly eroding norm of homosexual life, and they remain firmly in place for most queers in many parts of the world forty years later.

Also important was the development of lesbian and, particularly, gay publishing, as mainstream publishers started talking of the 'pink dollar', and a network of gay and women's bookstores and newspapers created space for marketing and publicity. Again, the United States led the way: Rita Mae Brown's *Rubyfruit Jungle* was originally published by a small feminist press in 1973, then was picked up by Bantam Books a few years later, and by the time Edmund White published *A Boy's Own Story* in 1982 (with the mainstream house Dutton), there was a network of gay bookstores at which people queued for his autograph at readings. The revived women's movement created a network of small publishers and shops, and the Dr Duncan Revolution Bookshop in Adelaide opened in 1975. A decade later, The Bookshop Darlinghurst started in Sydney; along with its Melbourne counterpart, Hares & Hyenas, it remains in business today, when almost all of its American counterparts have collapsed.

For a time during the 1970s Adelaide seemed at the forefront of social change in Australia: Premier Don Dunstan and the Adelaide Festival, which he turned into the premier arts and literary event in Australia during that decade, were synonymous with what we felt was a cultural renaissance. It was under Dunstan that South Australia became the first Australian jurisdiction to decriminalise homosexuality, and while his sexuality was complex and not openly discussed, he represented in some way the gradual erosion of heterosexual hegemony in our public life.[13] The best general discussion of Dunstan's sexuality comes from former federal minister Neal Blewett, who has pointed to the dislike generated by his 'sexual ambiguity, highlighted by a sartorial flamboyance unusual among politicians of his time'. Kerryn Goldsworthy, in her recent book on Adelaide, also points to the shock caused by Dunstan's famous parliamentary appearance in pink shorts. Overall, as Blewett writes: 'Much of the personal calumny ... vicious character assassinations and gutter-level smear campaigns circulating through Adelaide during [Dunstan's] years in power thrived on this questioning of his sexual identity.'[14]

It is likely that the reactions to Dunstan showed the limits to tolerance that existed in the 1970s; it would be several decades before one could imagine an openly gay politician being really accepted in the mainstream. Again, it was South Australia that led the way, with the first openly lesbian federal cabinet minister, Penny Wong, who became Minister for Climate Change in 2007. Since the arrival in the Senate of West Australian Liberal Dean Smith in 2012, there are now openly gay politicians from every significant political party except the Nationals in all federal and state parliaments.

This development seemed a long way off in the early days of the gay and lesbian movement. Like all identity movements, we had to work on a number of fronts simultaneously. Most importantly, there was a need both to change general public attitudes and to remake those of its own participants. For women and men who had grown up believing themselves inevitably marginalised and excluded from mainstream possibilities, the most important achievement of the time was to remake those assumptions from within – to remove the sense that our lives, our relationships were somehow less meaningful than those of 'normal' people. The gay movement borrowed 'consciousness raising' from the women's movement, and we sat in earnest circles discussing our lives and our lusts.

Change did come – slowly, in fits and starts – but in general there was less resistance than we had imagined likely. Distrust and even hatred were not uncommon reactions to those of us who sought change, as my colleague Lex Watson experienced when in 1976 he spoke at a public forum in Mount Isa organised by the ABC television program *Monday Conference*, but the vicious backlash against homosexual assertion that was evident in parts of the United States was less common in Australia. Although some grumbled that they wished people would keep their sex lives to themselves, most showed a surprising willingness to see overt discrimination disappear; nevertheless, politicians and, particularly, the churches lagged behind popular sentiment. Violence against people perceived to be homosexual remained a real concern. Every few weeks one read accounts of gay men, and occasionally lesbians, being accosted and beaten, and it was only gradually that police could be relied upon to take such events seriously.

Changing social mores also allowed for an explosion of a gay and, to a lesser extent, lesbian commercial world. Thus, in North America, northern Europe and Australasia there was a sudden expansion of lesbian and gay businesses, newspapers and organisations, many of which were resolutely apolitical, except for their insistence on homosexual visibility. This was less true of the gay media in Australia, where early papers – above all, the Sydney-based *Campaign* – clearly aligned themselves with the new political movement. Radical gay liberationists felt an ambivalence about commercial culture, and there were frequent attempts to create community institutions, some of which persist even today, such as the lesbian and gay centres in a number of US cities. In Sydney the youth drop-in centre Twenty Ten was established in 1982, and counselling services emerged in a number of Australia's capital cities.

One of the consequences of the growth of gay venues was a decline of private parties and street cruising, both of which I regret. I far preferred going to Lex's New Year's Eve parties, with views from Balmain of the Sydney fireworks, to the expensive commercial and large dance parties that took over. Equally, I share with many men of my generation a nostalgia for the casual cruising that took place, often in major streets such as Toorak Road in Melbourne's South Yarra. It now exists far more obviously in developing countries, often, as is the case in even the richest parts of South East Asia, in shopping malls.

As the lesbian and gay world became more visible, it also became a target for certain commercial enterprises, which saw a potential market. Glossy gay magazines came to carry advertisements for alcohol, airlines, cars and real estate, which helped shape particular images of the homosexual as a wealthy and sophisticated consumer. As Alexandra Chasin warned: 'The capitalist market makes possible, but also constrains, social movements whose central objective is the expansion of individual political rights ... the market eventually undermines the radical potential of identity-based movements.'[15] In an episode of the Scottish television police drama *Taggart*, filmed in 1996, there is constant reference to the power of the 'pink dollar' as a force for social and economic change.

At the same time, gay activism developed in a number of trade unions, and Australia is interesting for the extent to which both blue- and white-collar unions have often given support to homosexual causes.[16] The fourth national homosexual conference in 1978 took as its theme 'Homosexuals at work: highlighting discrimination against homosexuals in employment', which would have been an unusual issue for the American movement to have adopted at the time.

As homosexuals came to be viewed through the lens of markets rather than morals, we did indeed became increasingly acceptable. In 1978 *The Australian* proclaimed in a cover story that 'gay power is a fistful of dollars' and identified Sydney as lagging behind only San Francisco and Amsterdam as a centre of gay power.[17] But *The Australian* also has a record of making extreme claims about the gay population; when Max Pearce became the first openly gay candidate to be endorsed by a major party to run in a federal seat in 1983, an article in *The Australian* predicted that 'the estimated 35,000 homosexuals out of 65,000 voters in Wentworth should be able to topple the incumbent Liberal MP, Peter Coleman'.[18] In fact, only 20,000 people voted for Max Pearce, an increase of 1.6 per cent on the previous Labor vote. One suspects that the journalist was deeply wrong about both the figures and the assumption that being gay would be the decisive factor for most homosexuals when voting.

The shift from a small radical movement to a much larger and more amorphous 'community' is encapsulated in the story of how Sydney's Mardi Gras became the central institution of Australian lesbian and gay life for several decades. The original march in 1978, which was organised to commemorate the ninth anniversary of Stonewall – and so took place in midwinter – involved a few hundred people and led to mass arrests when marchers refused to obey police orders to disperse and continued from Oxford Street to Kings Cross. Those arrests – and the general brutality of the infamous Darlinghurst police – mobilised a new group of activists and increased pressure on the right-wing Labor government of New South Wales to move towards decriminalisation. Three years later, a small group decided to move the march from commemorating Stonewall to the end of Sydney summer, and around 5000 people joined that parade. Within a decade the parade had become an annual fixture in Sydney's calendar, drawing up to half a million spectators, who line the streets of the inner east to watch the parade.[19]

Over the years, the parade has become a celebration and now includes large numbers of floats that are paid for and organised by commercial interests, and even though there is always a political element – helped for many years by the strident opposition of morals crusader Fred Nile – most of those who participate do so to party rather than to demonstrate. But for thirty years Mardi Gras remained the most visible single manifestation of gay and lesbian life in Australia, an event of simultaneous subversion and inclusion.

During the worst period of AIDS deaths, the parade's survival was important as a testament to the resilience of a devastated community, while its ability to include groups from across the spectrum of gay, lesbian and transgender communities made it an important measure of the reality of queer life. While the television cameras linger on the drag queens, the dykes on bikes and the beautiful boys in leather, Mardi Gras is really a cross-section of Australian life: suburban mums with their homosexual children, middle-aged women and men in gay religious and sporting groups, Asian and other ethnic community floats. One of my fondest memories of an early Mardi Gras is helping a group of Sydney Brazilians set up their float for the parade.

In the lead-up to the 1983 Mardi Gras, *The Sydney Morning Herald* ran a major story on 'how the city came out', even though male homosexual activity remained illegal.[20] Mardi Gras is now largely accepted as part of the diversity of Sydney life, although as late as 1994 John Hewson's message of support was a factor in his losing the leadership of the Liberal Party, and in the party's subsequent shift to the right on social issues.[21] Mardi Gras has also become a sizeable tourist attraction, and may well serve as an introduction to queer life for not inconsiderable numbers of curious and perhaps sexually uncertain visitors from Asia, who line Oxford Street to watch the parade.

Mardi Gras was equally important as a demonstration that there was an Australian way of being gay, which was less determined to become a respectable pressure group than in the United States, where the movement created political arms such as the National Gay & Lesbian Task Force and the Human Rights Campaign Fund. Perhaps because acceptance was easier in a country far more secular than the United States, there was less interest in building mainstream institutions, which have become the basis for considerable political and economic clout in the USA. The far greater importance of fundraising in American politics is also a factor that has no real counterpart in Australia, and gays and lesbians have become important contributors to Democratic Party funds.

No other Australian city has matched Mardi Gras for size and colour, but the founding of the Midsumma Festival in Melbourne in 1989 introduced an event that has since become solidified in the calendar. It includes a large range of social, artistic and sporting events stretching over three weeks, while Adelaide's FEAST, which also contains a large range of events, has now been running for fifteen years. *The Age* estimated that 100,000 people attended the opening Midsumma Carnival on the banks of the Yarra in 2013, and the program for that year included 130 events spread across the city.

In a period of two decades, homosexuals were repositioned from perverts to citizens, and those who opposed equality seemed both old-fashioned and bigoted, despite remaining hostility from a number of more traditional churchmen. By the beginning of the 1980s the success of Mardi Gras symbolised the extent to which cultural and social space had opened up, and what Graham Willett argues was a real community began to develop, at least in the major cities. Graham points to the growth of venues, social groups and publications by the mid-eighties, which were defining a sense of identity not unlike that of an ethnic group, though I think he overemphasises the commonalities between women and men.[22] Activists came together at the National Homosexual Conferences, which had existed periodically since the mid-1970s, while large numbers of others found a place in sporting clubs, religious groups and organised social events. A Melbourne collective founded a magazine called *Gay Community News*, but after a few years a split between women and men led to it transforming into the far more commercial and male-oriented magazine *Outrage*.[23] The first few issues declared *Outrage* to be 'a magazine for lesbians and gay men', but by issue ten the publication's women staff and board members had largely withdrawn.[24]

At the same time, there was a marked expansion of gay and, to a far lesser extent, lesbian public space, usually defined by commercial venues. Some people came out through movement activities but many more did so through bars, discos and clubs. In the very telling phrase of Michael Hurley, 'socialising was associated with a re-forming of self'.[25]

The few years around the turn of the decade from the 1970s to the 1980s saw a significant shift in Australian culture, one that is less discussed than the earlier 'time of hope', but one where clear social changes were established and cemented. We have been accustomed to thinking of the Fraser years – 1975 to 1983 – as a grey period, bookended by the excitement of Whitlam and the reforms of Hawke, but in fact they were a period of creativity and change. The period of the Fraser government saw a remarkable flowering of the Australian movie industry, with local films including *Breaker Morant*, *Gallipoli*, *My Brilliant Career* and *Newsfront* drawing large audiences. Many of the films of that era – think of *Picnic at Hanging Rock*, *The Devil's Playground*, *The Getting of Wisdom*, *Gallipoli* – were largely about homosocial relations, and among these was the first Australian film with explicitly gay themes: *The Clinic* (1982), set in an STD clinic in inner Sydney.

In 1977 the remarkable singer, director and writer Robyn Archer produced her album *The Ladies' Choice*, in which she was open about her sexuality. David Malouf published his first novel, *Johnno*, in 1975, and it was followed by Helen Garner's *Monkey Grip* (1977) and Peter Carey's *Bliss* (1981); homosexuality was a theme in at least the first two of these. At times, it seemed as if it were heterosexuality that was in the closet.

The first explicitly lesbian novels appeared, among them Elizabeth Riley's *All That False Instruction* (1975) and Beverley Farmer's *Alone* (1980). Dorothy Porter, who would become widely known for her verse novels, started publishing poetry. In 1979 Patrick White's *The Twyburn Affair* was published, a remarkable exercise in crossing gender and sexual lines, and he followed this with a 'self-portrait' – *Flaws in the Glass* (1981) – in which he 'came out'. (Sumner Locke Elliott, best known for his novel *Careful, He Might Hear You*, who had spent much of his adult life in the United States, published his semi-autobiographical 'coming out' novel, *Fairyland*, in 1990.)[26]

Some of Elizabeth Jolley's novels from the period have been read as lesbian – indeed, she was already exploring emotional ties between women in one of her earliest works, *Palomino* (1965). Frank Moorhouse produced one of the most striking 'gay novels' in *The Everlasting Secret Family* (1980), where the 'family' in question is a politician's sexual involvement with two generations of men. Even so, the American Neil Miller, after visiting Australia in the early 1990s, commented: 'I met any number of gay men in Australia, New Zealand and South Africa who had come out after reading gay American novelists like Edmund White and David Leavitt, but had virtually no one to chronicle their experiences.'[27] Perhaps Miller was reflecting the failure of Australians to recognise our own writers, a continuing example of the 'cultural cringe'.

In 1974 the Chilean artist Juan Davila, whose work is infused with homoerotic imagery, moved to Australia, and he, along with people like James Gleeson and David McDiarmid, would bring a certain gay sensibility to the forefront of art. The first major exhibition of 'homosexual and lesbian artists' took place at the Frank Watters Gallery in Sydney in 1978. There is a major study to be written of the relationship between homosexuality and art in Australia, not only through the work of significant artists but also through the influence of galleries, both public and private, and the ways in which art was often a medium for expressing ideas about sexuality and gender that subverted the existing order. The photographer William Yang's first solo exhibition, 'Sydneyphiles', debuted in 1977, with its images of the Sydney gay scene; Yang would go on to become one of Australia's most established performance artists, drawing on both his Chinese and his gay identities.[28] Davila's very political and often sexually graphic paintings were often the cause of considerable controversy, as when his multi-panelled work *Stupid as a Painter* was removed from the 1982 Sydney Biennale after complaints about its so-called blasphemy and obscenity.

For me, the late 1970s are remembered in flashes of hot summer nights in Sydney, where the Paris Theatre Company had been established by Jim Sharman and Rex Cramphorn, with backing from Patrick White, to promote new Australian plays. The company attracted some of the hottest names in Australian theatre, but I remember mainly the building itself, on the corner of Whitlam Square. It's now demolished, but it had been built in 1915 to a design by Walter Burleigh Griffin, and was home to a very successful gay film festival in May 1978. A prelude to what would become the famous first Mardi Gras, the festival featured some classic movies, along with the Australian film *Journey Among Women*, in which a group of convict women break away from their prison to establish a women's settlement in the wilds of Tasmania – I suspect a film best forgotten. The Paris Theatre Company was probably seen by the theatrical establishment as far gayer than it actually was, but it did reflect a new willingness of people as yet uninvolved in gay politics to come out.

Of course, not everyone approved of the cautious assertion of homosexuality in theatre. Indeed, in the early 1980s there were consistent attacks on what was seen as too much gay influence on Australian, and particularly Sydney, theatre. When Jennifer Claire's play *The Butterflies of Kalimantan* was produced in 1982, the venerable theatre critic H G Kippax wrote, with some relief: 'This is a comedy about men and women, not men and men.'[29]

While those of us who saw our sexuality as a master identity developed a new self-assurance and sense of affirmation, there were also other signs of much larger shifts in attitudes towards sexuality generally. Indeed, many of the literary explorations of homosexuality at the time came from authors who were not themselves part of the new community – or who may have been using literature to explore their own homosexuality. There was some angst when the writer and critic Robert Dessaix included a number of ostensibly 'straight' writers in his anthology of 'Australian gay and lesbian writing' in 1993, arguing that what mattered was the subject, not the subjectivity of the author.[30]

One of the greatest barriers to full acceptance was that few people who were not themselves homosexual saw the issue as serious. Discrimination based on sexuality was rarely conceptualised as an issue of basic human rights until the late 1980s; the draft human rights bill considered by the Hawke government, for instance, totally ignored sexual identities or expression.* While there is a long and distinguished history of human rights, this was not the language of the early gay movement, and indeed it was not until relatively recently that international bodies concerned with human rights have conceded any space to sexuality. The enthusiastic support of so many

---

* One exception in the 1970s was the willingness of the Royal Commission on Human Relationships, an initiative of the Whitlam government and chaired by Justice Elizabeth Evatt, to consider homosexuality.

Liberal heterosexuals for same-sex marriage in the 2010 election, when it became a high priority for many on the Labor Party's left, is in marked contrast to their general disinterest in earlier homosexual concerns, such as decriminalisation. The way in which sexual rights have developed is part of a much larger story of globalisation and its interaction with existing ways of thinking about sex and gender in very diverse societies.

An awareness that homosexual rights might be part of a broader concern for social justice emerged in the 1980s, and in part was a product of the new openness and affirmation that had developed in the twelve years since CAMP was founded. But it was also a reflection of shifts in Australian political culture. With my romantic attachment to the United States, I overlooked the extent to which the political cultures of the two countries were changing, so that Australia would increasingly become the more accepting and progressive of the two.

The coming to power of the Fraser government seemed to suggest a return to some of the pre-Whitlam conservatism, but in 1983 Australia re-elected a Labor government, while the United States was being reshaped by the reborn Republican Party of Ronald Reagan. This was to prove enormously important in the very different responses the two countries made to the emergent AIDS epidemic, and also inspired a major shift in social attitudes towards homosexuality. In large part this was because Australia is a far less religious and divided country than the USA.

BACK IN THE US OF A

Between the late 1970s and the mid-1980s I moved frequently between Paris, New York and Sydney, living out fantasies of love, writing and the exhilaration of the new gay world. In retrospect, I see the truth in the comment of French author Tristan Garcia that: 'The eighties were a cultural and intellectual wasteland except when it came to TV, free-market economics, and Western homosexuality.'[1]

My first real experience of a non-English-speaking gay world came in 1977, when I used another sabbatical leave to spend ten months in Paris. The history of gay activism in France dates back to the founding of the social and literary group Arcadie in 1957 and the radical eruptions of 1968, out of which emerged the Front Homosexuel d'Action Revolutionnaire. The central figure of FHAR was Guy Hocquenghem, who became the most visible symbol of the new gay affirmation after the publication of his book *Le desir homosexual*. Guy, who was a loyal friend during my time in Paris, clung to a romantic vision of the homosexual as outlaw, a view that persisted somewhat longer there than in the English-speaking world, which by and large raced to embrace respectability.

Equally importantly, French culture was far more resistant than that of North America to notions of identity politics, which clashed with the strong ideology of universal citizenship. That attitudes persists even today; the French novelist Herve Claude complained in late 2010 about 'the very Anglo Saxon stress on coming out'.[2] The strong emphasis on a single national identity made it difficult for French homosexuals to adopt the model of de facto ethnic identity, which underlay the American – and Australian – creation of strong community organisations.

Even allowing for this, I am struck by the commonalities in building gay movements across different cultures, as in some ways I relived then in Paris what I had previously encountered in New York and Sydney – and would several decades later observe occurring in Manila and Mumbai. Producing a magazine is often the foundation of a movement (although in the age of the internet this is unlikely to remain the case). The collectives and groups of writers who gathered around publications like Boston's *Gay Community News* (a name later adopted by a Melbourne collective), Toronto's *Body Politic* and New York's *Christopher Street Magazine*, and the energies that produced a series of small lesbian presses and journals, were central to the new homosexual affirmation, as were the various women's publishing houses and musical festivals that became spaces for both communal and sexual affirmation.

In Paris I floated on the edges of the collective that was beginning to produce *le gai pied*, the most significant radical French gay publication, though my knowledge of French meant I barely followed the passionate debates that surrounded the production of every issue. We usually met in a large apartment off the Boulevarde Voltaire belonging to the founder of the magazine, Jean le Bitoux, and over the next few years *le gai pied* became a central institution of the growing French movement. Gay and lesbian film festivals are also usually significant, both in western and non-western societies; the excitement I recall during the 1977 Paris Gay Film Festival is now matched in events like the annual KASHISH Mumbai International Queer Film

Festival. And there are common tensions across borders, in particular around gender and attitudes towards the commercial world.

Of course, there had been lesbian and gay spaces in major European cities long before the social and political movements of the 1970s, but except for a couple of moments – Paris and Berlin in the 1920s are the most obvious – they were largely shadowy and deeply scarred by constant fear of exposure, corruption and scandal. One still finds remnants of the older-style homosexual world in the neighbourhood gay bars of Amsterdam, which I remember as small, smoky and full of overweight women and men who liked to sing along to Dutch popular songs. But with new affirmation came new commercial spaces, whose patrons seemed to flaunt their acceptance of sexual diversity as bars opened up to the streets, while, ironically, the creation of new commercial venues for sexual adventure killed off street cruising.

In 1978 I went briefly to Brazil as a guest of the journal *O Lampião da Esquina* (literally, 'the street lantern'), which had been established by a small group of activists in Rio de Janeiro and São Paulo. I think it was the first serious gay publication in a developing country, and its politics were clearly of the left; already the paper had published a long interview with a union leader, Lula da Silva, who in later years, as President of Brazil between 2003 and 2010, would lead his country to an unprecedented place in global affairs.

In Rio I stayed in a small flat belonging to a man who still lived with his mother but kept the apartment for sexual encounters, and I was taken to an extraordinary evening at the Cinema Iris in downtown Rio, a known homosexual space since the 1950s. Late at night the cinema was an exuberant mixture of disco and samba music, drag queens and go-go boys, packed with men of ambiguous but highly flaunted sexuality.

In Brazil one could see the ways in which different models of homosexuality overlapped and sometimes collided with each other. Brazil in 1978 was still in a period of military dictatorship, considerable inflation and remarkable inequality, so that class, race and sex all interconnected in palpable ways. As in much of Latin America, gender largely seemed to define sex, so that a 'real' man could have sex with other men without compromising his heterosexual masculinity; homosexuals saw themselves, as the character Molina puts it in Manuel Puig's novel *Kiss of the Spider Woman*, as '[a] hundred percent female ... We're normal women, we sleep with men.' That book and Puig's novel *Betrayed by Rita Hayworth* were reminders of the ways in which American culture seemed ubiquitous throughout the world.*

Now there is a considerable literature available in English on the emergence of gay politics in Brazil (less, as usual, on lesbians),[3] but thirty years ago I had few sources other than my hosts and my immediate impressions with which to make sense of the worlds I was discovering. In an article I wrote after my trip, I claimed: 'If homosexual *sex* is widely available and acceptable, the only form of homosexual *identity* that is acceptable is that of the *bicha*, and outside certain prescribed contexts, even that is open to constant abuse and contempt.'[4] My own sense of identity may well have been affronted by my recognition that, in Brazil, as indeed in most cultures, the performance of masculinity and femininity allowed for far more variation in sexual behaviour than was officially acknowledged.

One can see in many parts of the world a similar mix of assumptions around homosexuality as both a reflection and a rejection of rigid gender roles, and most large cities now contain examples of 'traditional' and 'modern' forms of homosexuality. This is symbolised by the gap between the luxurious 'western-style' gay saunas of Bangkok and Mexico City and the old bathhouses used by poorer locals, where there is a great deal of homosexual activity that remains unnamed and unacknowledged. At a more institutionalised level, Mexico City now recognises same-sex marriage, whereas much of rural Mexico retains very strong prohibitions against homosexuality in any form. At the time of writing, it seems likely that the Mexican courts will legitimise same-sex marriage across the country.

---

* I will admit to experiencing a feeling of great pride when Puig footnoted *Homosexual: Oppression and Liberation* frequently in *Spider Woman*, a particularly unusual device in a novel.

The enthusiasm of emerging 'LGBT' movements – to adopt the language of North American activism – denies the rather different ways in which most societies have understood gender and sexuality. It is hard to see why the LGBT community in São Paulo – or, for that matter in Chennai, India – should see Stonewall as central to their assertion of sexual diversity, but the riots continue to be commemorated in those cities. The 2009 Equality March in Poland took as its slogan '40 years of equality, 20 years of freedom', apparently equating Stonewall with the collapse of the Berlin Wall, which surely was a far more traumatic and meaningful event for all Poles. Even the French seem to have bought in to the myth: the Marseilles webpage for lesbian and gay pride events in 2012 relates the story of Stonewall with no mention of France's own homosexual histories. Imitation can lead to absurdities, as in an article on Colombia, which depicted Bogotá as being 'a little provincial' because it lacked 'some elements of gay culture' such as 'a bear community, an S/M community and exotic sexual practices'.[5]

By 1980, the lure of New York, which was deeply conflated in my head with the lure of being gay, led me to abandon my position at Sydney University and move to New York. This was the period when gay culture seemed at its peak, and for a few thousand of us – mainly male, white, young – the city offered a giddy mix of sex, intellectual stimulation and a sense of living, suddenly, in technicolour. We could not know how quickly a new disease would throw that whole world into turmoil, killing off so many important figures of that epoch.

Many fantasies have now been created of that time, and for some younger gay men (though far fewer women, I suspect), the early 1980s seems a golden age, when it suddenly became possible to live out of the shadows in a constant round of parties, drugs and sex, while still building a career. This world has been mined by a generation of gay writers, of whom Edmund White is the most successful, who have explored the creation of a self-confident culture that seemed to embody the ambitions of gay liberation. Being gay or lesbian had indeed become the equivalent of belonging to an ethnic community, and a new assertion took hold, celebrated in street parades, raucous dance parties and womyn's music festivals. Gay men, in particular, began to consciously remould their bodies, as the gym culture exploded in inner cities. The 'genderfuck' of the counter-culture was replaced by an exaggerated masculinity, as the androgynous look of David Bowie was superseded by that of the super-macho Village People; a similar retreat to more conventional femininity took longer to impact upon the lesbian community. Somewhat amazingly, the Village People were still performing thirty years later, and had retained their original clone look. I recall an editor dismissing my proposal for the book that became *The Homosexualization of America* because I used the Village People as an emblem of how gay styles were changing. 'Who will remember them in three years?' he commented.

While in retrospect the 'clone' look seems slightly grotesque, it marked an important shift in how gay men imagined their masculinity, which would in turn impact upon fashion and body images across society. The new gym-toned, pierced and moustachioed gay man rejected the association of homosexuality with effeminacy, just as 'lipstick lesbians' – a term that also emerged in the 1980s – suggested that women could be lesbian without rejecting conventional ideas of femininity. (Ellen DeGeneres publicised the term in a 1997 episode of her show, *Ellen*, commenting that she would be called 'a ChapStick lesbian'.) Women had an extra layer to work through during these fashion changes, as many lesbian feminists regarded wearing make-up or even dresses as a compromise with sexism.

From the 1980s on, homosexuals became both more visible and less easily identified, as styles that began in the gay world – buffed bodies, earrings, tattoos, goatees – were quickly taken up by younger men, while fewer women dressed in stereotypical 'feminine' styles, and straight as well as gay women were as likely to experiment with a wide range of clothes, hair and body ornamentation. More recently, numbers of younger lesbians and gay men have rejected any one style of presenting themselves, so it becomes more and more difficult to identify a person's sexuality from their appearance.

Inevitably, the growing visibility and affirmation of homosexuality affronted supporters of the old order of gender and sexuality, and produced a political backlash. Already the new politics of sexuality had played themselves out on the streets of San Francisco – where else? – after the election to the City Board of Supervisors of openly gay activist Harvey Milk and his assassination within a year by a disgruntled former co-Supervisor, who also shot City Mayor George Moscone. That tragedy took place as issues around homosexual rights became matters of national political concern, and campaigns were launched against those few cities that had instituted anti-discrimination ordinances. In 1977 voters in Miami overturned an anti-discrimination ordinance after a very effective campaign led by a fundamentalist Christian singer, Anita Bryant; the following year, however, an initiative to fire homosexual teachers failed in California, after both Ronald Reagan and President Jimmy Carter opposed it. Questions of homosexual rights were now taking centre stage in American politics.

Backlashes tend to occur when major social changes are succeeding, and there were echoes of the Bryant campaign in Britain in 1988, when Prime Minister Margaret Thatcher introduced a provision (Section 28 of the Local Government Act) that prohibited the 'promotion of homosexuality', particularly in schools. No prosecution was ever brought under this act, but it did lead to the closure of a number of gay and lesbian support groups in schools and colleges, and it was broadly seen as state-sponsored homophobia. The clause was repealed, first in Scotland in 2000, then altogether in 2003. The current prime minister, David Cameron – who had vocally supported the bill – has since formally apologised for it.

My infatuation with New York and the new gay culture that seemed to be sweeping aside all other ways of being homosexual resulted in a book, *The Homosexualization of America*, in which I argued that as homosexuals followed the ethnic model of developing community institutions, we were also changing the nature of American social mores. Thirty years later, it's revealing to read the first person quoted in that book, the then leader of the New York Gay Men's Chorus, who claimed: 'We show the straight community that we're just as normal as they are.' My argument was that normality itself was being remade by the new gay affirmation, which in turn reflected the larger shifts being brought about by new social and economic forces that were shaking up old assumptions around sexuality and gender, most evident in the dramatic opening up of career possibilities for women. As western societies came to depend more and more upon consumption rather than production, the old rigidities were giving way to a new commercialisation, in which the market's lack of concern for morality of the old sort displaced the puritanism that had characterised the period of industrialisation.[6]

Already the gay movement was mobilising to affect mainstream US politics, and luring politicians, primarily big-city Democrats, with the promise of money and votes. In 1982 I attended a large fundraising dinner organised by the Human Rights Campaign Fund at the Waldorf-Astoria in New York, at which the guest speaker was Vice President Walter Mondale. My notes from the Waldorf-Astoria dinner record that the closest Mondale came to acknowledging his audience was to refer to 'some of the people in this room'. As I wrote at the time: 'One wonders just who is co-opting whom.'[7] Earlier that year I had been at another fundraising event – held in a mock-Italianate Beverley Hills hotel for Gore Vidal's campaign for the Democratic nomination for the Senate – which had seemed full of lesbian and gay realtors, lawyers and therapists. This new professional and business class was becoming a force in southern Californian politics, and would in 1985 mount a successful campaign to incorporate West Hollywood as a separate city. Vidal, of course, did not win the nomination.

The story of West Hollywood is now largely forgotten, although it represented one of the most striking successes – and perhaps limitations – of the new movement. A coalition of gay and Jewish activists, many of them renters, sought city status to escape the neglect of the Los Angeles County authorities, and created a new city in which openly lesbian and gay politicians were central figures. West Hollywood, which runs for a few miles in a narrow strip along Santa

Monica and Sunset Boulevards, and includes both rich areas and large numbers of less lavish apartment complexes, would become a leader in enforcing rent control, anti-discrimination ordinances and special care for seniors and those with HIV.[8] It remains a highly visible centre of gay and (although less overtly) lesbian life in southern California.[9]

All of these movements were heavily white, and in retrospect the extent to which the emerging homosexual world was racially marked is more shocking than it appeared at the time. In the exuberant days of gay liberation there were attempts to identify with militant African American groups, and a small group of gay radicals travelled to Philadelphia in 1970 to join the Black Panthers for a 'Revolutionary People's Constitutional Convention'. The Panthers were a small group of young black militants who rejected Martin Luther King's insistence on non-violence, and they were ambivalent, to say the least, about their embrace by radical gay liberationists.

As the small radical gay movement gave way to a much larger and more commercial world, I had glimpses of the ways in which racism seemed omnipresent. At one point, in the early 1980s, I dated a black lawyer in San Francisco, and I noticed the extent to which he was 'carded' – asked for proof of age – at venues that admitted far younger white folk without a glance. Back in the late 1960s, the sociologist Ned Polsky claimed that the homosexual world was more integrated than the heterosexual, but there seemed little real evidence for this.[10] Even today, the gay bars of most American cities remain largely segregated, so that in the Dupont area of Washington DC, a city that is predominantly black, the gay businesses – and what is not in some way gay in that part of Washington? – seem whiter than inner-city Melbourne. The extent to which the gay world remains segregated is exemplified by the much greater incidence of HIV amongst African American homosexuals than among any other racial group in the United States. Although the reasons for this are complex, however interpreted they clearly suggest an ongoing racial gap that has disastrous consequences.[11]

Perhaps the two most successful and continuing gay institutions of the early 1980s are the Metropolitan Community Church and the Gay

Games. Both grew out of California, the former when the Reverend Troy Perry set up a church that would welcome lesbians and gay men in Los Angeles in 1968. It has since grown to have 250 congregations in countries as varied as Argentina, Nigeria, the Philippines and Romania. The church has had several congregations over time in Australia, but has been fairly peripheral here, even for gay Christians.

The Gay Games were inspired by former Olympic decathlon athlete Tom Waddell, who had a vision of sport as a means of strengthening community. Tom wrote:

> We need to discover more about the process of our sexual liberation and apply it meaningfully to other forms of liberation. The Gay Games are not separatist, they are not exclusive, they are not oriented to victory, and they are not for commercial gain. They are, however, intended to bring a global community together in friendship, to experience participation, to elevate consciousness and self-esteem, and to achieve a form of cultural and intellectual synergy ...[12]

They were not, however, to be known as the Gay Olympics, which was his original desire, after the US Olympic Committee took court action to prevent the name being used.

Since the original Gay Games, held in San Francisco in 1982, the event has become quadrennial and has been held on several continents, drawing participants from across the world. The list of original participants includes twelve Australians, the most of any country outside North America. I was lucky enough to attend the 1982 Games, and no memory of them is sweeter than the ironic curtsey of the heavyweight wrestler when he was awarded his gold medal during the closing ceremony in the Castro Theatre. Remarkably, one visiting European journalist complained to me of the absence of 'obvious' gay events, such as handbag-tossing.

A version of the Gay Games now takes place every few years in the Asia/Pacific region, and in 2012 a South Asian Games was organised in

Nepal. Although the games have been tarnished by complex disputes over their ownership and control, they remain able to draw thousands of participants, who often relish the opportunity to explode the myth that gay men are sissies, uninterested in sports – or, indeed, to relish in the stereotype of athletic lesbians.

For some Asian friends of mine – admittedly, middle-class and English-speaking – the Gay Games are an enormously important opportunity to revel in their sexuality in the company of other queers. At the 2010 Cologne Games at least one Chinese woman runner was able to take part as an avowed lesbian because of the event's scholarship program. An Indian participant wrote of his experiences at the opening ceremony of the Gay Games in Sydney 2002:

> I could see the distance we have to travel back home before we get to a point of celebrating our sexuality without fear or repression. I could also feel the euphoria of freedom where it exists, and the desirability of it, for it is inherently good. But most of all I could feel a validation of what I do back home, for unfolding before my eyes was an ideal that could be had, and playing at the back of my mind was the actual oppression I witness every day I live and work in India.[13]

By the time the Games came to Sydney that year, Australia could claim to be far ahead of the United States in the community's acceptance of homosexuality, with most jurisdictions moving towards abolishing all remaining discrimination. As the quotation above suggests, many homosexuals in the region saw Australia as a place where they could live openly; there was a certain irony in the two-way traffic that saw white gay men flock to Thailand and other Asian countries in search of sexual adventure, while many Asians sought to live in Australia because they could live openly as homosexuals. In 1985 Australia had become one of the first countries to accept same-sex relationships as a basis for immigration, although most homosexual immigrants probably come to Australia through other categories.[14]

From the beginning of the 1980s there was a growing move to bring gay and lesbian studies into American universities, following the trajectory established by women's and black studies. While a few institutions made room for new subjects by and about homosexuals – San Francisco State College and the City University of New York stand out, followed by Yale, after a major endowment by writer Larry Kramer – the attempt to introduce 'gay studies' into the curriculum was very ad hoc and piecemeal. Even the flourishing of certain sorts of queer scholarship from the 1990s on never really established what some of the early attempts to create a new field of scholarship had envisioned.

But although homosexuality remained tangential in most college and university curricula, a considerable body of research was developing, and it has now made its mark in almost every academic discipline. By the late 1980s there was a healthy debate about how best to both study and teach homosexuality, and several large and important conferences in the United States and the Netherlands helped create rich and continuing networks of scholars. (The Dutch took the lead at this time in developing gay and lesbian studies.) Unfortunately, the rich literature of that period seems largely to have been forgotten, including a very important defence of 'gay studies' by the philosopher Martha Nussbaum.[15]

Nussbaum's article was important because she wrote as someone who was not arguing from her identity, but rather as a philosopher who recognised the significance of sexuality for all, and the importance of coming to terms with homosexuality as an integral part of the human experience. Yet the move to incorporate homosexuality into curricula across subjects has now largely been discarded, and the modern-day emphasis on 'queer studies' has tended to create a very specialised discourse around homosexuality that seem irrelevant to the great bulk of homosexuals themselves.

As various forms of queer communities, identities and politics have developed globally around homosexuality, the influence of the United States remains significant. While queer movements across the world are fascinated by US political and cultural developments, the reverse is largely not the case.

WHERE WERE THE WOMEN?

The very framing of this question suggests that there is a story that needs to equally represent women and men, and that there is sufficient commonality between lesbians and gay men – and, in other narratives, 'bisexuals', 'transgendered' and 'intersexed' – that it is the fault of the author if this is not reflected in his (or her) text. I am not convinced this is the case.

A few years ago I was part of a panel discussing gay male writing at the Brisbane Writers Festival. A couple of lesbians in the audience were very indignant that all four of the speakers were men, and that we spoke almost exclusively of male concerns. They were, of course, right in arguing that there are considerable lesbian themes in Australian literature worth discussion. I was less convinced that such a discussion should automatically be linked to a panel set up explicitly to discuss recent writing by gay men. Indeed, given the strong evidence from studies across the western world that women are more fluid in their sexual desires than are men, one wonders whether there may be greater differences between male and female homosexuality than is often acknowledged – and, if so, how far this is biologically or socially determined. As Rosemary Pringle warned us some years ago: 'Though homosexual men and lesbians occupy vastly different worlds they are still lumped together.'[1]

Historically, many women managed to develop close friendships that were clearly emotional and sometimes sexual in nature, but that often went unobserved. Over thirty years ago, Carroll Smith-Rosenberg drew attention to these 'passionate friendships' in an important article about the nineteenth-century United States.[2] Writing of Australia, Graham Willett has noted: 'Because lesbianism was never illegal, and because women appear to have been less in the habit of having sex in public parks, they rarely came to the attention of the law.'[3] The bigger question is whether the differences between male and female sexual behaviour, hinted at here, are biological or social in nature; until very recently, the opportunities for women to escape their social and financial restrictions were clearly far fewer than for men.

Because I am writing out of my own experience and observations, this book is unable to properly encompass the full range of developments among lesbians over the past few decades. By their nature lesbian spaces are less visible, as women are more confined by economic disadvantage, fear of violence and responsibility for children. Moreover, many lesbians have chosen to work and socialise within feminist networks, making it harder to track specifically homosexual relationships and politics than it is for gay men. Yet the last few decades have seen an ebb and flow of women and men coming together with a sense of commonality around oppression and prejudice, only to be thrust apart (perhaps too phallic an image) by their clear differences. Often we are too scared to admit that these differences mean that a co-sexual and gender-diverse movement is more aspiration than reality.

Certainly, women were crucial in the early days of gay liberation, which took much of its intellectual and political energy from the reborn women's movement. Like many others, I was enormously influenced by Kate Millett's book *Sexual Politics* (1970), which used literary criticism to unpack the sets of ways in which gender and sexuality were regimented in western society. (I particularly remember the charged atmosphere of an early public meeting at Columbia University at which Kate acknowledged her attraction to women.) Indeed, many of us read the emerging literature of second-wave feminism with great excitement. Peter Fisher, who was a founder of the Gay Activists Alliance in New York, thanks his 'brothers and sisters' on the title page of his book *The Gay Mystique*, published in 1972.

Nevertheless, despite its apparent concerns for sexism and its flirtations with androgyny, gay liberation in most of its manifestations was largely a male business, and those women who did take part soon disappeared, frustrated by the overt male sexuality of the movement. The gender realities are epitomised in the change of the title of *The Gay Liberation Book* (1973) to *The New Gay Liberation Book: Writings About Gay (Men's) Liberation* (1979).[4]

The 1970s saw increasing tensions between women and men in gay politics across most of the western world, as the radical impetus of the early movement gave way to both greater institutionalisation and commercialisation. While a few organisations maintained the idea of a common purpose, the lives of most lesbians and gay men intersected far less as the decade progressed. Perhaps it was only among the most politically or intellectually committed that enough commonalities seemed to exist to hold together a coalition based on shared social disapproval. While many homosexuals enjoy the company of the opposite sex, the logic of being homosexual is to seek the company of one's own, and as new communal and commercial spaces opened up at dazzling speed, only a minority of homosexuals maintained strong social links across gender lines.

Of course, homosexuals have always had close friendships with non-homosexuals; the trope of the straight woman whose best friends are gay men is a recurring one in television and films – think *Will and Grace* or the rather cruel stereotypes in *The Devil Wears Prada*. There is even a term, 'fag hag', to describe women who hang out with homosexual men, although the reverse seems less common as a cultural type.* For women, a gay male friend is often a safe escort and confidant; for lesbians, there is less obvious advantage in bonding with straight men, except perhaps as a means of concealing their sexuality.

Sydney's early gay liberation meetings were held in an old house on Glebe Point Road, at the building in which the women's movement magazine *Mejane* was sometimes produced. Of the women who participated, several were clearly fluid in their sexuality, a reflection of a period in which newly energised feminists were often experimenting with lesbianism.[5] Women were central to events such as Melbourne's first Gay Pride Week, held in 1973, and the subsequent movie made by Barbara Creed, titled *Homosexuality – A Film for Discussion*, was the first such documentary to be shown in local schools. A number of women were important in the early days of CAMP, but they started to withdraw as they felt pressured by male demands for social and sexual space.

For women, there was a constant tension between identifying with other women on the basis of shared gender oppression and making sexuality the primary basis for politics and community. The same idea underpinned the idea of 'women identified-women', which some more traditional lesbians saw as de-emphasising their sexuality at the expense of an asexual view of 'sisterhood'.[6] Lesbians were the driving force behind many of the women's initiatives that flourished in this period – which, ironically, added to our inability to recognise them as lesbians. Lesbian activity ranged from specific separatist cultural institutions to working within the state, in that particularly Australian form known as 'femocrats' – namely, women who entered the bureaucracy, often in roles specifically created to improve women's position.[7]

Reading the massive documentation of feminist radical activism in Australia in the 1970s compiled by Jean Taylor, I am reminded of the extent to which many lesbians were determinedly separatist; even though men are mentioned in the collection, there appears to have been an editorial decision to not include them in the index.[8] Women

---

* I have come across the term 'lez-bros', but it is hardly in common use.

were increasingly aware of the male bias in most discussions of sex, whether heterosexual or homosexual; as one group, based in the Leichhardt Women's Health Centre, argued in a 1974 publication:

> Female sexuality is largely invisible and unexplored. Our ignorance of our bodies and our lack of freedom to explore our own potential in our own way renders most women unaware of the dimensions and possibilities of female sexuality.[9]

There is an important study to be written of the fluctuating relations between homosexual women and men – from the early days of the movement, when 'gay' was understood to embrace both, to the often bitter struggles around sexism. I can't do justice here to the full range of lesbian activisms that emerged in this period; some women even made attempts to exclude all contact with men from their personal and even professional lives. Many lesbian separatists were particularly hostile to transgendered women, denying them access to what was proclaimed as women's space.[10] Only a woman with contacts in both feminist and gay circles could chronicle the full story of these movements.

The ideological separatism of the late 1970s now seems largely to have disappeared, even if the worlds of homosexual women and men still remain separate for most purposes. Indeed, even during a period marked by bitter divisions between women and men, some still identified a shared purpose. Elaine Noble, the first open homosexual to be elected to a state or federal office in the United States – she served in the Massachusetts state legislature from 1975 to 1979 – recalls that: 'By the early 1970s, politically oriented gay men and women began to seek out each other and formed local gay caucuses that focused on legislation within their cities and states.'[11] Such developments came a little later in Australia; looking back at the writings of the time, I am struck by the ways in which politically active lesbians constantly negotiated their relations with both gay men and straight feminists.

I suspect that, at times, we tried too hard to maintain a commonality between women and men that never really existed organically. Without resorting to biological essentialism, it is possible that female and male sexuality is sufficiently different that the apparent greater degree of bisexual desire and fantasy amongst women is not merely a product of social conditions. Simone de Beauvoir remarked that, for women, lesbianism can be both a mode of flight from her situation or a means of accepting it.[12]

With the growth of feminism, different spaces opened up in which women could express themselves sexually that had no true equivalents for men, while men had access to a growing range of sex-on-premises venues that had no real counterparts in either the lesbian or heterosexual worlds. Occasional attempts to hold women's nights in gay male saunas have had mixed results; one participant complained to me that the women who showed up were more interested in the sandwiches than the sex. It is also true that the priorities for gay women and men often diverged: male homosexuality was criminalised, while lesbian behaviour was not, and the dominance of AIDS from the mid-1980s meant that men became caught up in a major health crisis, following paths already charted by the women's (and lesbian) health movements of the 1970s, though usually without realising it.

A renewed interest in theories and politics of sexuality – which, ironically, coincided with the beginning of the AIDS epidemic – also pulled small numbers of women and men together in what were called 'the sex wars', which bitterly divided feminists around issues such as pornography, sado-masochism and sex work. I was one of a very small group of men who attended the infamous 1984 Barnard College Conference in New York on 'the scholar and the feminist', which saw very angry divisions acted out around attitudes towards sexuality, some of which continue to reverberate today. Not surprisingly, pro-sex feminists, as they saw themselves, often found staunch allies amongst gay male activists.

While the American debates were on a larger and more heated scale than in Australia, they were echoed here: one group around the magazine *Wicked Women* clashed with others such as those associated with *Lesbian News*, which at one point claimed that lesbianism means 'women-loving-women: it has nothing necessarily to do with sex'.[13] But most women were less enthusiastic about sexual 'freedom' than were the men; as Jill Matthews warned us, sex entailed obligation as well as both 'pleasure and danger', to use the term that had been the title of a famous anthology on female sexuality edited by Carole Vance.[14] Jill wrote that women were 'embedded in a network of power relations, and their position in that network is usually incoherent'.[15] Gay men, too, were often caught up in obligation, especially when seeking sexual adventure as well as maintaining long-term partnerships, but for us the illusion that sex could happen with few consequences beyond immediate gratification was very strong until the onset of AIDS.

When I came back to Australia in 1985, lesbians seemed less prominent in the AIDS response than they had been in the United States, and while there were many in the AIDS Councils that started to spring up, most played traditional female roles of carers, social workers and health providers. But during the 1980s a new willingness to work together developed, at least between activists. Lesbians became central to a number of political campaigns, such as former Mardi Gras President Susan Harben's attempt to win the inner-Sydney state seat of Bligh for the Labor Party in 1995, and often took leadership positions in community institutions. Already organisations such as Mardi Gras and the various states' rights lobbies had become determinedly 'lesbian and gay', although new battles broke out around how far they should acknowledge bisexuals and trans as separate identities. But although women were prominent as community leaders, the organisations tended to remain largely male-dominated, as was true of the community press – even when, like Melbourne's community newspaper *Brother/Sister*, it sought to signal its openness to women.

Other issues emerged as significant for lesbians, above all those of parenting and pregnancy. Even as the lesbian sex wars seemed to grab attention in the 1990s, probably many more lesbians were thinking about children than they were about leather or multiple partners. By the 1990s, about twenty per cent of women who identified as lesbians either lived with children or intended to have children.[16] Gay male couples started seeking to adopt and raise children also, but their numbers were considerably fewer.

While gay men were dealing with the complications of safe sex and HIV infection, many lesbians were fighting for access to reproductive technologies that would allow them to bear and raise children. There is a large literature around the complexities of assisted reproductive technology, and the ways in which it has been significant in breaking down assumptions about the relationship between heterosexual coupling and parenting, which goes beyond the scope of this book. Gay liberation had not paid much attention to how families might be reconstituted if homosexuality became acceptable, other than to speak in vague, utopian terms of new sorts of communal living and child-rearing arrangements. But during the 1980s new critiques of hegemonic family structures developed, usually initiated by lesbians, which in turn began to be reflected in writings such as Kath Weston's *Families We Choose* (1991) and, in Australia, a collection edited by two Sydney lesbian poets and activists, Louise Wakeling and Margaret Bradstock, *Beyond Blood* (1995).[17]

Margaret's and Louise's story is particularly interesting, as it brings together a number of themes: women in heterosexual marriages with children who build new partnerships with other women, the beginnings of artificial insemination as a way of women having children independently of a male partner, and the involvement of gay men as potential partners at a time when HIV was becoming a serious concern.[18] Over the 1990s the idea of same-sex parents started to move from the almost unimaginable to the merely unusual, and by the 2000s it had entered mainstream popular culture through television shows like *Modern Family* and the film *The Kids Are All Right*. The possibility of infection by HIV clearly complicated the role of gay men as sperm donors, but now that sperm donations are legal, advertisements for 'the ultimate altruistic gift' are reappearing in the gay media.

Rather than a linear development, the history of interaction between lesbians and gay men is a complex set of moves, rather like an intricate board game. For different individuals – often, indeed, for the same individuals at different times of their lives – similarities or differences could loom as more important. In the same way, the tension between working within or without the system is not easily resoluble. The tendency towards a new coalition across gender has been most marked in recent years by the same-sex marriage campaign, which by its nature de-emphasises any difference between homosexual and heterosexual relations, and thereby avoids many of the sex debates that had previously divided women and men. Indeed, proponents of same-sex marriage now extol monogamy in ways that would have shocked most early gay liberationists.

Perhaps the sharpest sexual debates among feminists have revolved around sex work, an area in which Australia took a very different path to that of the United States or some European nations such as Sweden. While even leftist historians of social movements usually ignore sex work, or accept the particular feminist line that defines it as inevitably a product of patriarchal oppression, some feminists have seen the prosecution of people – usually women – for selling sex as a similar infringement of human rights to that of the anti-sodomy laws.

'Prostitution' had been outlawed in all Australian jurisdictions through a variety of British-derived laws, with some exceptions, such as the tolerance for brothels in the mining town of Kalgoorlie. Growing concern about police corruption and some changes in attitudes led to debates about decriminalisation from the 1970s on, often aimed at removing street prostitution in favour of regulating it through brothels and massage parlours. The situation varies from state to state, but a system of legalisation rather than decriminalisation now operates in the larger states, meaning that sex work is highly regulated. Sex workers can avoid penalties only by operating in quite specific ways; for example, Victoria requires them to operate in licensed brothels, and they are subject to certain forms of mandatory testing.

While some feminists hailed any moves that would reduce harassment and danger for sex workers, others believed that nothing short of total prohibition – with the buyer rather than the seller criminalised, as would become the case in Sweden – would address the issue satisfactorily. Women who disclose as sex workers often face considerable hostility from feminists and lesbian communities. While sex worker movements have usually included men, the feminist debates are largely oblivious to the existence of homosexual sex work, and generally ignore – or are too embarrassed to mention – the existence of heterosexual male sex work, which is often connected with tourism in poorer countries, with 'beach boys' making themselves available to wealthy female tourists. Australians have been particularly prominent in building international networks of sex work advocates, which may reflect our somewhat less repressive laws, compared to those of most countries.

Of course, the majority of commercial exchanges for sexual favours are not declared as 'sex work'. There is a refreshing lack of hypocrisy in a movement that declares that some people will always want to sell and buy sex, and that this should be recognised – and that the safety of workers and clients should be properly recognised and the workers recompensed. A great deal of commercial sex does not involve intercourse – think of lap dancing or erotic massage – but it can still provide instant intimacy without obligation, which, with a mutual understanding between worker and client, can be of enormous benefit. The sex worker movement deserves considerable praise for its consistent pressure to create awareness of what is a reality in virtually all contemporary societies, and for its attacks on the mindless rhetoric that confuses consensual exchanges of sex for money with the worst abuses of 'sex trafficking'.

As I have already mentioned, data suggests that more women than men are comfortable with sexual fluidity, but also that they are less dependent on commercial venues for sex and company. There are few places in the world where homosexual women are more visible than men, which does not mean there are fewer women who are attracted to and form relationships with other women. But it does mean that the social and political expressions of homosexuality remain different for women and men, and there are therefore limits to their common interests. At queer film festivals, despite their inclusive titles, it is striking how many audiences are almost entirely gendered, depending on what film is showing, and organisers generally recognise this by creating simultaneous 'boys' and 'girls' programs.

The lesbian world has been affected by a similar growth of consumerism and affluence to that which has marked the male world, and in the eyes of many older radical lesbians, this means that younger women are no longer at the cutting edge of rethinking gender and politics. Certainly, the gap between the womyn's festivals of the 1970s and a sleek party event such as Aqua Girl, Miami Beach – 'At Aqua Girl there is something for everyone, from dance parties, to comedy shows, to live music, to pool parties, to a bowlathon, a jazz brunch, dine-out event, vip reception, an art show to celebrity meet and greets and so much more' – seems striking.

Nonetheless, even party lesbians seem to have a very different view of sexuality to men. For the 2012 Mardi Gras, for instance, there were flyers around Sydney advertising Dirty Talk – 'a party for girls who do girls' – with no suggestion that this would be more than a hot evening of hip hop and dancing. An equivalent male event would almost certainly feature a back room for instant sex.

Some of the issues that sexual radicals raised thirty years ago seem to have largely evaporated. Debates over the morality of sadomasochistic role play, for example, are no longer particularly salient – and in fact this seems to have become a staple of heterosexual fantasy, if we can read anything into the extraordinary success of the novel *Fifty Shades of Grey*. Pornography by and for lesbians is made by small groups of enterprising women, but it remains a tiny sliver of the enormous pornography market, and most porn involving women having sex together continues to be aimed at heterosexual male fantasies.

While HIV has been responsible for an enormous boom in researching male homosexual behaviours, there has been remarkably little research about lesbian behaviour or social and commercial networks. Increasingly, however, younger queers mix socially across gender lines, often sharing houses and going out together, and women direct many of the major queer festivals. Maybe a new form of coalition is developing that in some ways harks back to the early days of gay liberation.

THE 1980S: HIV/AIDS AND WORKING INSIDE THE SYSTEM

It is impossible to reflect on the homosexual world over the past quarter-century without mention of HIV/AIDS, just as it is impossible to discuss the global epidemic without acknowledging the extent to which our perceptions of what is not predominantly a 'gay disease' remains marked by its particular connection with male homosexuality, even in countries in which HIV transmission occurs primarily through heterosexual intercourse or shared needles.

The first diagnosis of what was briefly called 'gay-related immune deficiency syndrome' came in 1981, when otherwise healthy young homosexual men in Los Angeles presented with cases of Kaposi's sarcoma, a cancer previously associated with the elderly and infirm. Gradually, news spread through community networks that a new disease was threatening gay men, whom the first reports linked with haemophiliacs, needle users and, at least in the United States, Haitian immigrants. It took several years for it to become clear that whatever caused the new disease was spread through intimate contact, and passed through blood and semen. HIV, the retrovirus that causes the collapse of the immune system, was formally identified in 1983 by scientists working at the Pasteur Institute in Paris.

Of course, HIV was not confined to homosexual men. Globally, as became apparent in the latter 1980s, its greatest impact was in eastern and southern Africa, where the primary route of infection was through heterosexual contact. This is not the place for a full history of the epidemic, which has been told elsewhere,[1] but rather for reflection on how it affected the changing perceptions and understandings of homosexuality. HIV spread through sexual networks, but so too did advocacy and care, and across the world gay communities were the basis for early responses to the disease. The initial reactions, a compound of denial and ignorance, gave way to a sense of shared responsibility, as large numbers of gay men and lesbians, along with heterosexual friends, signed up to become carers and peer educators in a remarkable display of communal altruism.

In the first years of the epidemic, when I was still living in New York, awareness, fear and denial spread simultaneously through the networks of gay men that had been forged over the previous decade. The first organisations that developed to fight the new disease grew out of the gay community: Gay Men's Health Crisis (GMHC) in New York, and the Terrence Higgins Trust in London. I recall an early attempt to raise funds for GMHC in the gay summer resorts of Fire Island, where most of the men going to the famous late afternoon tea dance avoided any contact with the handful of activists rattling cans for donations. Some men and a few women threw themselves into the new organisations, while others withdrew from the homosexual world altogether, even leaving the larger cities for the imagined safety of small towns. I first became involved in the response to AIDS, like many gay men in that period, because of my personal fears and anxieties, then through knowing people who fell ill, and then as a writer and activist.

As increasing numbers of young men sickened and began to die, the experience of AIDS reinforced a sense among many gay men that their lives didn't matter; as one activist remarked to me, we looked after ourselves because no one else would. This was the message of

Larry Kramer's play *The Normal Heart*, which was first produced in New York's Public Theatre in 1985 and became a symbol of gay anger and frustration at neglect by the larger world and apparent indifference even within the gay community. Kramer had a long history of both leading and attacking his community, and his demands for sexual restraint had first surfaced before HIV, in his novel *Faggots* (1978). That book outraged many for its attacks on promiscuity – the Oscar Wilde Bookstore in New York refused to carry it – but a decade later the world had changed. Kramer would become one of the most contentious figures in the AIDS world, prone to attack his allies even more fervently than he attacked his enemies, but his influence on American AIDS activism was remarkable, both as a writer and as a founder of GMHC and, later, ACT UP.

Before ACT UP grabbed media attention for a few years in the early 1990s, the epidemic saw a remarkable burst of creative energy, as thousands of people established organisations designed to educate, lobby and provide care and support for people with HIV. Often this meant hands-on care, with the training of 'buddies' (the term used by GMHC) to help care for people with AIDS, who did everything from shopping and cleaning to being there when pain and dementia drove family and friends away. Adam Mars-Jones gives a sardonic picture of a 'buddy' from the point of view of the man with AIDS in his 1987 story *Slim*, while David Leavitt wrote a story based upon falling in love with someone to whom he was delivering meals as a volunteer.[2]

In the United States, where the Reagan Administration seemed remarkably unconcerned by the threat of the new epidemic, it was largely the gay community that lobbied consistently and successfully for attention, research and funding – which reinforced the myth that AIDS was inexorably linked to homosexuality. Similar mobilisation occurred across the western world, and in a few countries – notably Denmark, Switzerland, the Netherlands and, to our surprise, Australia – governments not only saw the need to respond to the disease, but did so by working directly with gay community organisations, as well as with representatives of sex workers and injecting drug users.

The first diagnosis of AIDS in Australia came at the very end of 1982, and the first community organisations were established in Sydney and Melbourne in 1983. The early cases appeared slowly; I remember one woman, a volunteer with one of the first support groups, telling me ruefully that her group was trained to provide care but had no one yet to care for. Of course, that changed by the late 1980s, and for over a decade my life revolved around the micro-politics of an epidemic that was sweeping through my community, with very little real impact on the larger society.

Even so, the early years of the epidemic saw extraordinary scare stories around AIDS, which simultaneously demonised homosexuals and portrayed the disease as an imminent threat to everyone. 'Society in AIDS Crisis' trumpeted the front page of the Melbourne *Sun* in August 1985. Perhaps the lowest point came when the federal leader of the National Party, Ian Sinclair, linked the death of three babies from infected blood transfusions to the ruling Labor Party because it had 'encouraged homosexuality'.

For several years panic produced large numbers of irrational cases of discrimination against men perceived as homosexual, fed particularly by some religious figures who invoked the wrath of God.[3] AIDS was apparently divine punishment for the sin of homosexuality. (Some American religious figures later claimed to explain the terror attacks of September 11, 2001, in much the same way.) For a short time the hysteria around the new disease prompted the two major domestic airlines to ban travel by HIV-positive people, and as late as 1989 a survey of GPs suggested that a quarter did not want to treat people with AIDS. Leadership from community, some key medical figures and government turned these attitudes around, leading to a response that, as the historian Paul Sendziuk has argued, was based on an ability to trust.[4]

In Australia the epidemic brought forth a maturity in policy-making that few would have predicted, which led to the decriminalisation of sex work and the establishment of needle exchanges in ways matched only by a few European countries at that time. It was possible – indeed,

I experienced this – to sit between an archbishop and a sex worker at national advisory committee meetings. Partnerships such as this were far less likely in the United States, where a combination of resurgent right-wing rhetoric and deep religiosity meant a profound discomfort in directly dealing with those most vulnerable to HIV.

In fact, Australia managed to harness the scares around AIDS, in particular through the infamous 'Grim Reaper' ads in 1987, which portrayed a gothic figure of death striking men, women and children dead with bowling balls as they stood like tenpins. The campaign was misleading, in that it implied a much broader vulnerability to HIV infection than was the case, but it did bring a shift in attitudes, as the worst sort of homophobic sensationalism seemed to decline thereafter.

At first, the connection between AIDS and homosexuals threatened to undermine all the gains that seemed to have been made by the gay movement over the previous two decades. Some commentators and politicians used the epidemic to attack any acceptance of homosexuality, believing it responsible for the new epidemic. 'Did homosexual activists deliberately poison Australia's blood supply?' asked one article, written by a philosopher who went on to become vice-chancellor of Central Queensland University.[5] A *Four Corners* program on AIDS in 1987 drew responses such as this from Liberal MP Jim Cameron (against whom CAMP had demonstrated fifteen years earlier), who complained that he was prevented from making 'a forthright defence of the orthodox majority regarding its need for insulation from the entwined threats of AIDS and homosexuality'.[6]

A combination of effective and largely bipartisan political leadership and a savvy gay movement meant such attacks had remarkably little traction, and indeed both Queensland and Western Australia decriminalised homosexuality in the late 1980s, leaving Tasmania as the only state to resist these changes. (New Zealand had decriminalised in 1986, after a major political battle.) While they were not much commented upon, except in the gay press, the West Australian changes of 1989 were deeply discriminatory, with an age of consent of twenty-one and a provision that made it illegal 'to promote or encourage homosexual behaviour'.[7] It was not until this century that the state included homosexuality in the provisions of its anti-discrimination laws.

AIDS both legitimised and changed the nature of the 'gay community', as it had developed up to the 1980s. Indeed, the Australian author Michael Hurley has claimed that: 'We might also say that what died with AIDS was the notion of an authentic gayness, if by that is meant a single, fixed way of being gay.'[8] Michael's comment presumes a monolithic understanding pre-AIDS, which seems overly romantic, but against expectations the tragedy of AIDS has, overall, contributed to the mainstreaming of gay life, which in turn has meant the decline of sexuality as a master identity.

As AIDS became the dominant issue for gay men and mobilised increasing government and private attention and resources, it also complicated relations between women and men, with some lesbians becoming leaders in the new movements but others expressing resentment at the emphasis on one issue. Ironically, many of the demands of AIDS activists echoed feminist analyses of the health system, as gay men came into contact with similar problems of medical hierarchy and financial constraints that women had long experienced. Unlike in the United States, most of the women who became leaders of the Australian AIDS movement were probably heterosexual, and there remains a lingering bitterness amongst some older lesbians that AIDS activists seemed to ignore the heavy rates of fatal breast cancer.

But AIDS also meant a shift in how we imagined the possibilities of working within the state. For gay men, the tragedy of an epidemic opened up the sort of possibilities women had found through affirmative action and state services, and many gay activists moved slowly from street activism through organisation-building into positions within large community bodies, and government and international agencies. In health departments, in development agencies, in a few research centres, even in some small areas of the United Nations, it became possible to build a career out of one's involvement in the gay world. Because of the Health Minister, Neal Blewett, his advisor Bill Bowtell and a few determined politicians on both sides of politics, Australia in the 1980s pioneered a partnership between government, community and researchers that has endured, although it has changed somewhat as the partners have become institutionalised and, to some extent, ossified. One consequence of the government's early funding decisions was an expansion of biomedical and social research on HIV, in which Australia continues to play a significant role.

Blewett visited San Francisco in early 1985, and returned determined to develop a policy that embraced the affected communities – a policy that even as conservative a politician as Tony Abbott (who was Minister for Health from 2003 to 2007) was not prepared to fully abandon. Blewett's own account of the period makes clear just how significant good political leadership can be. 'Prejudice is always present in any community,' he wrote, 'but it only becomes dangerous to marginalised groups if the prejudices are made respectable by political elites.'[9]

Thus, AIDS produced a new integration into the state, but at the same time reinvigorated a sense of community and political organising amongst gay men. Lex Watson, the central figure in the Sydney gay movement for several decades, wrote to me at the beginning of 1985 that:

> The community, we all, are growing up so fast. I don't mean just the sobering effect of relatively young men suddenly having to come to terms with mortality and death, though that is slowly but surely starting to happen around some quarters, but more the overnight maturity of people taking on roles and responsibilities, thinking about structures and issues, developing ways of handling organisational conflicts which was virtually inconceivable even three years ago.[10]

The 1980s were times of great sorrow and considerable jubilation; as I write this, I have flashbacks of both. I remember the first time I visited someone with HIV in hospital, a former student from the University of California, Santa Cruz, who was bitter and in pain, facing death before he had really faced life. But I also remember the extraordinary sense of togetherness of the early days of the Victorian AIDS Council, in which I was immersed for the second half of the decade, the endless meetings and the rural retreats at which relationships were forged around a remarkable sense of shared urgency and commitment.[11] Hundreds of people, mainly gay men, committed themselves to caring for strangers, and peer support and home care was particularly important for men who had lost contact with – and, in some cases, any support from – their biological families.

Within a few years, people living with HIV and AIDS (the original term was 'People with AIDS' or 'PWAs') were declaring their status publicly, a move based on the earlier idea of coming out, and taking over leadership of the AIDS movement, demanding that they be seen as prime stakeholders and experts rather than as patients and subjects.

By the time of the Third National Conference on AIDS, which took place in Hobart in 1988, the Australian PWA movement was loud and visible. That conference was particularly memorable for the homophobic prejudices of then opposition health spokesman, Wilson Tuckey, who claimed that 'AIDS is very much a disease that results from deliberate and possibly unnatural activities'.[12] Tuckey was replaced in his position some months later.

The Final Victory of Law Reform

The 1988 conference was important, as well, in drawing national attention to resistance within Tasmania to the decriminalisation of homosexuality, which increasingly seemed both archaic and inimical to the basic tenets of public health. I went to Hobart for that conference and was impressed by the two remarkable leaders of the Tasmanian campaign, Rodney Croome and Nick Toonen, both aged in their twenties, and by the bravery they demonstrated in coming out in a state whose entire population was less than that of a few suburban councils in Sydney or Melbourne, and where there was an articulate homophobic movement. Soon after the conference a law reform stall was set up at the famous Salamanca Markets, on Hobart's waterfront, which the city council moved to ban. 'It is right,' said the Lord Mayor, 'for there to be one law for heterosexuals and one law for homosexuals.'[13] The rules governing the markets required that anyone who persisted in staffing the stall should be arrested, and over a period of some months over 100 people were arrested and charged with trespass.

The Lord Mayor's comments seemed mild when compared with the vitriol that was unleashed during the debates across Tasmania, and it is unclear why such deep hostility was expressed there when other states had already decriminalised without much concern. From March 1989, when a small demonstration for law reform took place in the north-west town of Burnie, the Tasmanian activists confronted extraordinary prejudice, hatred and real danger. Several attempts to change the law were blocked by an obdurate (and unrepresentative) Legislative Council, Tasmania's upper house, and a small group of activists succeeded in bringing the issue into the public arena.

They decided on an innovative strategy, which was to appeal to the United Nations Human Rights Committee, possible only because the federal Labor government had signed a protocol allowing citizens to follow this route once all domestic avenues had been exhausted. Nick Toonen would eventually become the victorious plaintiff in what was a ground-breaking case in international law, and one that remains a benchmark for international attempts to overturn laws prohibiting consensual homosexual activity. In 1994, in the case *Toonen vs. Australia*, the Human Rights Committee held that the references to 'sex' in Article 2, paragraph 1 (non-discrimination) and paragraph 26 (equality before the law) of the International Covenant on Civil and Political Rights should be taken to include sexual orientation. Thus, the Human Rights Committee created a precedent within the UN human rights system, although it has not extended it universally.

Six months after the UN Commission's decision, the Australian government invoked its external affairs powers to prevent 'arbitrary interference' with any consenting sexual act between people aged over eighteen, but the Tasmanian government remained obdurate. At this point, Nick and Rodney, along with several others, sought to test the law by demanding they be prosecuted for unlawful intercourse, but the Tasmanian Department of Public Prosecutions refused to do so. The need to publicly declare their sexual relationship – which, ironically, was then ending – was an extremely confronting act for both men; as Rodney said a few years later, it was an action that confronted not just the law but also a set of 'much more profound, irrational fears'.[14]

Three years later, the Tasmanian parliament finally decriminalised homosexual behaviour. Tasmania has subsequently become a leader in supporting gay and lesbian rights, with Premier Lara Giddings introducing legislation to recognise same-sex marriage in 2012. That legislation was defeated in Tasmania's upper house, but it was the first of similar moves within several state parliaments, although any successful state law would be open to challenge as being overridden by existing federal legislation.

Why has homosexuality aroused such passions in Tasmania? There have been a number of claims for Tasmanian exceptionalism, which are often linked to its convict history and low rates of population growth in the past century. I have never believed this, and indeed when I wrote *The Comfort of Men*, which grew out of the fantasy of a fictitious Tasmanian independence movement, my thesis was that Tasmania was essentially much more like the rest of Australia than either its supporters or detractors believed. Certainly, its small size and relatively few non-British immigrants were factors, but similar conditions are found in many regional areas of Australia. Indeed, the greatest difference may have been the power of the unrepresentative Legislative Council, which blocked law reform for years. A similarly constituted upper house in Queensland – which is unique amongst Australian states in having only one chamber – could easily have produced a similar impasse.

The Tasmanian law reform campaign was the last significant moment in Australian history when hostility to homosexuality was politically important. (Before the proponents of gay marriage scream, be reassured that I shall return to this issue.) This is quite unlike what happened in the United States, where debates around the legitimacy of homosexuality remained an issue of mainstream contention for much longer, with powerful lobbies mobilising voters against anything perceived as acceptance of 'sexual deviance'.

In 1992, and with relatively little public fuss, the Australian government decided to end discrimination against homosexuals in the military. Cabinet was divided – the first attempt, in June, led by Attorney-General Michael Duffy, failed, but cabinet returned to the question in November and, with the support of Prime Minister Paul Keating and a number of senior ministers, the change was made.[15] Despite concerns from the Liberal/National opposition of the time, the policies were not reversed when the Howard government came to power.

The fight over law reform in Tasmania was in some ways a harbinger of what would occur in an increasing number of countries, as the public health imperatives of preventing the spread of HIV clashed with ignorance, prejudice and denial. The continuing illegality of homosexuality in many countries remains a major barrier to effective prevention – and a contributing factor to the high rates of infection amongst homosexual men.[16]

AIDS Activism, AIDS Professionalism

A new phase of AIDS activism began with ACT UP, which exploded from its origins in New York in 1987, fuelled by apparent inaction and disinterest from government.* ACT UP borrowed some of its tactics from the street radicalism of the early 1970s, but it was infused with the desperate anger that came from increasing numbers of young people that were either dead or dying, apparently without concern from the larger world: thus the slogan, which still appears on T-shirts, 'Silence Equals Death'.

---

* ACT UP stood for 'AIDS Coalition To Unleash Power'.

ACT UP came to Australia with an American accent, but groups soon developed in Melbourne and Sydney from 1990 on, fuelled by frustration at the slowness of drug approvals and, I suspect, a more general anger that what was a crisis for those immediately affected seemed to be of so little concern to the larger society. The combination of fearless commitment and imagination meant that a small group of people were capable of staging dramatic protests, which helped push AIDS somewhat higher on the agenda of government action than might otherwise have been the case. Incidents such as the 'defacement' of the famous floral clock in Melbourne's Botanical Gardens, when flowers were replaced with small crosses signifying death, were guaranteed to attract press attention, even if it was largely unsympathetic. Equally, ACT UP created a sense of community and support amongst its members, many of whom were dying, and worked 'to support those AIDS activists who were on the inside, sitting on committees and advising the government'.[17] I was one such person.

The toughest period for those of us living in the rich world was the early 1990s, when the first generation of AIDS drugs promised false hope and the gay newspapers were filled with obituaries of men in what should have been the prime of their life. By the end of 1997, over 5000 deaths from AIDS had been registered in Australia, overwhelmingly among gay men. That period is caught particularly well in William Yang's extended monologue with slides, *Sadness* (1992),[18] and in Tim Conigrave's memoir *Holding the Man* (1995), one of a number of books that reflected the experiences of disease and death amongst young men. Conigrave died in 1994, before the development of effective AIDS treatments, and two years later Robert Dessaix published his novel *Night Letters*, which speaks of his HIV far more indirectly, through letters written by an Australian travelling through Europe after he has been diagnosed with an incurable disease.

Those who were not infected – or who lived long enough to benefit from more effective drug therapies, which were able to control if not eradicate the virus – were also deeply affected. While HIV was always most concentrated amongst homosexual men in Australia, the bestselling memoir of the period was Bryce Courtenay's *April Fool's Day*, written about his adult son, who had died after receiving an infected blood transfusion.[19]

The impact of AIDS on the generation of men who lived through its first decades was permanent, and it has created a gap in experience between us and younger gay men. For many of us, it has meant a hollowing-out of our own intimate worlds, as lovers and friends died. For much of the 1990s Paris was for me a painful vacuum, as almost everyone I had known well in my halcyon days there at the end of the 1970s, including one lover, was dead from HIV. Even today I am conscious of how much smaller is my social world than it might have been, had so many of my generation not died; Facebook too often brings news of yet another person who died too young. There are, of course, many men far younger than me who are positive (although the belief that young men are particularly vulnerable is, at least in Australia, a myth), and their experiences of coming to terms with HIV are often painful and complex, despite the medical advances that have been made.

The radicalism of the early 1990s was fuelled by anger, rather than the youthful exuberance of gay liberation. As large numbers of people were dying from AIDS, there was growing anger, which sometimes morphed into militancy but was sometimes expressed through outbursts against other parts of the AIDS community, as when a couple of disgruntled activists threw bricks through the windows of the Victorian AIDS Council. There were communal expressions to mourn the losses of the epidemic, such as the Memorial Quilt, which began in San Francisco in 1985, and the Candlelight Vigils, also an American import, but often men – and in Australia they were overwhelmingly men – died alone, unreconciled to their families and without any acknowledgment of their sexuality.

Sometimes there were large and moving funeral ceremonies, but often men were buried almost in silence by estranged families who sought to cover up the cause of death – as is true even today of many people who die of AIDS in parts of Africa and South Asia. In his still moving article about the impact of the epidemic, Douglas Crimp wrote in 1989 of the mood amongst gay men:

> Frustration, anger, rage, and outrage, anxiety, fear, and terror, shame and guilt, sadness and despair – it is not surprising that we feel these things: what is surprising is that we often don't ... To decry these responses – our own form of moralism – is to deny the extent of the violence we have all endured; even more importantly, it is to deny a fundamental fact of psychic life: violence is often self-inflicted.[20]

Small events could trigger paranoia, fear and anger, reminding us of the extent to which homophobia and fear of a new disease were intertwined in the public imagination. In 1989 I spent a day with friends in Montreal, who had decided to drive across the border into Vermont. At the border, US immigration authorities stopped us, suspicious of four presumably gay men – one of whom was bald, for reasons of fashion rather than health. The authorities carefully inspected his scalp, were deeply concerned that another in the group was carrying information literature on AIDS, but finally and reluctantly conceded that they could not diagnose our HIV status on sight and let us through. The United States would retain bans on the entry of people with HIV until 2010, despite a consensus among public health officials that the ban served no purpose.

As with every phase of activism, AIDS activism had its casualties, people who became so caught up in their passion and anger that their own lives derailed. Some people with AIDS were veterans of the gay movement and became leaders of the new activism; this was true of my own friends Terry Bell and John Lee, who had been comrades in early gay liberation. Another friend, Vito Russo, the American film historian, followed a similar itinerary, now captured in both a biography[21] and the film *Vito*. Others who had not been political were radicalised through their experiences of the epidemic, while some of the men who were caught up in activism were infected relatively late, and had to negotiate the painful transition from being advocates for others to becoming those for whom they had been fighting. Other gay men who remained negative seemed to have become emotionally cauterised, permanently scarred by the deaths of so many of their friends and lovers.

By the time of the 1996 Vancouver International AIDS Conference, scientists were speaking about 'triple therapy combination' and 'protease inhibitors', which promised to turn AIDS into a chronic rather than a life-threatening condition, and suddenly there was a sharp decline in the death notices in gay papers across the rich world. From the latter part of the 1990s, the anger that had fuelled ACT UP started to dissipate in rich countries after rapid developments in antiretroviral therapies, and it would be replaced by new forms of activism in resource-poor countries, above all South Africa. The combination of a genuine pandemic and a government that first prevaricated and then, under President Thabo Mbeki, denied that HIV was the underlying cause of AIDS – and thus rejected expanding coverage of antiretroviral therapies – created huge anger amongst large numbers of South Africans. The experience of organising within South African civil society, dating back to the anti-apartheid struggles, and the political space for protest created the most significant and inclusive AIDS movement in the world. Over time, the Treatment Action Campaign was able to bring about reversals in policy – especially after 2008, when Mbeki was replaced by President Jacob Zuma.

For gay men in the rich world, the African AIDS pandemic had unsettling echoes. On several trips to South Africa I found myself walking through the streets of Durban or Cape Town, where one in three or four adults were HIV-positive, and I was eerily reminded of the gay areas of Sydney or San Francisco a decade earlier. That extraordinary woman Noerine Kaleeba, one of the founders of Uganda's major AIDS organisation, once told me of visiting San Francisco and noticing its parallels with Uganda. In 2003 I was at the Adelaide Festival of Ideas with the Botswanan novelist and judge Unity Dow, who spoke of the stream of funerals her mother was attending, almost all from AIDS, though this was rarely acknowledged.

The AIDS epidemic would become my path into 'gay Asia', as almost by accident I became involved in several of the founding networks of people starting to build responses in South East Asia. The Australian government provided small amounts of funding for emerging community organisations there, and some of the leaders of these groups came to Australia on study tours at the end of the 1980s. Some of the leaders from developing countries were extraordinarily inspirational, such as Dominic d'Souza, who, when he was diagnosed as positive in Goa in 1989, was incarcerated – the polite term was 'isolated' – and confined in a solitary and unsanitary former sanatorium for two months. Following his release, Dominic established India's first PWA group, despite enormous prejudice and discrimination from all levels of government; he died in 1992. At the second regional AIDS conference in Delhi in 1992, the convention centre refused to allow gay men to meet on its premises, so an informal group was held in the park across the street from the Ashok Hotel – which, ironically, was known as a cruising area for men seeking each other.

At the 1994 International AIDS Conference, held in Yokohama, a young man, Toshihiro Oishi, came out as both gay and HIV-positive on stage alongside the Crown Prince of Japan; that was bravery of a sort that the current round of entertainers who proclaim their sexuality well into mid-career cannot emulate. I remember going back to my hotel that evening and seeing Oishi's image on channel after channel as I surfed through the television in my tiny bedroom. By 2012, in a sign of how rapidly things have changed, the Global Forum on MSM and HIV was able to hold a welcome reception for delegates to the International AIDS Conference in the ornate headquarters of the World Bank in Washington DC.

The historical accident that allowed me to combine activism and an academic career, which I shared with a few others of my generation, has become more difficult in the contemporary world. Now that AIDS has become an industry, with its community organisations staffed largely by full-time professionals, there is decreasing room for what Gramsci would have called 'organic intellectuals' – people who are able, through a knowledge of both theory and lived experience, to articulate a particular critique that goes beyond either academic convention or the rhetoric of special groups.

In rich countries with good health systems – to which the United States remains the great exception – the great majority of people with HIV now live largely normal lives on increasingly sophisticated drug regimes, which ensure that AIDS has become a manageable condition, if not yet a curable one. But this does not mean the stigma or psychological distress associated with HIV has disappeared.

Overall, the response to AIDS in Australia has been a remarkable display of partnership between researchers, health professionals, the gay community and government. More effectively than most countries, this partnership has limited new infections and provided good care to almost everyone in need. But the partnership is also fragile; when a conservative government was re-elected in Queensland in 2012, it quickly moved to defund the Queensland Association for Healthy Communities (the former AIDS Council) because it was seen as too much of an advocacy body.

At the same time, the epidemic has created its own closed, corporatist world of AIDS professionals, which reminds me of the comment (I think made by the troglodyte American commentator William F Buckley) that every great issue begins as a cause, becomes a movement and ends as a cabal. The energy and enthusiasm that mobilised thousands of people in the early days of the crisis has largely given way, perhaps inevitably, to a highly organised industry, which acts as both effective pressure group and service provider. One of the lessons I have learnt from AIDS is that people acting out of the best of motives can do great damage, not least because of the strength of their convictions. There is little room in the AIDS world for people who disagree with the current consensus, and too often personal ambition and altruistic commitment are confused.

The world of AIDS has become one in which celebrities are seen as central spokespeople; when Australia hosted a regional conference in Melbourne in 2001, one of my roles was to act as escort to one of the Queens of Bhutan (there were then four, all sisters), as well as a number of 'first wives', some from countries with rather dubious governments. As former Victorian premier Joan Kirner observed, none of the women who were being featured in a special session had been elected to anything.

The International AIDS Conference has become a massive trade fair, drawing over 20,000 people, including activists, researchers and officials – and enough pharmaceutical display stands that a smart conference-goer quickly learns where to get the best free cappuccinos and ice-cream. When I asked some former activists who are now working for state governments why they wanted to host the International AIDS Conferences in Australia, the responses were largely couched in statements about what it would do for the government and tourism, not about how it might actually affect the larger global struggle to contain the epidemic. Increasingly, community-based AIDS organisations see themselves as service-providers, with less and less of an organic connection to the communities they claim to serve.

& Sex

There is probably no ontological reason why HIV spread to the western world at a point in history when there was an explosion of sex venues for gay men, accompanied by an ideology of sexual adventure and frequent 'tricking' – instant sexual hook-ups, often in semi-public spaces. The impact of gay liberation was to unleash libidos in ways that had not been possible for most men before then, because they lacked the space for multiple sexual partners within safe (if not always clean) environments.[22] As one of the founders of the People Living with AIDS movement, singer Michael Callen (who died from AIDS in 1993), said: 'Every time I threw my legs in the air it was a blow for sexual freedom. Now I'm dying from it.' Michael had dragged me with him on a visit to one of Manhattan's dingier homosexual saunas, where he was trying to insist that the management promote safe sex at a time when the use of condoms and lube still seemed unnecessary to many.

The 1980s saw considerable bitterness as gay men both recognised and denied the implications of the new disease for our newly won sexual freedoms. In the very early stages of the epidemic, there was confusion and naivety, as a variety of reasons – too many drugs, pre-existing sexually transmitted infections, 'lifestyle' – were all blamed or ignored as possible factors in infection. Once it was established that HIV was the cause of AIDS, and that it could effectively be avoided through the use of condoms and appropriate lubricants, prevention efforts could be targeted, and most men in the gay world adapted accordingly.

Indeed, much of the early work of the Australian AIDS Councils was around the promotion of 'safe sex', which led to occasional clashes with governments as graphic materials were produced to encourage men to use condoms when fucking. A lot of this work took place within gay venues, where 'safe-sex sluts' distributed condoms and information; more difficult were attempts to reach men whose sex lives took place outside defined 'gay spaces'. In 1988 the Tasmanian and Queensland governments ordered the withdrawal of a brochure, headlined 'Safe', which they claimed was indecent, and even the progressive Victorian Labor government objected to the production of a poster entitled 'Two Boys Kissing'. But in general Australians accepted that frankness about sexual practices was preferable to spreading infection; I still recall an early AIDS Conference at which Ita Buttrose – perhaps the best known woman in Australia at the time, and someone who would play a leadership role as chair of the National Advisory Committee on AIDS in the 1980s – sat polishing her nails while listening to a discussion of the possible dangers of anal sex. AIDS opened the way for condoms to be advertised on television, and for them to become part of the apparatus of at least a certain amount of homosexual pornography.

While Australians seemed to adjust quickly to the new imperatives, this was certainly not the case universally. I remember being in Paris in the late 1980s, when sex venues continued to thrive without any sign of the sort of prevention information and interventions already common in Australia; some French radicals insisted that 'safer sex' – the term usually used in the United States – was another sign of American moralism. Despite a few tentative moves, the dominant Australian policy was to keep sex venues open and use them as sites for prevention outreach, although some American cities, notably New York and San Francisco, reacted to the epidemic by closing such premises.

In North America and Australia men developed a whole range of new non-penetrative tactics to allow for continuing, but safe, sexual adventure. Most famous were the 'jerk-off clubs', established in a number of cities, where naked men engaged in group masturbation and body play with strict rules – sometimes patrolled by 'monitors' with torches. These allowed a sense of physical intimacy, which had become even more important because of the threat of early illness and death.[23]

One often hears comments that the impact of HIV has reduced the acceptance of sexual adventure amongst gay men, who have become more judgmental of what used to be called 'promiscuity' – a word best defined as anyone who has more sex than you. In the early days of the epidemic, some men certainly retreated from sex out of fear, and it became less acceptable to boast of orgies and multiple partners. Nevertheless, my sense is that, over time, attitudes to sex amongst gay men returned to being a celebration of constant sexual possibilities. While greater social acceptance and the push for marriage may promote ideas of monogamy, it is equally true that the internet, and locative digital technologies, with their multiple sites for instant hook-ups, have created new spaces for sexual adventure.

While heterosexual attitudes are also changing, gay men retain a rather different set of mores around sexual expression, which allow for instant connections with no expectation of anything other than a one-off sexual encounter. For heterosexual men, the equivalent is probably to visit a sex worker – and, given the ease of casual sex for homosexual men, it is interesting how much commercial gay sex flourishes, even if it is often negotiated very informally.

Sex-on-premises venues have not declined significantly over the past decade, despite the growth of internet sites. It is now possible to use a simple smartphone application to find men in one's immediate neighbourhood who are ready for instant sex, something which few women would find attractive (even though I sometimes hear them speak with envy of the possibility). Gay men still allow for sexual pleasure to occur anonymously, without conversation either before or after, even if the means for cruising are constantly changing. In short, casual sex retains a quite different resonance in the gay world to anywhere else.

The assertion of sexual pleasure, and a recognition that under some circumstances this is a very political demand, remains an ongoing legacy of gay liberation, even if it is now countered by other, more conservative and assimilationist demands.

THE QUEER MOMENT AND REBORN RADICALISM?

The April 1992 issue of *Outrage* posed a question on its cover: 'Queer, Gay or Homosexual?' The accompanying story was written by the British cultural critic Simon Watney, who pointed to the emergence of groups such as Queer Nation in the United States and Outrage in Britain as signs of a reborn activism, critical of the more accommodationist style that seemed to have taken over the lesbian and gay movement.

Interestingly, Simon read this as, in part, a generational debate, a rejection by younger 'queers' of older men and women. Indeed, there was in the flush of radical enthusiasm in that period an element of 'slaying the father', as I experienced rather unpleasantly when I was booed while speaking at a Sydney Gay Lobby dinner in April 1991. It was never clear why this incident occurred, and it probably meant no more than that a group of diners was uninterested in an after-dinner speech, but it epitomised a time in which the community was both tense and angry. There were echoes of this mood in Melbourne the following year, when drag queen Barbra Quicksand ran for state parliament as an independent and was repudiated by a number of 'community leaders', who were quickly termed 'ALP daddies'.

Perhaps unconsciously, I acted out Simon's analysis, rejecting queer as anything but useful for aesthetic reasons, and arguing strongly that it undermined the need to organise specifically around our common homosexuality. Ironically, given my own history, I was also troubled by the unproblematic import of an American fashion, which to me seemed less relevant in the local context. (Looking back, I recognise that the same could have been said of the desire to insist on a specific 'gay liberation' movement in the early 1970s, as distinct from the groupings around CAMP.)

In any case, 'queer' quickly took on a variety of uses, united by the desire to escape specific identities while retaining a sense of opposition to the dominant sexual and gender order. It remains useful for avoiding the ever-growing 'alphabet soup' terminology (usually cut back to 'LGBTI'), and it's a term that I have used throughout this book.

For a number of younger homosexual intellectuals, queer theory was an electrifying revelation, offering a new perspective from which to interpret the ways in which their sexuality intersected with broader social and cultural streams. It built on the radical ideas of gay liberation (often without acknowledgment), but melded them with other strands; post-modernism and deconstruction, were, after all, the dominant themes of the humanities in the 1990s. Steven Seidman summed up the aspirations of queer theory as seeking 'to transform homosexual theory into a general social theory or one standpoint from which to analyse social dynamics'.[1]

Now, a couple of decades later, it is easier to see that queer theory was far more useful as a theoretical and scholarly device than as an organising principle, even though the term remains in events such as queer film festivals, where it acts as a catch-all term for sexual and gender dissidence. At another level, 'queer' became a marker of a new type of social world, in which younger people who were either sexually or gender non-conformist felt comfortable socialising outside the more segregated worlds of big-city lesbian and gay life. Parties and pubs developed in which people feel less pressure to live up to any particular image of how a lesbian or a gay man or a trans person should be present themselves.

The idea that 'queer politics' could produce new and broader alliances seems to be born of the same utopian impulse as was my original formulation of 'the end of the homosexual', and to carry the same traps. As the founding manager of Melbourne's Gay Men's Health Centre (herself a 'straight' woman) pointed out, if you abandon your base in the gay community, there will be no base at all. For some, 'queer' was a term that stretched far enough to include heterosexual sadomasochists or polyamorists, thus risking the creation of a new invisibility for homosexuality through queer's claim to combine everyone who might be viewed by conventional society as perverse. One lesbian friend of mine snorts at the idea that anyone with multiple piercings should feel qualified to claim 'queerdom', irrespective of their sexuality.

At the same time, queer opened up new ways of understanding that conventional ideas of sexuality and gender could be questioned without necessarily employing the language of gay and lesbian liberation. Closely related to Judith Butler's concept of gender as performance, queer allowed us space to show the extent to which what seemed taken for granted in matters of sexuality was often less fixed than it might appear.

It was this understanding that lay behind the presentation the poet Dorothy Porter and I devised called 'Queering Agatha', in which we read Christie's novels through a queer optic; we first spoke of this at a large gathering of Sisters in Crime in Melbourne in the late 1990s. Of course, there are homosexual characters in some of Christie's novels: in *A Murder is Announced*, for instance, there is an obvious lesbian couple. In the later book *Nemesis*, a lesbian relationship lies behind the murder itself, and at least one of Christie's minor detectives, Mr Sattherwaite, cries out for a queer reading. What else is one to make of a man who 'is an admirer of Kew Gardens and was once in love in his youth', who gave 'definitely "queer" parties' and who 'had a large share of femininity'. Sattherwaite was killed off in 1936 in *Cards on the Table*, thus meeting the typical fate of homosexual characters of his era.

In most of her writings Christie seemed to echo Virginia Woolf's cry in *Orlando*: shortly after Woolf's character awakens as a woman, she writes: 'But let other pens treat of sex and sexuality; we quit such odious subjects as soon as we can.'[2] Of course, we hardly saw such subjects as odious, but 'queering' Agatha Christie's novels allowed us to speak of homosexuality in ways that suggested the fragility of conventional sexual and gender norms. Here, the term 'queer' brought together both its contemporary sexual meaning with its older sense of something that disturbs what is taken for granted.

Simultaneously, queer represented a new sort of activism, largely inspired by the impact of AIDS and an attempt to break down the stereotypes of respectable gay/lesbian leadership that seemed to have a stranglehold on the movement. Some of the problems of queer were summed up for me in the much-cited anthology of lesbian and gay studies edited by Henry Abelove, Michèle Aina Barale and David Halperin in 1993, which, despite its title, marked a shift in American academic focus towards the new 'queer studies'.[3] The first section of *The Lesbian and Gay Studies Reader* was entitled 'Politics and Representation', yet not a single selection actually dealt with mainstream political activity or institutions, nor with the lesbian and gay movements that had opened up the space for such a project. The activism of groups such as ACT UP was clearly intertwined with interest in queer theory, even if David Halperin probably exaggerated when he claimed that everyone in ACT UP carried copies of Foucault's *History of Sexuality* in their back pockets.

Arguably the high point of queer in Australia was a special issue of *Meanjin* in 1996, edited by Chris Berry and Annamarie Jagose, while Jagose went on to write perhaps the best introduction to the subject to date, *Queer Theory*, published that same year by Melbourne University Press. That book continues to be frequently cited today, and Annamarie, after some time back in her native New Zealand, now holds a senior academic position in Sydney.

At the time these publications appeared, I described queer theory as the bastard child of post-modernism and gay liberation, which was very reluctant to acknowledge its father, and I am still struck by how many contemporary queer theorists seem to have written out any discussion of the development of a gay and lesbian movement, seeming to imagine that the theory emerged as a purely intellectual exercise spawned by Michel Foucault, Judith Butler and Eve Sedgwick (this is not true of Jagose's book). It seems odd that people who see themselves as deeply radical seem so disinterested in the history of the movement that made their academic redoubt so attractive, but this seems to be the case in much contemporary queer academic writing, which sees politics as discursive rather than organisational.

The most significant impact of queer theory in Australia was probably on a small group of scholars who have worked on sexuality and gender in Asia, including Peter Jackson, Audrey Yue, Fran Martin, Mark McClelland, Mark Pendleton and Baden Offard. Australians like to claim that we 'punch above our weight', and in explorations of the diverse sexual and gender regimes in Asia this is certainly the case.

Queer theory still thrives in American universities, kept alive by a small band of journals, but it is no longer at the cutting edge of thinking about sex and gender. Indeed, it's remarkable how little impact queer theory has had on international understandings and discourses around HIV/AIDS, for instance. Much queer theory often appears to ignore the topic, as Gary Dowsett pointed out in his comparison of two European conferences, one on gay and lesbian studies in 1989 and one on homosexuality and HIV three years later.[4] As queer theory has become increasingly academic and specialised, the gap between those working on the social politics of HIV and AIDS and those working on theories of sexuality seems to have widened – although some scholars have certainly drawn on queer theory while exploring the impact of HIV, as I discuss below. It's true, too, that the fault lies equally in the difficulties of incorporating cultural critiques into the dominant discourses around the epidemic, which are increasingly defined by very biomedical models of what constitutes meaningful research.

While some of the most interesting American writing on responses to the epidemic have clearly been influenced by queer theory, this connection seems to disappear once one moves to other parts of the world. In part, this is because queer theory is extraordinarily parochial in its American-centrism, from Michael Warner's collection *Fear of a Queer Planet*, written only by North Americans, to a 2007 publication 'on writing since queer theory', which acknowledges the importance of globalisation and transnationalism but fails to go beyond North America for its contributors.[5] This is in fact a feature of most current American queer writing, which, for all its claims to transgression, is as determinedly parochial as most American scholarship.

One of the oddities of queer theory is that it is written in ways that are largely inaccessible to people unversed in its particular idiom; despite the very academic language, it often reveals the deeply personal preoccupations of the authors, through their fascination with terms such as 'abjection' and their heavy emphasis upon 'affect'. As sexuality has become an acceptable arena for scholarship, it has also been seduced by the attractions of the academically obscure, so that much of queer scholarship reminds one of medieval theology in its opacity and self-referential nature.

Outside the Anglo-American world, queer has had limited purchase, although it surfaces in a variety of ways, often as a mark of cosmopolitanism. In 2003 I attended the first (now annual) Queer Zagreb Festival, a remarkable mix of cultural and intellectual events in a city still recovering from the scars of the collapse of Yugoslavia. The conference included some remarkable people, including two young Serbian men, Bojan Đorev and Siniša Ili, who presented a performance piece, *Konstrukcija (queer) identiteta na istoku uz pomoc zapadnih (queer) slika*. This interrogated – with some irony – the use of pop (and globalised) cultural references in the 'identification and construction/ constitution of identity', and as part of this critique questioned the (largely American) concept of 'coming out', and by extension other (predominantly American) images of particular forms of gay identity that were on display at the conference. My memory is of two guys who had never lived outside Serbia but were capable of being ironic in English – an irony that indeed escaped some of the Americans present.

The organisers of Queer Zagreb expressed a desire to explore the particularities of their situation and, equally, to situate themselves within a global (essentially American) framework of queer theory. The use of the term 'queer', and the combination of theory, performance and activism, were both to some extent strategic decisions, which, through the apparently radical optic of 'queer', also provided space for people who were sympathetic to homosexual issues without wishing to declare their own sexuality. There is an irony in the way that queer simultaneously promises a radical sexual politics while denying any specific behaviours or identities, thus allowing anyone to proclaim themselves as queer, but in this case the term provided an important shelter. It did have a couple of bizarre consequences, such as the woman from Bosnia who spoke for twenty minutes about 'identity and transition' and barely mentioned homosexuality or indeed any form of sexual behaviour.

In actual fact, most of the locals spoke of 'gay and lesbian' identities, rather than 'queer' – and in private they were fairly critical of the utility of the term. Indeed, there seemed to be a de facto division: when international theory was invoked, so too was the 'q' word; when local conditions or activism was discussed, it was under the rubric 'LGBT'. Not surprisingly, the emphasis was on sexual identities rather than behaviour; the former is needed to create a political movement, the latter too easily feeds the prejudice that homosexuality is no more than a form of licentiousness. The most memorable judgment on queer came from the most distinguished of the Americans present, who commented that queer theory was invented by accident and had proved too lucrative to abandon.

Perhaps the lasting legacy of queer is that it reminds us that gender and sexuality are permeable and fluid, and it provides a corrective to the essentialism of identity politics, which deny what has been expressed through theatre, art and literature whenever there has been sufficient freedom to do so. In this sense, much of contemporary culture can easily be read as queer: think of the film *Shakespeare in Love*, of Anne Rice's iconic *Interview with the Vampire*, or the extraordinary science-fiction novels of China Miéville, all of which transcend heteronormative assumptions without being explicitly 'LGBT'. Equally, there are movies that seem best described as 'queer', such as Greg Araki's *The Living End* (1992) or Jennie Livingston's *Paris Is Burning* (1990).

In some intellectual circles, 'queer' has become a codeword for a certain sort of sensibility that recognises sex and gender as social constructions, capable of being reimagined and re-experienced in ways we have yet to discover. Indeed, 'queer' has come to signify the same sort of dissatisfaction with the sexual status quo as Susan Sontag's use of 'camp' did half a century ago.

THE EMERGENCE OF THE 'GLOBAL GAY'

*There is one small street in Tokyo's Shinjuku district which is the closest to
a recognisable gay district that one can find in Japan. I first went there in
1994, after attending the International AIDS Conference in Yokohama.
Sixteen years later, little had changed. There were more men hanging
around aimlessly than is usual on the streets of Tokyo, especially on a cold
winter's night. Almost all the gay bars remained hidden from view, and
the only recognisable gay signs were at one small shop that sold pornography
(which confirmed that there are other standards of desirable bodies to those
assumed in the west). I was taken by my host to Jannys, one of the hundreds
of tiny bars that dot the area, often with English names that make no
apparent sense.*

*Here one sees that very different ways of being homosexual exist, even
in the middle of one of the world's richest 'global cities'. The bar was no
larger than an average living room, and was filled with older men in suits,
a number of much younger men and a couple of people of indeterminate sex.
I was the only Caucasian in the room. There were four young men behind
the bar, all of whom stood when we entered, and apparently they needed our
permission to sit. One came and sat with us and offered us a menu, apparently*

of drinks. The 'menu' also contained photos and short biographies of about twenty young men, who were available for various activities both on and off the premises (there appeared to be a couple of even smaller adjoining rooms). I have seen similar menus at massage spas in Bangkok; what was unique about this one was that the men's statistics included their blood groups, which was apparently felt to be important when judging potential sexual matches.

The next evening I was taken to the campus of the University of Tokyo to lecture on gay liberation, to be followed by a small dinner. The lecture, despite being in a room that was outrageously overheated and being subject to the whims of simultaneous translation, produced considerable debate, and some speculation among the Japanese present about the failure of their own society to produce a significant homosexual movement.

As the street in Shinjuku suggests, homosexuality is managed rather differently in Japan, being neither illegal nor much discussed – outside pornography, where it appears ubiquitous. Apparently, there is a large market for homosexual-themed manga among young women, and the pornography produced for Japanese homosexual men is striking in that the gym-sculpted bodies so important in the west are absent.[1]

*

During the 1980s, there were various moves to create an international lesbian and gay movement, most notably through the International Lesbian and Gay Association (ILGA), which was established at a meeting in Coventry, England, in 1978. Although strongly western European in composition, it marked the first attempt to build international solidarity around sexual (and, later, gender) marginality, and to lobby international organisations for support. For instance, the ILGA was important in helping persuade Amnesty International to accept that penalising homosexual behaviour was a human rights issue, and for some time its consultative status with UNESCO became highly contentious because of its alleged links to organisations that promoted paedophilia – particularly the North American Man/Boy Love Association (NAMBLA).

A few Australian groups affiliated at various times with the ILGA, and in 1989, when I was spending a sabbatical period in the Netherlands, I attended one of its meetings in Vienna. I remember the discomfort of a somewhat dilapidated youth hostel in the inner part of the city, but also the sense of bonding between delegates from perhaps thirty countries, and the time we spent in the Rosa Lila Villa, a café and drop-in centre for the local queer community. But above all I remember a very traumatic visit to the former World War II concentration camp at Mauthausen, about eighty kilometres west of Vienna, where I started sobbing uncontrollably at the horrors conjured up by the sanitised grey buildings of the camp. A small group from the ILGA conference who were Jewish formed a circle of grief, but my main comfort came from a few Irish guys, whom I barely knew, but who somehow sensed the buried traumas the visit had unleashed in me.

From Vienna I went on to Budapest, then still under Communist rule, though this was only a few months before the fall of the Berlin Wall would see the collapse of Communism throughout eastern Europe. Gay life in Budapest was very different to that of Vienna, though there was one small and very smoky bar where drag queens lip-synced 'New York, New York' – in tribute, perhaps, to the imagined gay life across the wall. Far more interesting was the homoerotic atmosphere of the Sauna Gellert, set in the basement of one of Budapest's grandest, if decaying, hotels, a reminder of the persistence of the Turkish *hamam* in Hungary. As in other parts of the world, Budapest now has an overtly 'gay' sauna, even while surreptitious male sex continues in the old *hamams*.

The ILGA – now the International Lesbian, Gay, Bisexual, Trans and Intersex Association – has member organisations in most countries in the world, and is active in regions barely acknowledged in its early years. Over the past thirty years the influence of democratisation, global imagery and an international movement have broken down many 'traditional' assumptions about sexuality across the world. This has been most apparent in Latin America, where there has been a rapid growth of new sorts of gay, lesbian and trans organisations, which, in the case of Brazil, are well organised at a national level and with considerable support from and access to government.[2] The June Gay Pride parade in São Paulo now draws up to three million people, making it by far the largest in the world. The largest gay pride parade in Europe is usually the one held in Madrid; in thirty years Spain has moved from being one of the most sexually repressive to one of the most sexually open countries in the world. Just why the most dramatic changes in attitudes towards sexuality over the past few decades seem to have occurred in Spain and Latin America is not altogether clear, but it seems connected with the rise of democracy, a strong tradition of popular involvement and the collapse of the dominance of the Catholic Church.[3]

A combination of global images, a new interest in human rights and the AIDS epidemic have come together to stimulate a rapid growth of gay and lesbian groups across most parts of the world over the past three decades, often bringing long-established communities with traditional understandings of sexuality and gender into contact with imported concepts of gayness. Homosexual behaviour appears to exist across all cultures and historical periods, but what varies enormously are the ways in which it is acknowledged, understood and regulated. Many societies have allowed for same-sex relations when they were clearly linked to gender non-conformity, as in such variants of the 'third sex' as the Thai *kathoey*, the Indian *hijra*, the Native American *berdache* and the Samoan *fa'afafine* – all biological males who adopt traditional female roles, including sexual passivity.

There are fewer cases of specific roles for women who identify as masculine, but there are examples from Surinam (*mati*) and both east and west Africa.[4] In many parts of the world established transgender communities and roles exist, and hostile reactions are strongest against people who appear to adopt western gay (or lesbian) styles, thus flouting accepted (and heavily circumscribed) ways of expressing sexual and gender difference. This is evident in Iran, where gender reassignment is permissible, while brutal punishment exists for homosexual behaviour. Some Iranian women and men who in other societies would adopt homosexual identities do in fact undergo gender reassignment to meet these conditions.[5]

Some Australian Aboriginal societies appear to have similarly blurred sexual and gender roles, and in the Tiwi Islands, north of Darwin, there is a tradition of recognising such men as *yimpininni* (literally 'boy-girl'). Early anthropological studies by Carl Strehlow and Géza Róheim claimed there were homosexual overtones to traditional initiation ceremonies, but the evidence is unclear; more recently, the term 'sistergirls' has come into use to recognise sexually and gender diverse men within Aboriginal Australia.[6] There has been reluctance on the part of many Indigenous Australians and their supporters to acknowledge homosexuality. In the early stages of the AIDS epidemic, for example, when there were fears of a large-scale epidemic in Indigenous communities, one 'expert' claimed that: 'Homosexuality and bisexuality is an uncommon practice amongst Aboriginal and Islander people [relative to the white population].'[7] When an episode of the SBS television series *The Circuit* depicted a troubled sexual relationship between a white and an Aboriginal man, several viewers echoed these sort of prejudices in their responses to the station.

During the 1980s and 1990s I travelled to a number of South East Asian cities where one could see the collision between 'traditional' and 'modern' forms of homosexuality, which often led to bitter debates around what terms were appropriate. There was a clear difference between those who seemed to be defined as a 'third sex' and the increasing numbers of men (and some women) who took clues for their appearance and their identity from western images, however many of these were transformed and reinvented under local conditions. I recall several trips to Manila in the early 1990s during which I began to understand the complex intersections of culture, inequality and tradition in how people in the Philippines formed their sexual identities.

The centre of gay life in Manila at that time was the Library, a bar so named because it was lined with old textbooks. Like so many other places in Manila, it was occasionally guarded by young men with guns that seemed bigger than those holding them. Growing out of the bar was the Library Foundation, which established HIV-prevention programs for homosexual men and a drop-in centre that offered a range of activities. It mainly attracted young men from metropolitan Manila, for whom it was often the only space in which they could talk through their feelings about sexual identity. Almost twenty years later, the Library Foundation still exists.

One evening I sat with about thirty young Filipino men in a consciousness-raising group as they discussed their feelings about and experiences of coming out. 'Speak Filipino', one would urge another now and then, but these were educated men for whom English was an easier language in which to discuss sex and emotions. It was only afterwards, in private conversations, that it became clear that almost all of them lived with their biological families, and expected to do so unless they married and formed their own conventional families.

I was in Manila as part of a small research project that was seeking to better understand the ways in which western-influenced concepts of gay/lesbian community and identity were emerging across South East Asia – a project obviously limited to people with English skills and access to various sorts of middle-class resources. The research would not have been possible without existing links through the international movement, and especially the increasing visibility of homosexuality through the development of international AIDS organisations. It gave rise to a whole set of writings from the mid-1990s on, in which I tried to make sense of what was happening in the emerging world of global sexual politics.

I found similar developments unfolding in Kuala Lumpur, where there was a group trying to inform homosexual men about the dangers of HIV that called itself 'Pink Triangle' – a clear reference to homosexual oppression, but also a term that was almost unknown in broader Malaysian society. (Some guys even started using the term 'pinklets' as a shorthand term for 'MSM'.) Once again, western imagery and identities were being imported, and then, significantly, were being reinvented to fit local realities. Indeed, smart groups, like Pink Triangle, became adept at using international discourses to appeal to funders, while carefully adapting to the restrictions of their rather different home environments. Over the past twenty years homosexuality has become a major issue in Malaysian politics, and the national government has funded various initiatives to discourage sexuality diversity among young people.

By the 1990s the language of sexual rights had come into international discourses, and it would become an increasing focus for contention. It is generally accepted that the concept of 'sexual rights' developed out of debates focused on reproductive health, the need to protect women (but not exclusively women) from sexually related violence, and the early formulations of 'health and human rights' that grew out of attention to HIV and its impact on already marginalised and stigmatised groups.[8] Central to this expansion of human rights were the various large international United Nations conferences – on human rights (Vienna 1993), population and development (Cairo 1994) and women (Beijing 1995). Not surprisingly, the concept was more related to protection of women against various forms of sexual violence, including rape and forced sterilisation, but the idea of bodily autonomy was clearly threatening to many political and religious leaders. While most of those involved did not address homosexuality, the possibility appeared as a 'monster lurking behind' every mention of gender or sexual rights.[9] By the time of the Beijing conference, lesbians – and sexual rights – were visible, even though attempts to include the term 'sexual orientation' within the conference's Platform for Action failed.[10]

There are at least three ways of examining the development of sexual rights: through an examination of international law; through discursive shifts in the language of human rights; and through various attempts to institutionalise the protection of such rights. Over the past few decades, various international bodies have extended some protection to homosexual behaviour and identity. The European Court of Human Rights was the first international body to find that laws criminalising homosexual behaviour violate human rights (*Dudgeon v UK*, 1981; *Norris v Ireland*, 1988; *Modinos v Cyprus*, 1993), and it was followed by the ground-breaking decision of the United Nations Human Rights Commission in the *Toonen* case. In 1991 Amnesty International adopted a policy affirming that persecuting or discriminating against people on the basis of their sexuality is a violation of their basic human rights, and various international organisations now include sexual and reproductive rights within their framework for advocacy. In 1996 post-apartheid South Africa became the first country to protect 'sexual orientation' in a bill of rights, and in the last decade the language of sexual rights and citizenship has been adopted in a number of arenas, and is beginning to affect discourses in health, international development and other fields.

Some remarkable changes have occurred in seemingly unlikely parts of the world. In Nepal the success of the Blue Diamond Society has resulted in major legal changes, the election of an openly gay MP, and some pioneering legislation. A recent Nepali budget states that: 'The state will accord special priority to solve the core problems of Nepali people relating to sexual and gender minorities and a common house for 50 people will be provisioned to live together for their socialization.' The Blue Diamond Society has fought for the recognition of a 'third sex', which it defines as including both gender and sexuality.

India provides a particularly rich case study of the ways in which debates around homosexuality are now global. India has a large (and often fractious) gay movement and a vibrant debate on sexuality, and the decision of its Supreme Court to strike down colonial laws criminalising homosexual behaviour in 2009 echoed earlier battles in western countries with a similar heritage of British legislation. Most significantly, the Indian 'gay' movement has been the site of fervent debate about the applicability of western concepts of sexual identity and how best to reconcile the claims of traditional constructions of gender and sexuality, including the ongoing presence of a significant trans-gender (*hijra*) community, with those of a rapidly globalising media and culture.

The rapidity of social transformation in India is caught in the clash between 'modern' and 'traditional' definitions of sex and gender, which are constantly negotiated in everyday life. In addition to ending the country's sodomy laws, Indian authorities now list eunuchs and transgender people as 'others', distinct from males and females, on electoral rolls and voter identity cards. Indian gay organisations have played a significant role in developing regional networks; the Naz Foundation, in particular, is becoming a model for groups in other developing countries. Many Indian cities now host 'gay and lesbian' film festivals, and gay-themed tourist operations are developing, seeking to service a perceived global market.

Increasingly, the international language of sexual rights tends to speak of homosexual and transgender identities as if they are fixed and comparable to racial characteristics. There remain exceptions: a recent posting by Haneen Maikey on a Palestinian 'LGBT' site echoed early gay liberationist arguments while attacking 'western' ideas:

> Al Qaws believes that the Western definition of an 'exclusive heterosexuality' and consequently of an opposing homosexuality as an abnormal reflection of heterosexuality over the past century is a successful bourgeois attempt to impose structural division between straight (normal) and gay (abnormal), thus controlling gays by accepting them but under the condition of 'segregation' in the sense that 'we are here and you are there' ... And by dismantling the LGBTQ ghetto, which is more a 'reaction' to heterosexual capitalist domination rather than a genuine, effective, crystallized identity, we adopt the discourse which places the 'queer' at the center and not as an emotional or proactive case, but as an individual re-formulating social and political relations from their perspective, from the perspective of the 'formerly oppressed'.[11]

It is not fully clear what Maikey means by 'queer', nor is her attempt to cloak a critique that dates back to early gay liberation in an attack on western domination very convincing, but it is refreshing to see these arguments resurface in a very different political and cultural context.

In 2006 a meeting of the International Commission of Jurists and others in Indonesia drafted 'the Yogjakarta Principles' on 'the Application of International Human Rights Law in relation to Sexual Orientation and Gender Identity', which is the most serious attempt yet to establish universal norms around these issues. While there remains considerable division over the recognition of homosexuality, and over its inclusion within the purview of human rights, the UN Secretary-General, Ban Ki-moon, has spoken eloquently of the need for the complete and universal decriminalisation of same-sex acts between consenting adults.

I hope his plea succeeds, but at this stage homosexuality remains a deeply polarising issue between and within societies.

PART THREE

TWENTY-FIRST CENTURY: THE NEW POLARISATION

The closet is still with us, which is why so many people, gay and straight, could respond to the 2005 movie of Brokeback Mountain.

Christopher Bram (*Eminent Outlaws: The Gay Writers Who Changed America*, New York, Twelve, 2012, p. 51)

RECONNECTING WITH MY TRIBE

I am writing this in Melbourne, Australia, a city of about four million people which, over the past two decades, has become a major centre of gay and lesbian life in ways that seemed unimaginable forty years ago. Melbourne once symbolised a certain Victorian prudery; when *On the Beach* was filmed here in 1959, Ava Gardner commented that it was the perfect place to make a film about the end of the world. Yet Melbourne has now become a remarkably cosmopolitan and multicultural city, regularly rating among the 'most liveable cities in the world' in polls of varying validity. The state government recognises homosexual relationships for legal purposes, and although this is clearly not equivalent to marriage, it does mean that the most overt forms of discrimination based on same-sex relationships have been officially abolished.

For twenty-five years I have worked in an outer-suburban university, most of whose students are the first in their families to undertake tertiary study, and many of whom are of first-generation migrant backgrounds. There is not much visible gay and lesbian life on campus (most Australian students live at home, and commute in for classes and not much else), although the student union employs 'queer officers'. Nevertheless, over the past couple of decades I have noticed a gradual shift in attitudes towards homosexuality, which is less and less viewed as a major issue. One of the university's media staff, a young man whose background is very much like that of the average student, interviewed me several years ago about homophobia. He was genuinely shocked when I told him that homosexual behaviour had been criminal until the 1980s. 'But how could people think that?' he expostulated, and I realised that he was quite unaware of the rapidity of change in both laws and social mores.

In most ways, one could be in a comparable British or American city – Manchester, say, or Minneapolis – although in the latter, gay religious groups would be more prominent. Melbourne has the full range of 'gay' bars, restaurants, clubs and organisations, and is the home of radio station JOY-FM, which claims to be 'an independent voice for the diverse lesbian and gay communities', and that it is 'listened to by 216,000 people in Melbourne and more online'.

Every summer Melbourne hosts the three-week-long Midsumma Festival, followed by a major queer film festival, both of which attract a fair degree of mainstream press attention. The latter, in particular, might well seem an anachronism after the box-office success of films such as *The Kids Are All Right* and *Brokeback Mountain*, but the numbers who show up, year after year, suggests there is still a strong desire not only to see queer films, but to see them in a consciously defined queer space. A cynic might add that our sense of community has shifted from one of participation to one of consumption, but it is important to note that these festivals also involve a large number of volunteers.

For such a large city, Melbourne has less of a 'gay ghetto' than one might expect, with venues and businesses scattered across a number of inner-city neighbourhoods. In this, it is rather different from Sydney, which during the 1970s and 1980s saw an overt gay world develop in Darlinghurst, around Oxford Street, and more recently along King Street, in Newtown, as Oxford Street gradually lost its iconic status as the visible centre of gay life.

We know a great deal empirically about gay male life in Melbourne, in part because of extensive social-network analysis conducted by my partner, Anthony Smith,[1] but also because of a thriving gay media and, inevitably, the internet. Lesbian Melbourne is less well mapped, partly because there has not been the interest and the resources that HIV generated, but also perhaps because women depend far less on commercial venues to meet and socialise, even though they increasingly organise mixed dance parties that have a strong queer flavour.

Most Monday evenings see group sex parties in several venues in inner Melbourne, which are frequented by a few hundred men in ways that are both similar to the 'legendary' orgies of pre-AIDS Manhattan or San Francisco, but also different in that they feel less like self-conscious expressions of rebellion. Listening to the conversations in most sex venues, one is struck by the sheer ordinariness of homosexual life, even if there are moments of communal sexual expression of a sort largely unknown outside the male gay world.

On a very hot night in early February 2010 I was down by the bay along which Melbourne stretches – fifty miles of suburbia – at the tail end of the annual Pride March. There were two small performance areas, a number of stalls selling everything from leatherwear to real estate, and a crowd of about five or six thousand, the great majority of the marchers having disappeared because of heat and exhaustion. Most of the crowd were young and very queer – that is, without obvious markers of their sexual identity. There were women and women, men and men, and women and men all mixed up in ways that defied easy categorisation. On one of the stages a parade of tired drag queens trotted their stuff, interspersed with occasional references to demands for gay marriage. A young man played desultorily with a long, white snake that was entwined around his neck, watched with some interest by two young police officers. Of course, I thought, most of the crowd were too young to remember a time when a police presence in such a crowd was seen as threatening rather than protective.

My own experiences of 'gay Melbourne' have changed during the past quarter-century. I settled here just as the first cycle of AIDS was emerging, when men already connected through the gay movement had come together to form the Victorian AIDS Council. For a few years in the late 1980s, the VAC was a focal point for gay life for hundreds of (mostly) gay men, combining altruism with a renewed sense of community and personal engagement. Once HIV became a largely manageable condition, at least for those with access to appropriate resources, and as positive people began playing an increasing role in AIDS organisations, the centrality of AIDS as an organising trope for the gay community declined. The last two decades have seen a steady growth of social acceptance and the breaking down of taboos, but whether this means that sexuality has become irrelevant to identity and politics remains an open question. For a new generation of activists, the question of marriage has become a new rallying point. It symbolises what they would argue is continuing inequality, although homosexual relationships are largely recognised as equivalent to de facto heterosexual ones.

For much of the late 1990s and the early part of this century, I drifted away from engagement with the gay/queer community, although I remained very involved in the international AIDS movement. In part, this was a consequence of age, of living in a stable partnership, and of the pressures of my university career. In part, too, it was because – other than places for sexual adventure – the gay world seemed to offer little, and others were taking up new issues that felt less pressing for me. But it may also have been from a desire to seek out other connections, both social and political, that seemed far more possible in a world in which my sexuality set me apart less than it did in the tumultuous days of coming out and gay liberation. I was less forthright than I might have been in pushing to teach courses on sexuality, although for several years in the early 1990s I co-taught subjects on sexuality and gender with some remarkable women colleagues. One of them, the cinema expert Barbara Creed, once invited some of us to her house to watch female-centred pornography; being very squeamish, I fled to the kitchen as a certain 'Mistress Anne' dripped hot wax onto her male 'victims'.

Anyone who has been part of a political movement will find adjusting to ageing difficult: inevitably, movements develop in ways we could not foresee, and in ways with which we are not necessarily comfortable. There is always the risk of seeming to express sour grapes, particularly as new spokespeople take the limelight, often without any acknowledgment of those who went before. It seems easier to withdraw into a grumbling nostalgia. During the fortieth anniversary of Stonewall in New York, I was struck by some of the bitterness in postings from veterans of that era about the new generation of activists, who were resented for forgetting the earlier history of the movement.

Why, then, in my sixties, have I felt a strong need to reconnect to what in some ways has been my tribe for most of my adult life? In part, it is a personal recognition of one of the themes of this book: that sexual identities are not simply disappearing, even if there is now far greater acceptance than there once was. I remember coming back to Sydney some decades ago after a week in the country and rushing up to Oxford Street to be in a gay bar, for no reason than to be amongst other queers (though I probably would have said 'poofs' at the time). The need for ongoing communal reaffirmation is stronger than I'd recognised.

But there is also a political imperative, which has been strengthened by my consistent involvement in international AIDS politics for a quarter of a century. From the early days of the epidemic, when the new disease was often discussed as if homosexuality itself rather than the HIV virus was its cause, the relationship between AIDS and homosexuality has not been an easy one to navigate, with many gay leaders caught between stressing the lack of any inevitable link between homosexuality and HIV, and simultaneously arguing for greater resources for homosexually active men.

It has been frustrating to find, forty years after first entering the public arena, that the same dilemma remains for lesbians and gay men. Many of us have been caught between our feeling that we must assert our sexuality and our sense of weariness that no one else seems to care enough to notice blatant discrimination and prejudice. It's still true that if we don't raise the question of discrimination on grounds of sexuality, no one else will. Isherwood's comment of 'annihilation by blandness' remains the dominant trope, and extraordinary abuses of people on grounds of their sexuality in many parts of the world go largely unremarked upon, even by people who claim to care deeply about human rights.

As I was finishing this book, I met with a group of La Trobe University graduate students who are establishing a new journal around issues of gender and sexuality. It was exciting to recognise that new forms of activism and community are emerging, even if they will inevitably adopt new and unpredictable shapes.

NORMALISATION AND THE GLASS CEILING

I began my first book, *Homosexual: Oppression and Liberation*, with the words: 'To be a homosexual in our society is to be constantly aware that one bears a stigma.' The nature of that stigma has changed considerably – in western societies, at least, homosexuality is no longer criminalised, nor in most cases is it regarded as illness or pathology. (Amongst many religious believers, of course, it is still regarded as a sin.) In some ways, the central question of this book is whether the glass is half-full or half-empty. Clearly, much has changed since the days of the first gay liberation demonstrations, forty years ago. Yet, as the historian Shirleene Robinson wrote, only a few years ago: 'It might be easy to feel that homophobia is no longer an issue for the majority of the queer population, and that the gay and lesbian liberation movement has successfully eradicated prejudices once so strongly held ... this is not the case.'[1]

Even so, by the turn of the twentieth century, it seemed that homosexuality had been largely incorporated into mainstream society, although there was constant and uneasy balance between acceptance and disapproval. In *Homosexual* I wrote of the difference between tolerance and acceptance: the former is consistent with retaining disapproval and stigma, the latter is a recognition that difference does not imply any form of inequality. Over forty years, Australia moved from a general atmosphere of disapproval to a grudging tolerance, and then to the current mood of cautious acceptance. Homosexuals – at least, those who do not too blatantly break with other taboos – are now seen as part of the broader society, both as consumers and citizens. In a capitalist society, maybe the former leads to the latter. The 200th issue of *Outrage* (coincidentally published in January 2000), for example, contained advertisements for Yamaha bikes, Volkswagen cars and vodka, as well as more specifically gay businesses (sex venues, accommodation), along with lawyers, doctors, electricians and even carpet cleaners who catered to a gay clientele.

But the creation of a certain commercial space does not, in itself, mean the end of heteronormativity. Only last year, *mX* newspaper could still run a banner headline 'Open the Closet: Study Finds Coming Out Still Hard to Do'.[2] Both the language and the tone of the article are worth pondering. It followed a special radio program co-broadcast by JOY FM and the popular commercial radio station 3AW and hosted by Neil Mitchell, focusing on gay youth and depression, which drew on a study funded by the Beyond Blue Foundation, established by former Liberal Victorian premier Jeff Kennett to counter depression. Kennett now talks freely about the need for open discussion of sexuality, a considerable shift for a man who had previously been clearly uncomfortable with the subject; for some years he resisted acknowledging queer issues within his foundation. (Indeed, some years ago I hosted a film screening for the AIDS Trust attended by the then Premier, whose body language communicated a strong impression that the whole issue was deeply embarrassing to him.) In the radio program, one could see the contradictions at work: yes, there have been huge strides towards greater acceptance, but these have not eroded the idea of a separate and discrete set of sexual identities.

In thinking about (homo)sexuality in the current moment, several themes come together: the ever-changing assumptions about sex, gender and their interaction; the persistence of homosexuality as the basis for identity, even as certain forms of gay and lesbian identity become 'normalised'; the persistence of religious and cultural fears and prejudices while levels of acceptance are rising across the western world; and the globalisation of debates about sexuality, in which homosex itself is often the central battleground.

There is little doubt that public attitudes to homosexuality, and perhaps to transgender identities, have shifted in major ways in most western countries. Before the 2000 presidential election, the political scientist Alan Wolfe observed of the United States that: 'No other issue taps into ... potential conflict more than the issue of homosexuality',[3] although he did also see significant changes occurring that would make the issue increasingly less divisive. Gay rights – and specifically support for same-sex marriage – has become a fault line between Democrats and Republicans, but in the 2012 presidential election it turned out to be a minor issue. Even so, there were still attempts by some to make opposition to gay rights central to the Republican Party's campaign, and Mitt Romney was forced to demonstrate his anti-gay credentials by sacking an openly gay adviser.[4]

In Australia issues of discrimination remain, and legal battles have occurred over recent decades around parenting, adoption and marriage. But the ground has shifted: homosexuality is no longer widely regarded as sick, evil or deviant, even if it remains easy to find examples of people who still use that language. I noticed real changes over the past decade amongst my students, who spoke of gay and lesbian issues as if they were an unproblematic part of their world, and free queer newspapers showed up in local shops and cafés alongside rock mags and advertisements for gyms and health foods. What once could not be discussed in public is now part of general discussion, so that proclaiming one's sexuality no longer seems a particularly radical act, however difficult or even traumatic it might be for the individual.

Every week brings new evidence of major shifts in social attitudes towards homosexuality, at least in western liberal societies. In October 2010 the British Equality and Human Rights Commission reported that the biggest gains in tolerance over the past twenty years had been the 'dramatic shift in attitudes to homosexuality'.[5] Also in Britain, at least one researcher, Eric Anderson, claims that homosexuality is becoming largely accepted: 'Young people have disassociated themselves from homophobia the way they once did from racism.'[6]

I think Anderson is partly right, even though it is equally true that racism is not dead, nor by any means have all young people disassociated themselves from it. Perhaps the biggest change is the openness with which many people, at least in western urban societies, now discuss sexuality, so that being homosexual is no longer something shameful, hidden or, often, even remarkable. In contrast to older stereotypes, media representations now present a romanticised view of homosexuality, which is often more squeaky-clean than is believable – as in the movie *Beginners*, in which a married man in his seventies can, after the death of his wife, suddenly surround himself with new gay friends and find a boyfriend half his age. Would that my future were as rosy as Christopher Plummer's.

This growing acceptance also is reflected in public opinion polls, although tracking them is difficult because questions and samples vary dramatically over time. (A number of published studies seem to be based on surveys of American college students, which perhaps tells us more about the laziness of researchers than it does about genuine social attitudes.) In the 2002 national Australian survey of sexual behaviour, which does provide a representative sample of adults aged between sixteen and fifty-nine, a clear majority refused to describe homosexual behaviour as 'always wrong', with women more accepting than men, although men were far more accepting of two women than two men having sex.[7] However, a third of the men and a quarter of the women surveyed felt that male homosexuality was wrong – a far higher percentage than those always opposed to abortion – which suggested that change still had a way to go. This finding was supported by a somewhat different survey conducted by the Australia Institute in 2005.[8] Not surprisingly, acceptance of homosexuality in Australia is somewhat higher than in the United States, where white evangelical

Protestants remain strongly opposed to it,[9] although their opposition is weakening amongst younger respondents.

But it is easy to read too much into these figures, which may tell us more about superficial norms than lived realities. Few whites will today express overt hostility towards other races, but those who are black or Arab live every day with the reality of real and painful prejudice. It has become more difficult to express overt dislike about homosexuality, but this does not mean deeper hostilities have disappeared, only that it has become less acceptable to express them.

Indeed, one of the most fascinating responses to David Marr's claims in his *Quarterly Essay* about Tony Abbott's homophobia was the almost instantaneous claims from Christopher Pearson, himself openly gay but also a conservative Catholic, that Abbott is in no way homophobic – a recognition that such a claim would be politically damaging to Abbott.[10] Pearson ignored Abbott's own public admission on television two years earlier that he felt threatened by homosexuals, a remark which he later retracted, but which appears to be a view held by some of his conservative colleagues. In the final episode of the ABC talk show *Q&A* in 2012, the Nationals' Senator Barnaby Joyce clearly struggled with his discomfort in talking about homosexuality on a panel with the openly lesbian Senator Penny Wong.

Even so, homophobic prejudice is always a lurking possibility in mainstream politics. When the speaker of the House of Representatives, Peter Slipper, was accused of sexually harassing a staffer, James Ashby, in 2012 – a case that was thrown out by the courts, with a federal judge determining that Ashby's claims were vexatious and motivated by political aims – at least one observer saw the whole matter as a 'homophobic horror show'.[11]

I was less convinced; indeed, I thought that most commentary around the case was very conscious of not stressing the homosexual angle. Rather, what seemed to be played out was a clash between two men of very different generations, neither of whom came out of the affair well. Slipper, who was conventionally married, had fallen for a younger man and seemed clumsy and incautious in pursuit, making him easy prey for Ashby, who appeared eager to manipulate the situation for political and possibly monetary gain, having employed a legal firm that had won considerable damages in previous high-profile cases of sexual harassment. But despite some rather nasty attempts to smear both men through the media, including references to Ashby's earlier history with younger men, the matter seemed no different to many other attempts to destroy politicians – Bill Clinton, Silvio Berlusconi, a string of US representatives – for perceived sexual misconduct.

Like Eric Anderson, I would like to believe that hostility and prejudice have disappeared, but every now and then one is jolted by the extent to which it remains, often in unlikely quarters. When, during the same-sex marriage debate in 2012, the South Australian Liberal senator Cory Bernadi suggested that the next step would be to recognise marriage between people and animals, he was forced to step down from his party's front bench, yet that very evening an ABC radio interviewer tried to get me to discuss these comments as a serious argument deserving of airtime on what most conservatives regard as the most left-wing of our national radio stations. I was amused, rather than offended, but several people told me later that they found the whole style of questioning deeply offensive – and inconceivable if we were discussing any other group in Australian society.

In a similarly unthinking vein, when I was invited to deliver the Dunstan Memorial Oration in Adelaide in 2012, on the topic of forty years of gay liberation, it was only at my urging that any community leaders were included on the guest list for the dinner. Interestingly, too, the event organisers seemed to depend on me to indicate who would be appropriate, even though I have little direct knowledge of Adelaide's gay community.

It is not difficult to find far more direct and offensive attacks on any form of sexual diversity, often from members of parliament and religious leaders. As I write this, the current Victorian MP for Frankston is being reported as claiming that there is no difference between discriminating against homosexuals and convicted sex offenders and child molesters.[12] In the world of federal politics,

Liberal frontbencher Kevin Andrews' opposition to same-sex marriage clearly reflects a far deeper distaste for homosexuality. An American book called *A Parent's Guide to Preventing Homosexuality* has been in print for over ten years, with endorsements from a number of senior psychiatrists, and some psychologists still offer 'reparative therapy' to change sexual orientation, despite the admission of one of its founders, Robert Spitzer, that it is largely ineffective,[13] and the recent ban of the practice in California for minors. Since 2000, the Australian Psychological Society has recommended that: 'Ethical practitioners refrain from attempts to change individuals' sexual orientation.' Even if the practice is increasingly discouraged in western societies, it is finding new ground in other parts of the world, as Benjamin Law has described in Malaysia and India.[14]

For teenagers, coming to terms with their sexual feelings remains fraught, even if social attitudes appear to have changed enormously. There is considerable evidence that teenagers are frequently teased, and sometimes abused, if they are suspected of being homosexual, and that fear about their sexuality drives some to suicide.[15] 'That's so gay' can be a term used affectionately, but also as prelude to serious bullying. It's hard to get accurate figures, but American estimates are that up to forty per cent of homeless kids are gay or trans.[16] We don't have very good Australian data, but youth workers believe there are certainly more 'queer' youth amongst the homeless than their overall numbers might suggest. Even in the Netherlands, the country that most prides itself on acceptance of sexual diversity, recent evidence suggests that considerable numbers of teenagers are hostile to homosexuality, with a third of Dutch secondary students reporting that they would feel uneasy at too much contact with a homosexual classmate.[17]

'Poofter-bashing' remains a reality, and may be in fact increasing as homosexuality becomes more visible; as many incidents are not reported it is very difficult to get accurate figures for any sort of analysis across time. Only recently has it been acknowledged that there was a significant wave of murders of gay men in Sydney in the last part of the twentieth century, with one estimate suggesting about fifty gay-hate murders in New South Wales between 1985 and 1995, which may well be an underestimate.[18] It would be naive to assume such violence does not continue, and it doubtless remains underreported. Indeed, the awareness of those assaults followed a dogged private investigation of a supposed suicide, which almost certainly was a murder of a young man assaulted at an isolated stretch of Manly known for gay cruising.

There is persuasive research suggesting that depression, anxiety and substance abuse are more common amongst people who are homosexual or gender nonconformist.[19] Several people, most notably the Anglican Archbishop of Sydney, Peter Jensen, have tried to use these figures to suggest that the problem lies within homosexuality itself – which is to deny the known links between self-doubt, low esteem and social stigma and a tendency to self-abuse of various kinds.

Most significantly, the majority of organised religions maintain that homosexuality is unacceptable. At the time of writing, the official position of the Catholic Church remains that homosexual acts are 'acts of grave depravity' that are 'intrinsically disordered' and 'contrary to the natural law', and it has called on homosexuals to devote themselves to chastity. There is no reason to expect any change to this position with the elevation of Pope Francis in March 2013. The Salvation Army proclaims that homosexuality is 'unacceptable to God', while the Exclusive Brethren, who have played a significant role in supporting conservative politicians, are deeply hostile to any expression of homosexuality, regarding it as clearly 'against God's word ... people get themselves so perverted and they just can't think morally'.[20]

Similar views are expressed by fundamentalist Protestants, Orthodox Jews and almost all Islamic clerics, and in a country where increasing numbers of children are being educated in religious schools, these views cannot simply be dismissed. As long as exceptions for prejudice are allowed by law on the grounds of religious beliefs, and as long as state-funded institutions can refuse to employ homosexuals, it is hard to deny that homophobia continues to be protected through legal and institutional ways that would not be tolerated in cases of racial discrimination, for instance. The Australian government's support for 'school chaplains' – who are largely recruited from fundamentalist religions, even though they are not expected to provide religious instruction – leads one to ask how far our school system is promoting conservative religious views of homosexuality, while researchers have had considerable difficulty accessing the more conservative religious schools. There is considerable variation in the state systems, with Queensland seemingly lagging behind other states in its willingness to address issues of sexuality within its schools.[21]

A conversation overheard in a sauna from a young man: 'My parents were told either they throw me out of the house [for being gay] or they could no longer come to church.' That such sentiments can be held by people who profess a religion based on 'love' seems macabre – and sinister. But such stories are replicated over and over again in almost every organised religion, whether it is Hinduism, Catholicism, Islam, Mormonism or Orthodox Judaism (as portrayed so powerfully in the Israeli film *Eyes Wide Open*). The sad reality is that only those religious groups that are already largely secular in their outlook have been able to embrace an acceptance of sexual diversity.

Indeed, many religious people seem preoccupied with homosexuality in ways that demand psychoanalytic explanations. Australia may have few counterparts to the Islamic extremists who brand homosexuality as a reason for killing, or the powerful right-wing evangelical American Christians who preach hatred and, in extreme cases, rejoice over the death of homosexuals, or who explain natural disasters as God's punishment for acceptance of homosexuality. But in an era of globalisation, these views are as likely to be spread through mass media and the internet as are those aimed at accepting sexual diversity.

To simplify, there are two approaches to confronting religious-based bigotry: either we try to change institutions from within, or we accept that sexism and heteronormativity are fundamental to many religious worldviews and try to ensure that they cannot influence larger society.

When Acceptance, an organisation for Catholic lesbians and gay men, was founded in Sydney in the 1970s, I was invited to an organisation dinner and expressed my cynicism that the church's attitudes would change. Almost four decades later, unfortunately, my cynicism seems all too well founded, although the current members of Acceptance have found one local church in Sydney where they are welcomed to attend mass. But outside some parts of the Uniting Church and a few liberal Jewish congregations, genuine acceptance by organised religion remains extremely rare. For an unbeliever like myself, this is not surprising. I remain sufficiently convinced by a Freudian analysis to think that strong religious beliefs are based on the need to repress certain desires, which is why sexuality and gender are such difficult issues for believers to confront.

Certainly in Australia, the most overt discrimination has vanished. We have become accustomed to openly homosexual politicians, several of whom – above all Senators Bob Brown (Greens) and Penny Wong (ALP) – have become significant national figures, as has former High Court Justice Michael Kirby, who came out publicly by listing his male partner in *Who's Who* in 1999. As I have discussed, anti-discrimination laws began to include homosexuality from the 1980s on (remarkably, for a short period New South Wales forbade discrimination on the grounds of homosexuality and homosexual acts between men at the same time) and have largely been extended to all areas of social policy. There are still very few openly homosexual business leaders, although Alan Joyce, the controversial head of Qantas since 2008, is one exception. As late as 2012 there were no openly homosexual CEOs on *Fortune*'s Top 100 list of companies.

Increasingly in Australia, as in other western countries, refugees are seeking asylum on grounds of persecution for their sexuality in their home countries. Establishing both that one is homosexual and that fears of persecution are real can be very complex, and can founder on judicial interpretations of both an individual's sexuality and the fears of persecution in the country of origin.[22] I recently was asked to provide evidence to support what seemed to me well-grounded fears of people from gulf states that they faced considerable persecution were their homosexuality known back home and was shocked at the ignorance revealed in the original judgment denying asylum.

The Rudd/Gillard government can claim credit for systematically removing most remaining anti-homosexual discrimination from federal legislation and administration. Legal changes are important both because they create real benefits, in areas such as access to superannuation and health benefits, but also because they are symbolic statements of social attitudes. Other than marriage, which I shall deal with later, the only remaining area of legal uncertainty is around access to IVF for lesbians and same-sex couple adoption, which is only legal in several states at this time. However, despite Labor's achievements, proposed legislation will still allow religious institutions to discriminate against people on the basis of their sexuality; David Marr has called this anti-discrimination legislation 'a bigot's charter' because it exempts religious schools, hospitals and charities from hiring those whose sexual or marital status infringes church teachings, even when such institutions receive public funding.[23]

Media panics around homosexuality have largely vanished in western countries, although they are real in many other parts of the world. Some Australian states still allow an alleged homosexual advance to be argued as a mitigating factor in murder trials, and a 'gay panic' defence has been invoked as a mitigating factor in several trials this century.[24] Some older men still have criminal records for convictions under now repealed laws, and there is growing pressure to expunge these, as has been done in Britain.[25] But in general the panic that led public figures such as New South Wales Police Commissioner Colin Delaney to proclaim that 'homosexuality was the greatest social menace in Australia'[26] only sixty years ago has disappeared.

Some of the same sort of moral panic is now visible in the recurring hysteria around paedophilia, and there remains a general perception that it is closely related to homosexuality, although the majority of cases actually involve men molesting young girls. Recent high-profile attention to Catholic priests and child abuse has probably contributed to a somewhat distorted view of paedophilia, which is often acted out within families and goes unreported. But there is a long tradition of associating homosexuality with paedophilia, which has been true of certain societies – such as ancient Greece – even though the great majority of homosexuals are no more likely to see children as sexually attractive than is anyone else. There is a growing tendency to use sexualised images of teenagers – indeed, even pre-teens – in media and advertising, even while there remains huge social objection to any overt acceptance of the idea that adolescents might have sexual feelings and behaviours.

Panics around paedophilia often create great anxiety for gay men, because of the way the two are linked in the popular imagination – even the word 'paedophile' seems to invoke homosexuality. It is difficult for gay men to explain that often teenage boys will seek out older men. I recall being cruised very aggressively by two teenagers at a Sydney beach many years ago, and my fears that this could so easily be misinterpreted by anyone passing by.

All these examples suggest that, despite the undoubted progress of the past few decades, homosexuality has not been normalised in the ways that phrase 'the end of the homosexual' might suggest. On Easter weekend 2012, both major national weekend newspaper magazines carried cover stories relating to ambiguities around the place of homosexuality in modern Australia: 'the secret lives of gay Arabs' appeared in Fairfax's *Good Weekend*, while the public 'coming out' of Tony Abbott's sister was reported in *The Australian*. The following day, *The Sunday Age* ran a long cover story on the failure of Christian conversion programs aimed at 'saving' homosexuals. Homosexuality remains contentious even though in some ways it appears to have been normalised.

One of the most difficult issues thrown up by this apparent normalisation is how far one should talk about the sexuality of public figures in an assessment of their work. Clearly, there are public figures who are openly and comfortably homosexual, just as there are others – some prominent politicians come to mind – whose homosexuality is revealed through scandal and leads to deep embarrassment. Sometimes this is because they are people who have carefully preserved the appearance of conventional heterosexuality, at times – especially in the United States, it would seem – because they have aligned themselves with attacks on gay issues.

It would be comforting if one could take the high moral ground and argue that sexuality is a private matter that should not affect how someone is viewed, but it is impossible to reconcile that view with the experience of those of us who are publicly homosexual. A recent biography of the dancer Robert Helpmann that tried to slide over his sexuality was as deeply unsatisfying as would have been a work that condemned him as a pervert; getting the balance right is difficult. This is also evident in much of the literary criticism of writers such as James Baldwin or Elizabeth Jolley or Patrick White or Sumner Locke Elliott, which often, in a mixture of prudery and embarrassment, retreats from asking how far their sexuality influenced their writings. As Colm Tóibín noted in reviewing Mario Vargas Llosa's novelised life of Roger Casement: 'For a biographer there is a need for an understanding of his sexuality in all its energy and compulsion and its connection to the energy and compulsion he showed in other areas of his life.'[27]

With living artists, it sometimes remains difficult to discuss the impact of their sexuality upon their work. When *West Side Story* premiered, for instance, it would have been a brave critic who would have speculated upon the significance that a great heterosexual love story was being created by four gay men. Edward Albee has always protested strongly against those critics who claim *Who's Afraid of Virginia Woolf?* is really an account of a gay relationship, and Stephen Sondheim has prohibited gay interpretations of *Company*, even though its basic plot – a single man who lives in a world of married heterosexual couples – seems to allow such a reading.

With openly queer artists, now more common, there is an equal danger of assuming that their sexuality is all that matters. When I published my only novel, *The Comfort of Men*, I was angry – naively so, I now recognise – that it was not read as a story about Australia as much as about gayness, even though I had intended it to be a novel about how Australia had changed over the past thirty years.

In some cases, being homosexual may lead people to a deeper empathy with others who are oppressed, as is probably the case with Justice Michael Kirby. But there is no reason to assume this is always the case; there are nasty and xenophobic homosexuals, and increasingly they are playing a particular role in public life, however inconvenient the combination of homosexuality and repressive politics might be for those of us in the 'LGBT' movement – or indeed for their own conservative allies.

Sexuality is private and public at the same time. The specific pleasures and practices of an individual's sex life are rarely relevant to those other than his or her partners, and should be left to novelists and filmmakers. But how we understand and imagine our sexual identities, to whom we are attracted and whether we act on or repress those desires will inevitably impact upon how we behave in the world, and so are legitimate questions for public debate. In everyday life the reality that being homosexual still sets one apart to some extent from the mainstream reveals itself in two major ways: the continuing trope of 'coming out' and the need for separate queer spaces, where homosexuality is the norm.

Gay Life Persists

Every generation needs to come out in its own particular way, and many more kids are talking about their homosexual desires at a younger age, as networks of support have grown up in schools – in part because of government-backed programs to minimise homophobia. Coming out on Facebook has become common for teenagers, who often declare their sexuality before experiencing it. Our nephew came out that way while still at school, telling us – ironically – just at the moment that we were watching Kurt come out to his father on the television show *Glee*. Even so, the public announcement of one's sexuality remains an event, and often has unpredictable consequences for both one's self-image and how one is seen by others.[28]

The Olympic diver Matthew Mitcham writes about his experiences, both at school and then in the public arena, in very perceptive ways. He thought of himself as gay very young, and 'until I was 11, I wore a rubber band around my wrist, and flicked it every time I had a gay thought'. This gave way fairly quickly to acceptance, and to letting his friends and family know, but he then had to make a major public decision, and spoke frankly of his sexuality and his long-term partner to *The Sydney Morning Herald* on the eve of the Beijing Olympics. As he writes in his biography: 'When I try to pinpoint the course of my apprehension, I can only put it down to the subliminal message that I, and no doubt countless other young LGBT kids, picked up from society: that gay is not as good as straight.'[29] Mitcham also makes clear that teenagers do go out searching for sex, and suggests that the current hysteria, which always assumes the older man is the aggressor, even if 'older' means eighteen as against sixteen, is based on a desire to believe in a prolonged childhood naivety which is largely non-existent.

The term 'coming out' encompasses acceptance of one's own sexuality, disclosure to others, but also something as simple as first entering a gay bar, or having one's first passionate kiss with someone of the same sex. In *Homosexual* I described three cases of men whose sexuality was more complex than is allowed for in any simple binary divide between 'gay' and 'straight'. Forty years later, it shocks me that many people still want to believe in an essential sexual orientation, so that any ambivalence and uncertainty is seen as denying who one 'really is'.

That does not mean that there are not complicated issues for anyone coming to terms with their sexual feelings and desires, and coming out may include elaborate deceptions, by which people somehow persuade themselves that what they feel and desire is a passing phase, or not 'really' who they are. Many people still enter into heterosexual relationships in a desperate attempt to persuade themselves that they are not 'really' homosexual.

For men in particular, sex work is often a way of disguising their own sexual feelings. For many, being paid somehow means they are not 'really' homosexual, while for women attracted to women, the male client becomes a convenient source of income that is easily detached from any possible emotional connection. Research suggests that between a third and a quarter of gay men have, at some point or another, connected with another man who has wanted money for sex, sometimes as much to reassure himself that he is not 'really' gay as for the money itself. Indeed, sex for money is far more common in the gay world than is often acknowledged, and not a few men advertise for commercial sex as a way of finding sexual partners; it's also true that desire for both partners can actually be heightened by the exchange of money. (In one aspect, sex work could be a harder job for men – sorry for the pun – in that it is difficult to fake an erection.) Lesbian sex work seems far rarer, although sometimes women are paid by male clients to participate in threesomes.

There is an emerging literature on sex work as 'queer', with an emphasis on experimentation, new forms of intimacy and the breaking down of sexual taboos, mediated through a commercial exchange that need not necessarily be understood as exploitative or reinforcing inequalities.[30] My own discussions with young men who offer sensual massage suggests that many gain more than simply financial rewards as they experience their work.

We lack longitudinal comparisons in the data now being collected for various research projects, so it is impossible to make definitive statements about how far homosexuals' sense of self has changed over the past few decades. I suspect that there have been major changes in what certain psychologists call 'self-esteem', in that there are now large numbers of people who identify as lesbian, gay or queer and who are comfortable with their identity and feelings in ways that were very rare until the end of the last century.

I dislike terms such as 'self-hatred' or 'internalised homophobia', but they do touch on feelings that are raw and often difficult to discuss. Both female and male homosexuals have higher rates of alcohol, tobacco and drug use, and 'party drugs' are certainly common. Many men state on internet sites that they are – or seek to be – 'wired', or high on crystal methamphetamine. It also appears that there is a greater degree of depression and isolation among homosexuals – which is hardly surprising, given the ongoing realities of both family and community prejudice. It is revealing that, even in 2012, AIDS educators were still talking of 'internalised homophobia', even though they may have been born long after the concept was first formulated.[31]

Much of the famous bitchiness and brittleness of gay life – the stereotypes captured in, for example, *Boys in the Band* – seem a reflection of self-doubt and protectiveness, which should be disappearing as social attitudes change. My hunch is that almost all of us at some level still internalise a sense that we are not quite normal, though clearly large numbers of homosexual women and men are comfortable with their lives and have no desire to change their sexuality. 'I've been gay and I've been straight,' said the actress Cynthia Nixon in the interview referred to earlier, 'and gay is better.'

Perhaps being homosexual in the western world is now rather like being Jewish: one is different but accepted, even perhaps admired, yet there remains a sense of apprehension that at any moment the admiration could turn to envy or hatred. Unlike other minorities, most Jews and homosexuals can choose whether or when to disclose their identity: in neither case is one's identity instantly apparent unless one chooses to display it (through Orthodox clothing or a very nelly or butch appearance). Echoing a term that is much used in gay circles, the narrator of Howard Jacobson's *Finkler Question* asks: 'Is there a Jewdar that enables you to pick one another out?'[32] I increasingly find it more important to disclose my Jewishness – which is neither religious nor based on any real connections to the organised community – than my sexuality, but I have also been in situations where there is clearly more antagonism to Jews than to homosexuals. Indeed, someone who was not Jewish might find even making these comparisons politically fraught.

Like Jews, homosexuals can adopt many forms: the once popular stereotype of the Jewish intellectual, wimpish, nerdish and impractical, has after all been replaced by the image of the strong Israeli fighter, rather as the nelly queen has given way to the macho gay man. And again like Jews, homosexuals move unpredictably from strategies of assimilation to chauvinism. I remember one prominent activist, when I lived in New York in the 1980s, arguing that gays should emulate Jews in asking of every political initiative 'But is it good for us?'; similarly, the British actor Sir Ian McKellen says he is a one-issue voter – gay issues.[33]

The great difference, of course, is the family, and the need to negotiate identities with one's family that are perhaps similar to a child rejecting an Orthodox religious upbringing. Despite growing acceptance, strong tensions persist in homosexuals' needs to both remain part of their biological families and construct new ones that cannot really duplicate them.

Acceptance of homosexuality in Australia is clearly related to the development of multiculturalism, both as an official ideology and as a reflection of the rapidly growing diversity of Australian society. It is not surprising that the television channels run by the Special Broadcasting Service (SBS), which was established to cater to ethnic groups, are also the most likely to feature queer programs – a de facto recognition that, in many ways, the gay and lesbian community can be understood as yet another ethnic group, with its own culture, language and sacred sites. For some time I have suspected that most Australians would be more comfortable with a lesbian bar than a mosque in their neighbourhood.

There is, however, another side to multiculturalism, and that is the danger that increasing cultural diversity does not necessarily mean greater acceptance of others, as new arrivals often bring with them other attitudes and prejudices. When my life partner Anthony was hospitalised because of a major physical collapse, the medical staff had no difficulty in accepting me as his partner, with all the rights and responsibilities of the next of kin, but this was clearly not the perception of all the hospital employees. 'Is he your brother?' one Filipina orderly asked me in confusion when I came into Anthony's room. There is deeply entrenched ignorance of and hostility towards homosexuality in many immigrant communities, and if we cannot develop smarter ways of helping new arrivals recognise that mutual acceptance is required within Australian society, we run the risk of producing new tensions just when we seem to be achieving genuine acceptance of sexual diversity.

A concrete example of this came in a recent short series of webcasts that told the story of a Lebanese gay man and lesbian who decided to get married in order to hide their sexuality from their families. This is a familiar trope in many societies – it is the central plot line of *La Cage aux Folles* – but acquiescing to familial prejudices rather than confronting them raised uneasy questions for me. Too often multiculturalism is interpreted to mean we should accept the dominant power relations within migrant cultures, rather than insisting that respect for diversity needs to extend within as well as between cultures.

In the current mood of uneven acceptance, many homosexuals remain eager for legitimation, and so some will allow others to speak for them and become extravagantly grateful when known heterosexuals defend queer rights. To older liberationists, the thunderous applause for people whose coming out in the current atmosphere of official tolerance can seem a good career move, risking virtually nothing, grates, as does the eagerness of well-meaning supporters to offer public leadership rather than background support. When a senior but heterosexual university officer was asked to raise the rainbow flag at Gay Pride Week at my university a couple of years ago, I was genuinely shocked that someone openly queer was not asked to perform the ceremony, which seemed, after all, the essence of 'pride'. Can one imagine a man being asked to raise the flag at a celebration for International Women's Day?

But times have changed. At the 2013 Pride Parade, which ends Melbourne's Midsumma Festival, there seemed to be more non-queers marching than those who clearly identified as sexually or gender diverse. After the obligatory drive past of 'dykes on bikes', there was something of a gap, and then a group of largely straight footballers were followed by contingents from the police, Ambulance Victoria, Yarra Trams and several political parties. It took at least ten minutes before any clearly queer groups showed up; my favourites were the Melbourne Bears, who chanted enthusiastically: 'Say no to waxing!' We might welcome the support of Darebin Council and the ALP, but might it not be more appropriate for them to follow rather than march ahead of actual lesbian and gay groups? Whatever the intentions of the organisers, the ABC's television news that evening paid no attention and reduced the march to footballers and drag queens.

There remain moments when sexuality still creates a need for community, and contact with other queers. Contemporary gay activists tend to bemoan the disappearance of 'community', while theorists prefer to speak of 'affect' as a device for linking people through emotions,[34] but 'community' has always been a problematic term. In cinema it has usually been portrayed through images of bars and discos – it is hard to think of a gay or lesbian film that does not at some point flash to a bar scene, complete with pounding electronic music – but 'community' has usually been invoked to suggest something more solidly rooted, a sense of belonging and commitment to a particular group of people who share an important part of one's own sense of self.

I am concerned that the notion of 'affect' downplays the significance of actual institutions, which remain important both in coming out and in establishing a sense of comfort. Writing of himself circa 2000, the author Benjamin Law describes his experience as 'a newly minted homosexual' working with 'the country's longest-running LGBTI radio program' in Brisbane, and his subsequent visit to the city's gay bars, his ambivalence about these institutions but at the same time his need to seek out those spaces.[35] In the sudden explosion of web-based nostalgia for 'lost gay' Sydney, Melbourne, Adelaide and so on, a common complaint was that the sense of community forged through both gay/AIDS activism and a bar/disco culture was disappearing; people were increasingly becoming more private, with the web serving as a primary means of social connection.

The persistence of gay and lesbian organisations, events, newspapers and businesses suggests that, for many people, their homosexuality is something they want to reaffirm and experience with others who are like them, even if they are completely 'out' about their sexuality in other contexts. Indeed, greater social acceptance might well increase the need some feel for queer spaces. 'I always check how many other queers are around,' one woman friend told me of her experience when entering a new social gathering. One's 'gaydar' is not always accurate, of course: 'There is a visibility so tenuous, so different, or so discomfited that it is easy to miss,' observes Lisa Cohen in her fascinating book about three almost forgotten lesbian modernists.[36] Through social and sexual networking apps like Grindr and Scruff it is now possible to check for the presence of other queers when walking into a public event – indeed, one now sees young men busily searching their smartphones even when they're in the middle of obviously sexualised spaces such as bars and saunas.

Sometimes it is tiring to be part of a well-meaning liberal discourse in which both sides are expected to be on their best behaviour all the time. A few years ago my partner and I went on a cruise down the Rhine. As is the way of such cruises, the people aboard were almost all couples, only three of whom were same-sex. We quickly teamed up with a pair of lesbians from Brisbane, who became remarkably good at snapping up one of the few tables for four in the dining room. In an atmosphere dominated by married couples and their families, we felt a great relief in being able to escape the assumptions that all relationships are heterosexual. 'You boys have to eat with us tonight,' I remember one of the women saying. 'I can't bear any more talk about people's grandkids.'

Of course, increasing numbers of lesbian and gay couples not only want marriage but are having and raising children, and they presumably could have joined those dinner table conversations more happily. The turkey basters of cliché have now been replaced by sophisticated (and sometimes very expensive) IVF procedures and surrogacy,[37] and the topic is now appearing in television shows such as *The New Normal*. In writing this, I am not sure if I should admit to my own deep discomfort about surrogacy, which is a legally complex issue in Australia.[38] Despite all reassurances, I remain uncomfortable at what seems an exploitation of another person's biology to fulfil a need that may not be fully understood by those who express it.

But while many heterosexual couples now have children through IVF and surrogacy, some same-sex parents themselves organise support groups, because there is a need to be with others in a situation which remains potentially stressful. Same-sex parents have to manage a whole set of assumptions and explanations in how they negotiate their way through school and community encounters, which become tiring even where there is no maliciousness involved. Jaime Hovey has chronicled the ways in which, even as more positive images of lesbians appear in the media, lesbians still feel a need to meet together, in bars and private homes, to watch their lives on screen.[39]

I am reminded of my own experience during the 2010 football finals in Melbourne, when I dropped in at the Laird, a pub that has now been virtually exclusively gay for thirty years. The pub was full of men, of a variety of ages and looks, watching the game and occasionally cheering their teams. Most would have looked completely at home at any of hundreds of other pubs around the inner city, although the ambience was clearly that of a gay pub. What struck me most was that with only a few changes – thirty years earlier there would have been longer hair, fewer tattoos, perhaps a couple of bandanas – that afternoon in the Laird could have been taking place at any time over the past thirty years. The need for gay men to be together in their own space remained as strong as ever.

Not all younger queers agree. As one visiting American put to me:

Considering how integrated the gays and straights are in Australia, I don't see exclusively gay venues as lasting a whole lot longer, and with them some of the cultural glue that keeps the community cohesive and which is already fading away quickly.[40]

Yet queer officers and rooms remain on campus, and students tell me they are important aids to coming out and moving into a world that is quite different to the one they knew through home and school. In the student elections at La Trobe University in 2012 all three groups running for the position of queer officer stressed the importance of providing safe queer spaces on campus – although none, to my regret, made any mention of influencing what and how sexuality might be discussed in class. Moreover, counsellors at La Trobe tell me of students who are so traumatised by their sexual feelings that they feel suicidal; such students are unlikely to hang out in a 'queer room'.

At the same time, as if to remind us of Raymond Williams' point about residual and emergent cultures, new spaces are emerging, in which specific identities are less important, and many younger queers now go to 'mixed' bars and dance parties. With the development of the web as both a meeting place and a site for commerce, some of the central institutions of gay life are disappearing. In the United States gay bookshops are no longer flourishing, having become victims both of trends in the overall book business, as more and more is sold and published online, and of the mainstreaming of homosexuality. Announcing the closure of Washington's Lambda Rising Bookstore in 2010, its owner, Deacon Maccubbin, said:

> The phrase 'mission accomplished' has gotten a bad rap in recent years, but in this case, it certainly applies. When we set out to establish Lambda Rising in 1974, it was intended as a demonstration of the demand for gay and lesbian literature. We thought ... we could encourage the writing and publishing of LGBT books, and sooner or later other bookstores would put those books on their own shelves and there would be less need for a specifically gay and lesbian bookstore. Today, 35 years later, nearly every general bookstore carries LGBT books.[41]

Yet in both Sydney and Melbourne the specialist bookstores have managed to survive, and continue to play an important role. When we took our seventeen-year-old nephew and his then partner to Hares & Hyenas in Melbourne, they were enthralled by what the shop offered them, and a range of ages and genders attend the frequent queer events organised by the stores.

All large Australian cities have thriving queer film and community festivals, too, even if they have lost the cutting edge of early Mardi Gras and Midsumma cultural events, which included new plays, artworks and some engagement with ideas. The brochure for Pridefest in Perth in 2012 included three seemingly interesting plays, as well as parties, picnics and a fair day, and a quite remarkable assortment of commercial promotions. 'When it comes to being fabulous,' proclaimed Curtin University's advertisement, against an appropriately pink background, 'we're the campus.' Darwin Pride, on the other hand, was heavily party-focused, with an overwhelming emphasis on parties and dances. Every year thousands of 'queers' gather for the annual Tropical Fruits New Year's Eve parties in Lismore, which grew out of a desire to establish a gay and lesbian counter-culture in the northern rainforests.

Despite the ubiquity of the web, a queer press remains, with enough advertising for venues and gay-related businesses to ensure that a number of free papers are produced each week across Australia. Certainly, they do not speak to everyone who is homosexual, and more broadly it remains true that organised gay life reproduces the racism of everyday Australia. Ethnic divisions sometimes run deeper in Australia than those of class, but it remains true that homosexuality is often a means for people to move across class lines. I have sometimes told the apocryphal story of two working-class boys: the straight one becomes a tradesman, marries and remains in a somewhat more affluent version of his childhood milieu, while his brother, who is gay, starts work at an upmarket store such as David Jones, meets men with very different backgrounds, and ends up living with a wealthy partner in a posh suburb, even though he continues to earn less than his brother. As those sociologists who research class seem quite oblivious to the possibilities of how sexuality might influence social mobility, it's hard to go much beyond anecdotal evidence.

The gay world is no less racist than mainstream Australia. When I first visited Darwin in 1990 I was taken to a local gay bar, and was shocked by the misogyny and racism of the performers. Sadly, the gay press reported a similar incident at the Cairns 2013 Out! New

Year's Eve Party. Recently, a younger friend of mine told of going to a prominent gay pub, and his discomfort at realising he was the only non-Caucasian in the place. It is less than twenty years since Melbourne writer Christos Tsiolkas published his first book, *Loaded* (later filmed as *Head On*), which drew on his experience of being gay and Greek, but also insisted on the somewhat different experience of 'wogs' coming to terms with their sexuality. Rereading that book, which impressed me enormously at the time, I am struck by the anger he puts into the words of his character:

> Being a wog is a plus as well ... I hate the macho shit, period, but the truth is that the faggot scene is a meat market and the tougher the meat the bigger the sale ... I get a buzz out of faggots thinking I'm straight.[42]

In all of Tsiolkas's subsequent books there is a similar ambivalence around homosexuality, a mix of bravado, defiance and dislike of mainstream commercial gay life.

The imagery of gay and lesbian Australia rarely reflects the reality that Australia is a deeply multicultural society, and most clearly omits Indigenous and non-Caucasian Australians. It is still common to find personal advertisements in the gay press that specify 'no Asians', who are seen as soft and feminine. (It is, of course, an oversimplification to assume that in all inter-racial relationships the Caucasian is dominant; the assumption, which underlies sneering references to 'rice' and 'potato' queens, actually denies effective agency to the non-Caucasian partner.) Over the past two decades, Asian Australians have started confronting these stereotypes, as in Tony Ayres' ground-breaking film *China Dolls* (1998), while the photographer William Yang has toured the country with a series of personal narratives of growing up gay and Chinese in Queensland.

Through some of the AIDS Councils there has been considerable mobilisation of gay Asian Australians, allowing them to share their experience of racism within the gay community and entrenched homophobia within their ethnic and family communities – and, equally, to display impressively gym-toned bodies.[43] Gradually, similar assertion is occurring amongst Arabic and African Australians, although few of the agencies which work with newly arrived migrants appear to take the issues of sexual diversity seriously.

A few years ago the historian Robert Reynolds, echoing some of the sentiments already discussed, argued that, for a new generation: 'Gay life … is an auxiliary of the self, not a definitive reflection of who they are. And this, I believe, is good. We are more than who we choose to bed.' Robert structured his book *What Happened to Gay Life?* around the changing experience of three generations of gay men as social mores changed, arguing not only that gay life is being mainstreamed but also that: 'Kids still grow up believing it is unacceptable to have same-sex desires; tragically some will kill themselves before they discover otherwise.'[44] More recently, Robert has acknowledged that he might have overstated his case. One younger reviewer, Andrew Burry, wrote at the time: 'I don't see an end to activism and I don't see an end to gay life. I see a change and I see an infusion of new people with new ideas about what it means to be gay.'[45]

How far homophobia remains is a matter of judgment. At the end of 2012, the outgoing Australian High Commissioner in London, John Dauth, complained about the homophobia of Australian society – which he seemed to base on the failure to accept same-sex marriage – although one might equally argue that the fact he was in an openly gay relationship while representing Australia in London was a mark of acceptance.[46]

Too often, I suspect, we look for victimisation where it might not exist. Is Sarah Schulman right, for example, in seeing it in Obama's failure to appoint 'openly gay people' to his first cabinet – or, indeed, in her frequent complaints about the dearth of support for lesbian playwrights?[47] What does one make of the large numbers of internet postings during the 2012 election campaign that claimed Obama was secretly gay, along with all the other claims about his alleged closeted Islamism, socialism and non-citizenship? On at least one occasion I suspected a benign homophobia may have contributed to my failure to receive a research grant: the planned research on international polarisation around homosexuality was just not seen as sufficiently significant, but how would one establish that? And what does one make of an apparently 'scientific' article that tells us: 'As a rule, conservatives are more likely than liberals to prefer white people, straight people and high status groups'[48] – a sentence that appears to assume that all 'conservatives' and 'liberals' are both white and straight.

There are much stronger examples. In 2011 the Australian defence forces revealed that there had been a number of cases of homophobic abuse, many using social media, and military leaders are still struggling to deal with such cases. Sports, and particularly male sports, remain an arena in which coming out is still exceptional, and there has been considerable controversy about the ways in which the various football codes, in particular, remain deeply closeted. Since the Sydney rugby league player Ian Roberts came out in 1995, no professional Australian footballer has done so. (In general, the sport was supportive of Roberts, who went on to develop an acting career after retiring from rugby league.) Over the past few years, the AFL, which controls the now national code of Australian Rules football, has been the site of some controversy: although it has adopted an official policy of opposing homophobia, no AFL player has yet come out as homosexual.

A major breakthrough took place in 2012, when the AFL agreed to screen anti-homophobia advertisements on the big screens at its two preliminary finals, after a campaign led by a young outer-suburban footballer, Jason Ball, to eradicate homophobia from the game. Ball marched with some of his (straight) teammates in Melbourne's 2013 Pride Parade, and the AFL is currently planning that one of its regular high-profile matches should be declared a 'gay pride' game.

With luck, one AFL footballer will have come out between my writing this sentence and the appearance of this book. Symbolically, that would be one further crack in the glass ceiling.

GLOBAL INEQUALITIES

Debate around homosexuality has moved inexorably into the global arena, in part because of conflicting domestic pressures as nation states adjust to the globalisation of homosexual identities in very different ways. The contradictions are everywhere. In Singapore, Gulf Air advertises special fares to attend Sydney's Mardi Gras, even though in both Singapore and Bahrain (the home of the airline) homosexual behaviour remains illegal.

The spread of certain understandings of homosexuality is often linked to American models, both of gay assertion and of homophobia, so that both LBGT groups and American evangelicals export their views on sexuality. Of course, globalisation is not just about Americanisation; indeed, over the past decade the influence of non-western societies, especially of Islam and of China, has become increasingly significant. The assertion of 'Asian' or 'African' values as a counter to what is perceived as imported western individualistic values is a growing part of nationalist ideologies in a number of countries, and often includes claims that homosexuality is a 'western import', despite evidence of well established pre-colonial homosexual cultures and practices.

Nonetheless, western assumptions about homosexuality as the basis for identity are spreading rapidly, often in ways that displace or further marginalise more traditional assumptions about gender and sexuality. While theorists may see this as the imposition of western values, as has been argued by a number of scholars,[1] increasing numbers of people in the majority world assert 'LGBT' identities, self-consciously using terms taken from the west. For instance, Mark Gevisser has described a 'flowering of a working-class lesbian subculture' in South Africa: 'Sexuality has become a matter of identity ("I am lesbian") rather than mere practice ("I sleep with women"); an overt insistence on equality rather than a covert satisfying of desire. The result is social upheaval.'[2] When I started to write about new gay and lesbian assertion in South East Asia at the end of the 1990s, my conclusions were based on the visibility of new groups that used western (usually American) terminology and literature to make sense of their desire to assert identities that they could relate to in their contemporary urban societies.

Homosexuality has often served as a proxy for a whole set of anxieties in western societies around sexuality, gender and change, and it is now developing a similar role in global politics, as the push to recognise sexual rights is causing increasing polarisation between states that uphold particular concepts of human rights versus those that claim these rights cannot overrule tradition, culture and religion. Both former US Secretary of State Hillary Clinton and British Prime Minister David Cameron have declared that human rights protect sexual diversity, and have talked of making foreign assistance conditional on respect for this view. Not surprisingly, many governments have responded angrily to what they see as the imposition of 'western values' on their societies.

In September 2012 the United Nations Human Rights Council voted to support 'the traditional values of humankind', which appeared to be code for opposing sexual and gender equality; the resolution was introduced by Russia and supported by a range of countries from all parts of the world outside Western Europe, including some, such as

Ecuador, that had been supportive of gay rights in earlier votes. In this case, geopolitical considerations were clearly more important than human rights. Russia, in particular, has become a site of anti-homosexual activism, both nationalist and religious, and in 2013 passed laws prohibiting homosexual 'propaganda', which had eerie echoes of Margaret Thatcher's 'Section 28' from the 1980s, though they are likely to be enforced rather more draconically.

In an increasingly complex and interconnected world, where cultural conflicts exist within as much as between nation states, both the assertion of homosexuality and opposition to any claim for sexual rights are increasing. The naming of homosexuality as a specific identity, rather than as being part of a spectrum of human sexual potential, has had the consequence of creating a fundamental divide between those who claim that diverse sexual identities and behaviours are fundamental to human rights and those who argue that they represent degeneracy and a threat to the moral order. As this divide seems to parallel that between 'western' and 'non-western' societies, it also becomes a major terrain for competing views of individualism versus cultural and national identities, and a crucial point of reference for very different concepts of religion, freedom and human rights.

It appears sadly perverse when countries that claim to be strongly anti-colonial echo long outdated prejudices about homosexuality which could have appeared in British and American texts in the 1950s. In Malaysia, the Education Ministry has produced guidelines to assist parents to recognise 'LGBT' symptoms in their children; they include the rather strange comment that lesbians, 'beside their female companions, will distance themselves from other women'. The signs of male homosexuality are a wonderful mix of stereotypes: parents are alerted to watch out for men 'who have a muscular body and like to show their body by wearing V-neck and sleeveless clothes', but also who 'like to bring big handbags ... when hanging out'. Does one laugh or cry at the fact that this information is being circulated by an official government agency in a country with ambitions to be a modernising economic and political power in its region?

Often homophobia is more direct and violent. Nowhere has this been more obvious than in Uganda, where in 2009 legislation was introduced that would have mandated a death sentence for repeated acts of sodomy. After considerable international pressure, this law was temporarily withdrawn, but the following year a prominent gay activist, David Kato, was killed in Uganda. Kato was murdered shortly after winning a lawsuit against a local magazine that had published his name and photograph, identifying him as gay and calling for him to be executed. Even at his funeral the presiding minister preached against the gays and lesbians present, before activists grabbed the microphone from him, forcing him to retreat from the pulpit to Kato's father's house.[3] In Nigeria, where homosexual sex is already illegal, there are frequent calls to toughen up legal restrictions and punishments for any expression of homosexuality. In much of the Middle East the punishment for homosexual behaviour remains draconian, with five countries – Mauritania, Saudi Arabia, Sudan, Iran and Yemen – proscribing the death penalty, as have some regions of Nigeria and Somalia.

Reflecting on Argentina's decision in 2010 to recognise same-sex marriage, one writer observed that this is viewed by some in the west as 'the human rights battle of our times'.[4] I don't share this view, but it does seem true that acceptance of homosexuality remains almost entirely confined to countries that have democratic traditions, and that very different sorts of repressive regimes are agreed on restricting the open expression of homosexuality. To argue against including sexuality within the framework of human rights, its opponents invoke the concept of 'cultural rights', probably the most problematic of all rights.

Other issues of sexual regulation are less easily linked to broader concepts of tolerance and diversity. One can find that abortion, for example, is accepted in both repressive and liberal regimes, if for rather different reasons. In a similar vein, Aleardo Zanghellini has argued that, even more than debates around the *hijab* and veil, homosexuality has come to mark 'a discursive field for the ideological construction of

Islam and the West as two discrete, homogenous wholes irreducible to each other'.[5]

The apparent divide between the liberal west and intolerant Islam is most marked in the case of the Netherlands, which has the oldest continuous gay movement in the world and has long been seen as a pioneer in accepting sexual diversity. Over the past decade, tensions between fundamentalist Muslims and gay rights activists have been particularly acute, reaching crisis point with the slaying in 2002 of the openly gay Dutch politician Pim Fortuyn because of his attacks on Islamic immigrants. Indeed, it has been claimed that 'gay rights have become a proving ground for the Dutch social compact'[6] and homosexuality has become a symbol of Dutch tolerance against the perceived threats of Islamic fundamentalism. Such views ignore the reality that almost all organised religions are hostile to expressions of homosexuality, and the ferocity of some fundamentalist Christian and Hindu groups matches much of that found in Islam.

Acceptance of homosexuality is one of the values required of those who would take out Dutch citizenship. The Netherlands has had an important influence on developing European Union policies on the inclusion of sexuality within a human rights framework, and pioneered pressure for homosexual rights as part of its international development assistance, in which it was followed by Sweden, the United Kingdom and others. For some critics, this can become a new form of conformity, whereby a certain sort of homosexual respectability becomes linked to nationalist identity – perhaps the mirror image of the 'political homophobia' I discussed earlier.

This debate is clearest in the furore around 'pink-washing', whereby a number of queer activists have attacked Israel for using its relative acceptance of homosexuality to underline its liberal credentials in western countries. While I have no intention of defending the policies of the current Israeli government, it seems perverse to attack it for behaving better towards homosexuals than do the states surrounding it – though it's equally perverse to argue, as do some Israeli gays, that progress in one area can excuse the abuse of human rights elsewhere.

As the Israeli activist Aeyal Gross has written: 'Putting LGBT activism in a political framework that denies the rights of Palestinians, asylum seekers and others makes it hollow. It can only be accepted if one believes that LGBT rights take precedence over every other human right.'[7]

For many political and religious leaders who dislike what they see as the gratuitous freedoms and hedonisms of the west, homosexuality has become a crucial touchstone. We should not be surprised that regimes such as those of Robert Mugabe, Mahmoud Ahmadinejad and Vladimir Putin rail against homosexuality, which they invoke as a symbol of westernisation, rather than shopping malls or DVDs, which they embrace. In many parts of the developing world small groups of gay activists, often supported by western-based human rights organisations, come into conflict with deep homophobia, often voiced by those claiming to defend 'culture, tradition and religion'. Interestingly, as Bosia and Weiss point out, this means that state-sponsored homophobia may well precede much organising amongst 'gay and lesbian' activists.[8] One example is the move to ban same-sex marriage in Nigeria, which came in the absence of any movement that was in a position to advocate for it, and which led to the introduction of legislation that would imprison anyone 'aiding or abetting' homosexuality.

Indeed, reactions to homosexuality in many societies now resemble the classic definitions of 'moral panic', which, according to Stanley Cohen, occurs when a 'condition, episode, person or group of persons emerges to become defined as a threat to societal values and interests'.[9] There are parallels to the 'homosexual panic' that was common in western countries in the post-World War II period, above all in the United States during the McCarthyite period of enforced conformity.[10] In both cases, the threat was largely illusionary but remained politically potent nonetheless.

It is not surprising that the connections between nationalism and sexuality mean that male homosexuality is so much more contested than female, for the construction of a certain sort of nationalism depends upon rigid gender stereotypes in which masculine dominance must be maintained. Related to this are the anxieties about globalisation, so that gay and lesbian identities become symbols of modernity, which is simultaneously feared and desired.

In many societies organised religions play a crucial role in perpetuating hostility towards the acceptance of homosexuality, and the most extreme manifestations of homophobia are often cloaked in religious language. But it would be simplistic to see religion as the only cause of homophobic ideology. After a brief flirtation with ideas of sexual freedom in the early days of the Soviet Union, communist states have largely been deeply homophobic, even as they have also denied the significance of religion. Indeed, some of the worst examples of violence directed at open manifestations of lesbian and gay life have occurred in former Soviet Europe, and pressure from the European Union has supported the development of gay/lesbian movements and sought to modify state-sanctioned discrimination in a number of states. Over the past few years, Cuba – once known for its persecution of homosexuals – has seen a major shift in attitudes, in part because of a political movement led by Raúl Castro's daughter, Mariela.

Indeed, at a societal level there seems to be a correlation between state-supported homophobia and authoritarianism, and even today the most homophobic countries are largely those that are also the most repressive of social and political dissent. How far this reflects a fear by authoritarian leaders of sexual dissidence leading to political rebellion is difficult to assess – sexual permissiveness could, after all, also be a means of diverting political action into privatised satisfaction, rather as Aldous Huxley predicted in *Brave New World*.[11] Yet there are very few examples of authoritarian societies that are not deeply sexually repressive (one might make a partial exception for the Philippines under Ferdinand Marcos). Again, there could be differing explanations for the extent to which homosexuality seems to be so significant an issue for religious believers, although most research suggests that they are likely to hold more rigid beliefs about what is 'natural' than non-believers. There is a growing literature on religious attitudes towards homosexuality, especially those of fundamentalist Christianity and Islam.[12]

At the same time, some poor countries are deliberately cultivating gay tourism, as a means of encouraging investment. The tradition of white gay men (and occasionally lesbians) seeking sexual adventure in poorer countries has a long history, which is reflected in semi-official campaigns to attract the pink dollar. Businesses in Cambodia, Thailand and Bali all seek to attract gay visitors, and in 2010 Siem Reap in Cambodia was proclaimed a 'gay haven' by the travel section of *The New York Times*.[13] Not surprisingly, the promotion of sexual tourism based on economic inequality is likely to further inflame homophobic prejudice, as has happened in some Caribbean countries, where there has been strong hostility expressed to large cruise ships packed with gay men docking in local ports.

Homosexuality is politically charged because it becomes a proxy for anxieties around identity and modernity at both the personal and the political level. There is considerable evidence that much of the most violent homophobia comes from those who are frightened or in denial of their own homosexual feelings. At a societal level, homophobia becomes a way of displacing anxieties about rapid change and feelings of declining status and power, as it appeals to traditional beliefs and ingrained feelings about what is natural, which almost certainly equates to the perception of men as both dominant and necessarily heterosexual.

Over the past decade, the beginnings of global organising around homosexual identities and politics, discussed in earlier chapters, has been given a major boost by mobilisation around AIDS, and older groups such as the ILGA have been joined by groups more specifically focused on HIV, which have taken up the links between health and human rights. Most impressive is the Global Forum on MSM and HIV, which has become a major advocacy body within the international AIDS world and has recruited some quite extraordinary leaders from countries with emerging gay and transgender movements. At the same time, a continuing interest in global sexual politics at a more academic level is maintained through the International Association for the Study of Sexuality, Culture and Society, which has run successful biennial conferences on a number of continents since the early 1990s.

Moreover, activism amongst sexually and gender diverse groups is developing rapidly, even in countries that would seem unlikely to embrace such movements. The panics around homosexuality in countries such as Uganda, Nigeria and Russia are, in part, products of the growth of a new assertion amongst local sexual and gender dissidents, who are building movements that are influenced by their counterparts in the western world, although they operate within very different political spaces.[14]

There are real political dilemmas for an international movement in responding to what seems to be a growing political homophobia in many parts of the world. While many activists hail the statements of western governments, others see this strategy as provoking a counter-reaction. As one African wrote on the MSM forum: 'Foreign (western) intervention can only make it worse for sexual and gender minorities in many of these countries who pay for the intervention dearly with their lives.' Statements of support from American embassies, complete with rainbow flags and references to 'LGBT rights' may satisfy gay lobbyists in the United States but are not necessarily effective in countries such as Kenya or Pakistan.

Not all homosexual movements support the overt demands and militancy that seems to dominate global discourses; as one activist in Guinea wrote: 'The only way as gay to live without any harassment is to keep silence.'[15] In a similar vein, a statement from the Samoan Fa'afafine Association disassociated itself from calls for same-sex marriage:

> Even the idea of us having partners, it's discreet. We would do it elsewhere but never in our families or where our parents are at because we love them ... we can't bring partners in our families where our siblings are, it's not nice – our culture is too strong.[16]

There is a genuine danger that well-meaning activists in the west – often supported by international agencies – will push local groups to move too fast or in directions that are inappropriate, given the political and cultural spaces within which they operate. Consultants and donors can go home; local homosexuals have to live with the consequences of their actions.

SEX, LOVE AND SAME-SEX MARRIAGE

A poem from the period of gay liberation by San Francisco poet Pat Parker reminds us of the contradictions of liberation:

> Me, I am
> totally opposed to
> monogamous relations
> unless
> I'm
> in love

(Pat Parker, *Child of Myself*, 1972)

Throughout the period of writing this book, the issue of same-sex marriage has dominated discussions about the place of homosexuality in public life in Australia and several other countries, including France and the United States.

In September 2012 both houses of Australia's federal parliament voted down several bills to end the requirement that marriage need be between a woman and a man; the changes were sponsored by both the Greens and some sections of the Labor Party, but the Liberals and Nationals were refused a free vote, ensuring that there was no realistic possibility of the bills passing. While a majority of Prime Minister Julia Gillard's ministry voted for change, the bills were opposed both by Gillard herself and her predecessor, Kevin Rudd. There is constant speculation about why Gillard, an unmarried atheist, is so opposed to same-sex marriage, and whether this is due to political calculation, because of her support from the right of the party, or reflects her own lower-middle-class Welsh background (she has spoken about coming from 'a quite conservative family, in the sense of personal values').[1]

The following week, the Tasmanian upper house voted down a similar measure, but there are complex legal arguments about whether the states in fact have the constitutional power to rule in this area. While it is impossible to make an accurate prediction, the current political environment suggests that same-sex marriage is unlikely in Australia within the next few years, although some form of civil union may well be institutionalised.*

Arguments about the same-sex vote dominated much of the media for several weeks, and clearly became an important issue for large numbers of people, both 'gay' and 'straight'. Already same-sex marriage had emerged as a media issue in the 2010 election, to the embarrassment of both major political parties. As both Julia Gillard and Tony Abbott struggled to avoid the issue, it was raised persistently in public forums, most movingly by the father of a gay man in a live television interview with Abbott, who struggled to balance his own conservative views with his apparent sympathy for a father who felt his son was denied a basic right.

Labor was even more embarrassed by the persistent questioning of its openly lesbian minister, Penny Wong, who supported her leader's stance during the election campaign but has since become one of the most eloquent proponents of marriage equality. Wong was a key figure

---

* Queensland briefly allowed such unions, but the incoming conservative government in 2012 overturned the law.

in the adoption of support for same-sex marriage at the ALP Federal Conference at the end of 2011; because of Prime Minister Gillard's views, the party made the issue one of the very few in which Labor parliamentarians were allowed a conscience vote. This was probably the only time in Australian political history that Labor granted a conscience vote to its parliamentarians and its conservative opponent did not, although the Liberals and Nationals like to insist that they are less controlling of their MPs.

The Greens have used the issue effectively in their campaigning, especially in inner-city seats, and it was a factor, though not the decisive one, in Adam Bandt's success in winning the seat of Melbourne in the 2010 federal election.

Same-sex marriage has now become a crucial marker of acceptance for large numbers of young people. In March 2012 the television presenter Adam Hills hosted the first on-air mass same-sex marriage ceremony on his ABC program *In Gordon Street Tonight*, creating a very different television image of homosexuality from those earnest talk shows of the 1970s. His claim that viewers of the show saw it as the single most important legislative change needed in Australia seemed borne out by a parliamentary inquiry into same-sex marriage in April 2012 that received some 75,000 submissions, the majority in favour.

Increasingly, I find myself in the odd situation of hearing straight friends and politicians insist on the importance of an issue which, for me, as a gay man with a long history of activism, is at best a second-order political demand. Thus, Kevin Rudd's former advisor Troy Bramston wrote: 'Labor's leaders still talk of opportunity and equality, but they don't support marriage equality for all Australians.'[2] I applaud his support for equality, but I also contend that extending 'marriage' to same-sex couples is not necessarily the only way of achieving this.

I recognise that to argue this is to align myself with some of the most homophobic elements of Australian society, and it is an argument that is increasingly difficult to make in public. Indeed, when the bills were introduced I not only wanted them to pass but was infuriated that several left-wing Labor MPs who were fond of preaching tolerance and diversity actually voted against the measure.

For queer activists, the rise of gay marriage exemplifies the ongoing tensions between seeking respectability and asserting difference. The campaign for marriage first emerged as central to the gay and lesbian movement in the 1990s, and there followed recognition of same-sex unions in several European countries, beginning with Denmark and the Netherlands. Nowhere was the debate as heated as in the United States, where it echoed the particularly American mix of an assertive gay movement, a strong resistance to homosexual equality, and a culture imbued with religiosity. The issue emerged rapidly and marked a strange turn in the American movement away from the apparent radicalism of ACT UP in the early 1990s. It was as if, overnight, the assertion of radical difference was replaced by the desire for integration.

Of course, this is a somewhat lazy generalisation, and gay marriage had been mooted a number of times before it became a politically salient issue. The performance artist Yayoi Kusama staged 'the first homosexual wedding ever to be performed in the United States' in 1968, a year before Stonewall,[3] and as early as 1972 the American gay liberationist Pete Fisher discussed arguments within the gay movement around marriage in his book *The Gay Mystique*. In 1975 a county clerk in Boulder, Colorado, issued marriage licences to six same-sex couples; one involved an Australian, Anthony Sullivan, who otherwise would have been deported and separated from his partner, Richard Adams. The licences were overturned by the state attorney-general; after appealing, in order to allow Sullivan to remain in the United States, the pair received a letter from the Immigration and Naturalization Service that read: 'You have failed to establish that a bona fide marital relationship can exist between two faggots.'[4]

The American historian George Chauncey has pointed out that there were consistent moves for same-sex marriage, in particular through the Metropolitan Community Church, over the past few decades. Chauncey attributes the rise of interest in gay marriage to the losses from AIDS and the 'lesbian baby boom' that began in the

1980s.[5] I think there is a third significant factor: namely, the triumph of conservatism in the United States. After twelve years of Republican presidencies, the country seemed to have shifted to the right, and President Bill Clinton's failure to remove discrimination in the armed forces – all he achieved was the equally offensive 'don't ask, don't tell' policy – seemed to signal clear limits to acceptance. (Clinton has now said he was wrong to sign into law the Defence of Marriage Act in 1996.) Fairly quickly, military service and marriage became the rallying cries for a new sort of homosexual militancy, one that insisted not on difference, as had queer radicals, but rather on equal rights.

Marriage equality started to emerge as a theme in the Australian gay press by the mid-1990s, but there was comparatively little interest in the issue until 2004, when Prime Minister John Howard introduced the Marriage Amendment Bill, which incorporated the common law definition of marriage – 'the union of a man and a woman to exclusion of all others' – into both the Marriage Act and the Family Law Act, thereby giving the same-sex marriage movement its impetus.[6]

Howard had clearly been influenced by his Republican friends in the United States – Karl Rove would use the spectre of 'gay marriage' to rally voters behind George W Bush in the 2004 presidential election – but its impact in Australia was limited. The Liberal federal member for Adelaide at the time said it would cost her seat, and she was right, although there is little evidence that the issue won the Howard government additional support.*

Since then, there has been a rapidly growing movement in support of same-sex marriage, and public opinion surveys suggest that a majority of Australians now support it. Given this, the timidity of both major parties is somewhat surprising, although it is likely that politicians are somewhat more religious – or scared of religious criticism – than the population at large. Even supporters of same-sex

---

* Ironically, in that same year the Liberal candidate for the seat of Brisbane, Ingrid Tall, was openly lesbian; she claimed she lost votes as a consequence of her sexuality, although the only clear evidence of her claim is that the Family First party refused to preference her over the sitting Labor member, who retained the seat.

marriage are (privately) surprised by the way the issue has attracted so much interest and support. My hunch is that it has become a symbol of deep changes in social attitudes, and clever political leadership has been able to persuade large numbers of people that the question is a basic test of equal rights.

In the United States the battle over same-sex marriage is moving inexorably towards the Supreme Court, given that a referendum in California has overturned a state court ruling in favour of marriage equality, which in turn has led to further legal appeals. The confusion for many couples is summed up in Armistead Maupin's 2010 novel *Mary Ann in Autumn*:

> Michael and Ben had been married for the third time in August. The first wedding had been performed at City Hall but was thrown out by the state courts. The second had happened at a B & B in Vancouver but was valid only in Canada. The third one Michael had referred to as 'the shotgun marriage', since he and Ben had rushed to say their vows before the November election, when the voters would have their say.

The battlelines are not predictable: a top-level Republican lawyer helped argue the case for same-sex marriage at the Supreme Court of California, and even the commentator Glen Back, a supporter of the Tea Party, has indicated that he's not bothered by gay marriage.[7] When President Barack Obama declared in mid-2012 that his views had evolved to the point of supporting same-sex marriage, there was general agreement that this would not have a major impact on his political support in an election year; if anything, it may have helped mobilise his electoral base. At the time of writing it seems likely that the US Supreme Court will overrule the Defence of Marriage Act so that the federal government can recognise same-sex unions in those states that have legalised them.

Obama may have been reflecting a shift in views amongst many African Americans, even if some conservative church-goers were publicly critical of his statement. The shift was symbolised by the very public coming out of hip hop singer Frank Ocean, and was also caught in a casual journalistic comment about the black television comedian W Kaman Bell, 'whose gimmick is intersectional progressivism; he treats racial, gay and women's issues as inseparable'.[8] This had seemed a radical view when we suggested it in the early days of gay liberation; now, for a surprising number of Americans, most of whom strongly supported Obama, it is taken for granted. Obama himself took this position in his second inaugural address, when he linked Seneca Falls, Selma and Stonewall as pivotal moments in the struggles for equality. (Seneca Falls, New York, was the location of a women's rights convention organised in 1848, while Selma, Alabama, saw one of the civil rights movement's most notable clashes with entrenched racism in 1965.)

The gay liberation movement developed out of extreme alienation from a model of the family that was predicated on particular gender relations, the pretence of monogamy and the biological link between children and parents. This model remains, but it is increasingly distant from the experience of more and more people as marriages break down, living together outside marriage occurs more frequently, and new family structures, involving step-parents and children moving between two homes become more common. It is becoming easier to accept gay and lesbian family members within increasingly diverse family structures, just as more and more children are growing up in same-sex households.

A strong theme of gay liberation writings was the idea that we created our own families, so that friends, rather than biological relations, became the central reference point of gay and lesbian lives. Indeed, this is a trope of much of the literature of the 1970s, and was reflected in attempts to create communal households and to build close circles of friends. Perhaps the best-known example of this comes in the very complex relationships charted in Armistead Maupin's *Tales of the City*, in which a family is built around the lodgers in Mrs Madrigal's home on Telegraph Hill, many of whom have difficult and distant relations with their own parents. By the 1980s, some gay men were donating sperm to lesbian friends, partly out of a desire to break down assumptions that only heterosexuals could bear children.[9] But at the same time, relations between queers and their biological families were also changing.

For many gay and lesbian activists, the recognition of same-sex marriage has become the ultimate test of acceptance, with claims that its achievement will be a powerful blow against homophobia. As someone who was in a primary relationship for over twenty years, which only ended with the death of my partner, I appreciate the real importance of formal equality. But two doubts remain: does the institution of marriage really advance acceptance? And is there a danger that homosexuals are parodying an outmoded institution by seeking inclusion in the romantic myth of marriage?

The argument that gay marriage weakens homophobia is only correct if the great majority seriously accept same-sex marriages. The issue can too easily become a parody, as it is in the opening scenes of the film *Sex and the City 2*, which mocks a same-sex wedding while apparently endorsing it. Even the wedding in *Gordon Street* seemed simultaneously a celebration and an ironic send-up of the whole idea, as Hills altered the language of the traditional ceremony to include references to television ratings and viewers' complaints.

Campaigners for same-sex marriage claim that it provides 'role models, development paths and stability'; as Ryan Heath writes:

> Is there no connection between this and the disproportionate numbers of suicides and risky and addictive behaviours found in gay communities? Are we not denying the very best safety net of all to some of the people who need it most?[10]

Yes, perhaps. But the assumption that the answer to deep feelings of inadequacy and marginalisation will be met by the availability of a marriage certificate seems to me as yet unproven. There are many models of long-lasting same-sex couples who thrived in the absence of marriage. Surely it is more useful to offer a range of possible ways of living one's life than to buy in to the myth of monogamous marriage, whose record is generally not inspiring. Indeed, the desire to align the pro-marriage movement with monogamy was strong enough that whether to include polyamorists – who believe in multiple concurrent relations – in Sydney's Mardi Gras has become a matter of contention.

When gay marriage became a major movement goal, some radicals expressed unease about what they saw as accepting mainstream heterosexual values. 'Against Equality', a small but very active ginger group in the United States, proclaimed:

> In their constant invoking of the 'right' to gay marriage, mainstream gays and lesbians express a confused tangle of wishes and desires. They claim to contest the Right's conservative ideology yet insist that they are more moral and hence more deserving than sluts like us. They claim that they simply want the famous 1000+ benefits but all of these, like the right to claim protection in cases of domestic violence, can be made available to non-marital relationships.[11]

I am particularly uneasy with the frequent equation of the prohibition of same-sex marriage with that of interracial marriage. In the latter case, racism prevented marriages that were indistinguishable in any other way, prompted by deep fears of miscegenation. Same-sex partnerships are as valid and as significant as heterosexual ones, but they are also different, and maybe we should celebrate rather than deny that difference.

Feminists have long criticised marriage as the institutional basis for male supremacy and restrictive notions of monogamy, and sexual radicals have denounced it as a declining and oppressive institution. The notion of marriage implies a long-term commitment to both sexual and emotional commitment. Yet the two are not necessarily synonymous, and certainly many gay men incorporate a whole range of sexual adventuring within long-term, committed partnerships. There seems something hypocritical in the rush to embrace marriage vows, which were designed to emphasise that commitment was to be measured entirely by sexual fidelity.

Moreover, the constant stress on marriage as the ultimate test of gay equality risks making invisible those homosexuals who either do not want or cannot find a long-term relationship. The available research suggests that many more homosexuals live alone than is true of the general population – does the emphasis on marriage further marginalise them? The importance given to marriage risks excluding those people whose sexual and emotional lives do not fit a primary couple relationship.[12] (Judith Butler made similar points in an important article some years ago.[13])

There is an extensive feminist literature on the ways in which women are restricted by the emphasis on seeking a husband to the exclusion of all else. It would be ironic if the lesbian and gay movement ignored these warnings, and reified marriage as the only acceptable way of living one's life. Yet, as Gore Vidal once said, the only people left who believe in marriage are homosexuals, and who am I to deny them that pleasure? There are many homosexuals who believe passionately in marriage as the ultimate test of equality, and there is a danger of the worst sort of elitism in denying the agency of those gay men and lesbians for whom this is an important goal. Social movements do not always adopt the positions their intellectuals would prefer, but they are no less significant for that reason.

In this century the same-sex marriage debate has brought women and men together in a new coalition. But I suspect the alliances around same-sex marriage hide deeper divides around attitudes towards sex, which the movement seems increasingly loath to discuss. During a panel discussion at the Sydney Writers Festival in 2012, I upset a fellow panellist, the writer Jeanette Winterson – and some of the audience – by insisting that fidelity should not be measured by monogamy. Indeed, the emphasis on marriage seems to have bleached sex out of the discussion altogether.

The debate around gay marriage now extends even to societies where acceptance of homosexuality remains at best deeply precarious.

In 2011 a male couple in Malawi were imprisoned after they held a symbolic marriage ceremony, and they were released only after considerable international pressure, which included intervention by the Secretary-General of the United Nations. The President of Malawi, one of the few women heads of state in Africa, has now called for decriminalisation of homosexuality. The gay movement in Nepal is pressing for recognition of same-sex marriage, and in the Philippines it was part of the platform put forward by the party Ang Ladlad (or 'Out of the Closet'), which had formed to contest one of the three seats reserved for minority groups.

Cambodia's King-Father Norodom Sihanouk, when nearing the end of his reign in 2004, announced that he thought same-sex marriages should be allowed in his country. He said that, as a liberal democracy, 'this kingdom should allow, if they wish, marriage between man and man or between woman and woman', adding that '[God loves] a wide range of tastes'. There have been reports of same-sex marriage in Taiwan dating back to the 1990s, and marriage was a theme of the gay pride parade in Taipei in 2012. A move to recognise same-sex marriage has been submitted on several occasions to the Chinese People's Political Consultative Conference,[14] and more recently has been mooted by government officials in Vietnam and Thailand.

Talking to a few young activists in Tokyo and Kyoto last year, I was struck by their desire to find an appropriate form of activism that might better engage with Japanese reality. When I asked what issues might demand activism, one young man said that marriage was an important issue because only recognised family members could inherit under Japanese law. Despite my own reservations, I recognise that marriage has now become a potent symbol of equality, and that its acceptance in the United States, at least on a state-by-state basis, is now faster than in Australia.[15]

I have already discussed the claim by second-wave feminists and gay liberationists that 'the personal is the political'. Today, large numbers of lesbians and gay men are discovering the reality of this, precisely because they seek to live openly in ways that assert their role in conventional society. In the Swedish film *Patrik, Age 1.5*, two gay men move to a small town, marry and seek to adopt a child. They are taunted by the neighbourhood kids as homos; 'What's a homo?' asks one of the kids when he visits one of the men, who is also the local doctor. The very attempts of the couple to live 'normally' mean that they must constantly assert their right to inclusion in village life. As more homosexuals marry, raise children and move to suburbia, the need to negotiate relations with schools, neighbours and workmates means they constantly must confront the problems of grudging acceptance and lingering prejudices.

CODA: THE END OF
THE HOMOSEXUAL?

The gay movement has been one of the most successful of the cultural movements of the 1970s, both in achieving major changes in cultural mores and in its ability to continue to mobilise support, even if today's demand for same-sex marriage seems rather distant from the radicalism of early gay liberation. At the same time, it seems as if these changes often remain invisible, even to otherwise acute social observers, so that many of the recent books that talk about social change over the past few decades remain oblivious to sexuality, and especially to homosexuality. What has been of huge consequence to those of us who have lived it has had remarkably little impact upon the way the larger society tells the story of the last forty years.

A middle-aged generation of Australian male journalists and scholars has been writing in interesting ways about social change, but remains too heteronormative to notice the extent to which the perception, regulation and popular imagination of homosexuality has changed over the past few decades. I am thinking here of three writers I both know and admire – which is precisely why I think it worth criticising them – George Megalogenis, Gideon Haigh and Jeff Sparrow. All have produced significant books in the last several years:

Megalogenis's *The Australian Moment*, Haigh's wonderful (and well illustrated) *The Office* and Sparrow's narrative of his explorations in the world of commercialised sex, *Money Shot*.

While Megalogenis is very aware of the ways in which 'wogs and women' have changed Australia, he reveals no interest in sexuality; Haigh discusses sexuality in office politics but with the assumption that the story is exclusively heterosexual; and Sparrow is clearly supportive of homosexual equality but discusses the sexual politics of pornography and the commodification of desire in almost exclusively heterosexual terms.

In its first seven years of existence, *The Monthly*, which claims to be Australia's leading journal of opinion, has not published a serious story on queer politics – although it has run several on AIDS, including one I wrote. Heteronormativity remains dominant in most strains of social commentary, and in most books on sex and love, whose various permutations remain unproblematically heterocentric.[1] The literary critic Geordie Williamson's overview of 'good Australian novelists' includes three whom he recognises as homosexual: Patrick White, Sumner Locke Elliott and Randolph Stow. At no point does he reflect on how their homosexuality might have shaped their writing, nor does he discuss the homosexual themes in their novels.[2]

The assumptions of heteronormativity remain strong in some surprising quarters. Given her own history of disparaging remarks about homosexuality, who would have expected Germaine Greer to be the person to point to Naomi Wolf's 'incurable heterosexual' view of the world in her book *Vagina: A New Biography*.[3] Wolf, after all, has presented herself as a model of the contemporary feminist, sensitive to all forms of oppression. Other than in specific departments devoted to gender and sexuality, the movements these issues have generated and the political disputes that surround them are rarely taught within our universities, although Australia does have several centres and departments in which first-class research takes place in these areas.

Western cultures are now saturated with sexual images and an acceptance of behaviour that would have seemed startling even twenty years ago, and inconceivable twenty years before then. The vast quantity of pornography available on the internet, the use of increasingly explicit sexual images in advertising, and the increasing frankness – or crudity, depending on one's views – of sex in television and film have all changed cultural norms and created pressures for sexual performance that many see as eroding childhood and setting up exorbitant expectations for sexual gratification that few can meet.

In this context, complaints about homosexuality as degenerate or overly concerned with sex seem less and less convincing, and indeed there is an increasing overlap in the mores of the 'gay' and 'straight' worlds. There may be fewer claims today that sleeping around is revolutionary than were made in the 1970s, but as the film director John Duigan put it: 'When men and women go out at night, it's no surprise to them if they end up in bed and they don't think any less of themselves if they do.'[4] The internet has helped open up possibilities for heterosexual liaisons which are as fleeting and immediate as those often associated with gay men.[5]

Many young women now claim the right to be as sexually unconstrained as men, but equally to be free from potential sexual violence if they are perceived as 'easily available'. This claim was symbolised by a number of 'SlutWalks', which were triggered off in Toronto in 2011 by a comment from a policeman that women encouraged sexual assaults by 'dressing like sluts'.[6] The early feminist insistence that 'no means no' has actually been recapitulated in signs I've seen in gay saunas, where patrons are urged to accept rejection politely. What some observers see as an increasing 'pornification' of the culture – namely, a greater overt emphasis and discussion of sexuality – is also potentially liberatory, in that it helps make acceptance of sexual and gender diversity increasingly more common.

The mood of much current fiction, of which the French writer Michel Houellebecq is the most extreme example, is that sexual commodification and gratification is an expression of increasing alienation. There are strong arguments to be made against the increasing commercialisation of sex, and the pressures it places upon young people to measure up to unrealistic standards – as well as the equally oppressive fears of ageing and the loss of sexual options – but, moral judgments aside, some of these changes have been important in allowing for growing acceptance of sexual diversity. (One might also ask when sex has NOT been commodified: the forms may change, but the exchange of sexual favours for money and influence is common throughout most of human history.)

The growing separation between intimacy and sex, acknowledged in acceptance of 'one-night stands' or terms such as 'friends with benefits', is something gay men have always understood. What was once feared and regarded as decadent is now increasingly accepted as just another variety of sexuality, in a world in which sex is no longer defined as sacred or something confined to monogamous marriage.[7] Heterosexual women now go in groups to male strip clubs, and behave remarkably like the gay male patrons of similar bars in Los Angeles, Paris and London. (Other than when special shows are organised, usually at dance parties, go-go boys seem less common as background entertainment in Australian gay bars.)

These changes mean that many younger homosexuals find it easier to socialise and party in a pan-sexual world, even while retaining a strong sense of their queer identity. Many contemporary homosexuals would share the feelings of the Englishman Dan Martin, who, in a revealing blog entitled 'The Lady Gaga Backlash Begins', wrote: 'As we march towards true equality, the whole idea of a "gay culture" becomes more and more meaningless as the world accepts the truth that gay people aren't all the same.'[8] Martin's argument seems in almost total juxtaposition to that made by the American theorist David Halperin, who has argued for the continuity of a certain sort of 'gay culture', and the need to initiate men into it. Echoing some of what Sontag wrote in her famous, if somewhat coded, 1964 article about 'camp', Halperin argues that: 'Being gay would seem to involve an entire attitude and set of values, an entire *cultural* orientation.'[9] He goes on to link these values to 'Hollywood movies, grand opera, Broadway musicals ... as well as camp, diva-worship, drag, muscle culture, style, fashion and interior design'.

The limits of Halperin's approach are summed up in a story I've been told that someone applying for refugee status on the basis of his homosexuality was knocked back because he couldn't sing a Madonna song. It's probably true that more middle-class white American homosexuals can discuss, say, Stephen Sondheim, Judy Garland and *Lucia di Lammermoor* than their heterosexual counterparts, but to elevate this into some sort of requirement for being gay in the contemporary world strikes me as problematic. As Halperin ignores lesbians, it is unclear what cultural yardsticks he would apply to them: maybe a knowledge of netball and the best lines of Jane Lynch in *Glee*? But if his approach becomes hyperbolic, there are also some important arguments in his book *How to Be Gay* that recognise the ongoing connections between sexual and gender dissidence.

I would prefer an analysis that accepted that being homosexual may no longer mean feeling constantly stigmatised, but that there remains an awareness of difference which becomes a bond of sorts between all those who are sexually or gender diverse, however fragile these bonds may be in practice. Rather like another contemporary American gay theorist, Shannon Gilreath, Halperin seems convinced that there are deep and immutable differences between 'gays' and 'straights', and is concerned that the rush to acceptance will obliterate much of what is best about gay culture, although the two authors may not agree on exactly what that is.[10] Ironically, while I have been deeply critical of both books, I share Gilreath's and Halperin's underlying concern about the drive for assimilation. Halperin's argument is in some ways meant as a refutation of Daniel Harris's 1997 book *The Rise and Fall of Gay Culture*, which claimed that: 'The end of oppression necessitates the end of gay sensibility.'[11] I suspect that both sides overstate their cases.

Even so, there is a certain sense of shared exclusion from the mainstream that still unites queers; when I have coffee with my gay or lesbian colleagues, there is a different tone to the discussions than when others are there. A room filled with queers – even more, one that is completely lesbian or gay – remains different in the forms of its social interaction from a room of mixed sexualities. Sometimes I think the difference between gay and straight men (less true for women) is that gay men tend to embrace or kiss on meeting, whereas straight men rely on the manly handshake, though even that is changing.

Not all homosexuals seek integration and acceptance, and indeed new forms of assertion are emerging as I write. Suzanna Walters put this beautifully when she wrote:

> In the current mainstream 'pro-gay' zeitgeist, gay marriage plus gay parents plus gay genes plus gay soldiers=victory. This media-friendly version of sexual minority inclusion is predicated on an erasure of feminist and queer critiques of gender normativity and the nuclear family.[12]

Early in the course of writing this book, I read two remarkable first novels from Europe, Tristan Garcia's *Hate* (first published in French in 2008 under the title *La meilleure part des hommes*) and Max Schaefer's *Children of the Sun* (published in Britain in 2010). What is interesting about both books is that they reflect an equal contempt for mainstream gay respectability and for heteronormativity. The sexual mores of gay men remain rather different to those of the mainstream, as is evidenced by the continuing popularity of sex-on-premises venues and websites that allow instant hook-ups, even if this is rarely acknowledged in the public debates on same-sex marriage. Interestingly, many of the notices for hook-ups that appear on such sites proclaim men to be 'straight acting', as if to disavow the very homosexuality they are seeking.

Yet increasingly, many heterosexuals are likely to behave no differently to most homosexuals, as some gay men eschew 'promiscuity' and some heterosexuals embrace sexual adventure.* Perhaps the least likely group to use the web for instant hook-ups are lesbians; there are numerous accounts of attempts to establish websites like those available to gay men, and of their inability to attract users who are

---

* It is probably worth pointing out that the early episodes of the television movie, *Sex and the City*, produced at the turn of the century, depicted its women characters in ways that were clearly modelled on stereotypical gay male behaviour.

willing to accept sex with, as the standard abbreviation states, 'NSA' (no strings attached).

Even so, the rules for sexual connections remain rather different in the gay male world, and part of what Raymond Williams might term 'residual culture' is the persistence of certain forms of sex-on-premises venues that have no real counterparts for either lesbians or heterosexuals. But it is my sense that these are also spaces where men come together to feel a sense of community. One of Melbourne's biggest gay clubs, for instance, hosts a monthly sex party at which many men spend more time playing pool and catching up with their friends than they do playing upstairs in the naked sex zones.

I think that Halperin is right to see a shift in homosexuals' emotional attitudes towards their sexuality but wrong to lament it. Increasingly, there is a new persona emerging – in the sense that Jung saw the word, as a mask designed both to impress others and to conceal some of one's 'true nature'. Younger queers are more self-confident, more comfortable with their sexuality, and therefore more able to move easily between the queer and straight worlds. If this leads to a proliferation of different ways of being gay, that would seem to me a major achievement.

Currently, there is a strange tension between the language of 'sexual diversity' and an insistence on 'LGBTI people', which to some extent reprises older debates between essentialists and constructionists. For some of us, it is disconcerting to see a new generation of activists whose priorities seem to renounce the radicalism of gay liberation, and who seem unaware of and uninterested in the radical push shared by women's and gay liberation to challenge the 'common-sense' and taken-for-granted assumptions about private life.

Modern queer activists, at least in the western world, start from different assumptions than we did: primarily a solid sense of entitlement that comes from their inner certainty about the legitimacy of their desires. My generation protested too much because we needed to convince ourselves as much as others, and we veered between unnecessary timidity and assertiveness. We saw ourselves as growing out of the protest movements of the left, and desperately wanted to be radical: thus our claim that our sexuality was inherently political. This mood was quickly displaced in the United States as middle-class lesbians and gay men became active in mainstream politics; in Australia it took longer, although AIDS meant that many gay men had to learn how to work with the state, drawing on some of the lessons many lesbians had learnt as femocrats in the 1970s. It was only with the emergence of the marriage issue as central in the past decade that a large, professional and respectable gay and lesbian movement has emerged in Australia, one that has no compunctions about claiming that all it wants is inclusion. This can be seen as a conservative shift, but it is also a mark of a new self-assurance.

In secular western societies it is probably true that homophobia and hostility towards homosexuals has declined dramatically, to the point where it is difficult to imagine a return to the denials and repressions that were common half a century ago. In this sense, the utopian vision of sexuality ceasing to be a primary identity born of oppression seems correct, although the idea of a fluid and diverse sexuality that does not require categories is still utopian.

But here, too, reality becomes more complex. Back in the seventies, we had assumed that as gender roles became less rigid, and prescriptions for 'masculinity' and 'femininity' more fluid, so too would fewer people feel a need to change their sense of gender identity. The reverse seems to be true: greater acceptance of sexual fluidity is now accompanied by an equal emphasis on gender fluidity, which, on reflection, is a logical consequence of the constructionist emphasis on how much of what is taken for granted is in fact socially constructed. In part, this is due to greater medical possibilities for gender reassignment, but it's also because of more sympathetic media depictions and a greater willingness to experiment with a much broader range of gender performativities.

Raewyn Connell, who herself has made the transition, has pointed to our shared unawareness of the persistence of transgender feelings in the heady period of gay liberation, and tensions remain between those who see themselves as becoming the woman or man they have long felt themselves to be and those who declare a transgendered identity that denies a gender binary altogether. Some older women such as Germaine Greer have clung to a particular feminist view that transitioning is ultimately a delusion, which led to her being 'glitter-bombed' in Wellington in early 2012. 'Transphobic feminism is so 20th century,' declared Tracy of Queer Avengers. 'Women's liberation must mean the right to refuse imposed gender roles, to fight for diverse gender expression.'[13] To which one might retort: 'Does diverse expression require physical modifications?' But on balance I accept Connell's conclusion: 'Transsexuality involves deep gender disruption and reconstitution, in a historically specific form. But to *operate* this revolutionary possibility, many transsexual women and many of their doctors have relied on deeply conservative gender schemata.'[14]

The last decade has seen an explosion of awareness of transgender, whether it be though films such as *Transamerica* (2005) or well-known figures such as Chaz Bono coming out as trans. In Australia there is a small but vocal group of trans folk, who produce the magazine *Dude* and insist that the term 'trans' covers a variety of sexual and gender identities. Online, one can find men seeking men who are 'open minded enough not to mind boys with c-nts [*sic*]'.

We thought we'd separated sex and gender through the liberation sought by the lesbian and gay movement, but in fact the connection persists: macho men and lipstick lesbians are still playing with gender stereotypes even as they reject the idea that 'real' men and women are necessarily heterosexual. Indeed, some people today may be defining themselves as 'transgender' rather than as 'gay' or 'lesbian', which seemed the only possible identity in the recent past. There are even some examples of once butch lesbians who in recent years have decided to adopt trans identities.[15] Confusion between the ideas of sexual and gender diversity seems, if anything, more marked than it was several decades ago; even intelligent discussions tend to fall back on stereotypes and essentialist views of identity, as in much of the debate around same-sex marriage. And even sophisticated and progressive commentators, such as the grown-up adolescent boys who make up the Chaser television comedy team, still use effeminacy as a marker for homosexuality.

It might seem contradictory that there is an increasing interest in transgender at a time when there are increasingly diverse styles of presenting one's gender, irrespective of sexuality. At the same time, more kids, defying the expectations of earlier liberationists, are declaring themselves to be transgendered, which may or may not be associated with a desire for women, men or both – perhaps they simply have unspecified sexual desires. Certainly, it seems odd that, at a time when there is growing hostility towards any therapies that might change one's sexual orientation, there is increasing support for changing gender characteristics, which usually requires extensive hormonal, psychiatric and surgical intervention. Trans activists are caught in the dilemma of wanting to deny that theirs is a medical condition while remaining heavily dependent on medical intervention for physical modification.

It is probably true that no discussion of homosexuality can be divorced from a recognition of the malleability of gender, or from the complex ways in which sexuality and gender intersect. At the same time, it should be possible to have an intelligent discussion about how far there is a commonality between experiences based on sexual and gender diversity, which is occluded by the constant emphasis on 'LGBTI' politics. Raewyn Connell has claimed that: 'Support from other feminists is the most strategic resource for empowering transsexual women,'[16] and she has also questioned the assumption that trans people should be seen as part of, rather than allies of, a movement based on homosexuality.

The progressive narrative of 'LGBTI' rights assumes increasing assimilation of people with different sexualities into the mainstream, while at the same time asserting the importance of identity politics. In western societies – and particularly nations such as Australia, the United States and Canada, which are committed, at least rhetorically, to ideas of multiculturalism – this seems quite possible. But behind this optimism is a belief that the growing secularisation of society will lead to increasing acceptance of the blurring of distinctions around sexuality and gender, and for that the evidence is more mixed. Not all ethnic groups do, in fact, assimilate; often they reassert their separate cultural identities once a certain level of acceptance is possible. And while there is certainly a decline in the political clout of the religious right in the United States, the world is not necessarily becoming more secular. Margaret Atwood's consistently dystopian warnings in novels such as *The Handmaid's Tale* and, more recently, *Oryx and Crake* may be a necessary corrective against the too easy assumption that acceptance of diversity will increase to a point that we can dispense with a sense of sexually based identities.

Nor, indeed, should we assume that most people will want to dispense with such ideas of themselves. The enthusiasm for queer identities, which now dates back two decades, has not replaced a need for people to stress their particular identities within that umbrella term. What is at stake is when and by whom our sexuality is defined. 'Sexual liberation', a term that now sounds almost archaic, means the right to move between asserting that one's sexuality is central and equally asserting that it should not affect all parts of one's life or relationships. The current interest in what happens to 'LGBTI' people as they age – a 'LGBT-friendly affordable senior housing facility' has just been opened in Philadelphia, for instance, and there have been intermittent discussions of the demand for such facilities in Australia – suggests that the need for a sense of identity and community is not declining.

The current confusions between identity and behaviour, and between acceptance and discrimination, are rather different to those of forty years ago, but in some ways they remain just as intractable. It has become increasingly common to speak of 'LGBT' people as if we are a self-evident minority that should be recognised as such, while at the same time many homosexuals insist that we should not be defined by our sexualities. None of us can be identified solely by reference to one part of our identity, but at the same time we cannot pretend that something as central as our sexual desires, identities and behaviours is irrelevant to who we are and how we act in the broader world.

What we can hope for is greater acceptance that there is no one way of acting out human sexuality, and that society as a whole is enriched by recognising greater diversity. While writing this, I came across a column in one of my local gay papers expressing the hope that: 'One day a generation of kids growing up don't even care about the concept of sexuality. They aren't "gay" or "straight" or "lesbian" or anything – they just are.'[17] I believed this when I called the last chapter of my now forty-year-old book 'The End of the Homosexual', and four decades of change, politics and experience have not made me alter that basic conviction. I would not, however, now talk of homosexuality ending, but rather of an increasing blurring of boundaries, rules and stigma around sexuality and gender.

When I wrote *Homosexual* in 1971, I had no idea of the extent to which it would help define my life, my career and my friendship networks. As I moved towards the end of the first draft of this book, my partner, Anthony, died after a rapid deterioration of his condition – two months between diagnosis of cancer and death. In my grief and continuing sadness, I recognised that much really had changed in forty years: at no point did anyone I dealt with in the medical system question that I was his life partner, and while I had his medical power of attorney no one ever asked to see it. Of course, this was helped enormously by the fact that his biological family was interstate, and, more importantly, that they accepted that I was his partner, in the full sense of that term. But forty years ago it would have been inconceivable that a same-sex partner would have been treated effectively as a spouse in a Catholic hospital, by funeral directors and by our employers. The only official problem I encountered was that the death certificate had no provision to list Anthony as being in a de facto relationship, but this seems to be in the process of being corrected after I sought help from both gay and political friends.

At some level, I cannot imagine the horrors of dealing with death for a couple who were not 'out' to their family and colleagues, and how one would manage the complex personal and bureaucratic entanglements that follow the death of a partner in such a situation. This was in fact the opening premise of Isherwood's novel *A Single Man* (1964), and it was the experience of many of the homosexual men who have died from AIDS. In most parts of the world, the fundamental need to share one's grief at the loss of a life partner continues to be denied to same-sex couples. Nor does one need go far from central Melbourne to hear of continuing prejudice and discrimination; even in inner-city hospitals there are reports of homophobic remarks from staff, and sometimes of callous disregard for primary partners.

When gay liberation emerged out of the tumultuous social and cultural upheavals of the late 1960s, it saw sexual liberation as a necessary part of, and connected to, a broader change towards a more just and equal society. While we grossly underestimated the extent to which a certain sort of consumer liberalism could easily incorporate at least apparent acceptance of homosexuality, it remains true that full acceptance of sexual and gender diversity does seem to require social and cultural change on a large scale. Young queers today are caught in the same dilemma that confronted the founders of the gay and lesbian movements: do we want to demonstrate that we are just like everyone else, or do we want to build alternatives to the dominant sexual and emotional patterns?

In some ways, though not as I had originally imagined, homosexuality is now accepted as an integral part of human life, and I think we have come too far for this not to become part of the fabric of our social and cultural life, at least in western liberal societies. Some activists will claim that there is an inexorable march towards an acceptance of new forms of family, in which same-sex couples, surrogacy and adoption are becoming part of the new norm. I am less certain. It is equally possible that there will be a backlash from socially conservative forces, or, indeed, that a new generation of homosexuals will reject what currently seems most attractive – namely, the construction of gay versions of mainstream nuclear families. Indeed, why should we assume that the current emphasis on 'LGBTI' identities will remain as the defining ways of thinking about sexual and gender diversity? John D'Emilio has mused:

> Is it possible, I wonder, that fifty years from now, the reigning wisdom will argue that gay and lesbian proved to be relatively short blips on the historical screen and that transgender—or what I am referring to as gender crossing—provides the more robust framework for historical understanding?[18]

I am too attached to the need to see gender and sexuality as separate but interconnected to accept D'Emilio's hypothesis, and I suspect he is no more likely to be right than was my prediction of 'the end of the homosexual' forty years ago. What is clear is that, over time, what seems obvious can change dramatically. The period of Stonewall, Woodstock and the gay liberation movement is as removed from today as the apparent freedoms of Paris in the 1920s were for the generation that invented modern gay and lesbian identities. Likewise, the images of films about the 1970s, such as *Velvet Goldmine* or *Taking Woodstock*, are as removed from the immediate experience of someone coming of age today as were Isherwood's Berlin novels of pre-Hitler Berlin to those of us who became activists forty years ago.

But D'Emilio is right to point to the likelihood that future generations will think of sex and gender in ways we can't easily imagine. In another forty years time, the current emphasis on 'LGBTI' identities and same-sex marriage may seem no more than residual memories of another era. The one safe projection that can be made about the future is that it will not be what the conventional wisdom predicts.

ACKNOWLEDGMENTS

This book grew out of the experience of two major events over the year while I was writing, the organisation of a conference in honour of my first book, *Homosexual: Oppression and Liberation* (first published in 1971), and the death of Anthony Smith, my partner of twenty-two years. Both these events involved numbers of other people, without whom this book could not have been written. Indeed, the warmth and support that was shown, first in January around a celebration, and then in November around loss and grief, was the best encouragement a writer could imagine.

My first acknowledgments, therefore, are to the organisers of the 'After Homosexual' conference: Michael Connors, Graham Willett, Mark Pendleton and, above all, Carolyn D'Cruz, who became a special friend to both Anthony and me, and one of a small group of close friends who have helped me through a very difficult time. The conference brought together old and new friends, cutting across lines of age and gender, and many of the people whom I need to acknowledge wrote papers that are published in the collection *After Homosexual* (UWA Publishing, 2013).

My greatest thanks for the actual writing of this book goes to Dion Kagan, whom I tentatively asked to look at a draft – and who became a scrupulous and demanding editor, pushing me to rethink some of my assumptions and giving me more feedback than even a greedy author expects. Once there was a completed manuscript, Julian Welch provided the professional editing of which every author dreams.

I asked help on many questions of an enormous range of people, and the Australian Lesbian and Gay Archives – in particular, their archivist extrordinaire, Nick Henderson – were always willing and, more usefully, able to help. Others in Australia who were generous in supplying ideas and support include Barbara Creed, Raewyn Connell, Deb Dempsey, Gillian Fletcher, Leigh Hetherington, Dino Hodge, Michael Kirby, Ben Law, Finn Leach, Toby Lee, William Leonard, David Marr, Rosemary Pringle, Kane Race, Edward Reis, Robert Reynolds, Nick Toonen and Garry Wotherspoon.

The conference coincided with the re-publication of my first book, *Homosexual: Oppression and Liberation*, and my agent, Fiona Inglis, and John Hunter and the production team at UQP all played a major role in producing that book quickly. Alexandra Payne and Meredene Hill have been supporters of this project from its inception and a big thank you to Jacqueline Blanchard and Susan Hornbeck, who have worked tirelessly on the production and promotion of this book. Special thanks to the guys at The Bookshop Darlinghurst, who organised a launch party for the re-publication, and to those at Hares & Hyenas in Melbourne for involving me in some wonderful reading events.

But this is both an Australian and an international book, and it reflects the support of colleagues from many continents with whom I've been privileged to work now for thirty years. Special thanks to my friends and colleagues who came to Australia to help celebrate: Alice Echols, Neville Hoad, John Treat, Jeffrey Weeks and many others. I also reconnected in the course of writing with a few of the original gay liberation activists in the United States, especially Perry Brass, Steve Dansky and Martha Shelly. Several discussions with friends three years ago helped me shape a different book to the one I thought then I could write, so thanks to Doug Mitchell, Jakob Horstmann, Hector Carrillo and Steve Epstein for their input.

During the year, I was involved in working with colleagues in the International AIDS Society, and on a special issue on MSMs and HIV for *The Lancet*; again, this involved many collaborations, and special thanks go to Peter Aggleton, Chris Beyrer, Kent Buse, Greg Millett, Veronica Noseda, Richard Parker, Julie Pluies, Vasu Reddy and especially Michael Williams, who, like so many others listed here, is both collaborator and friend. I also have been working with a number of colleagues on related projects, especially Jonathan Symons. Thanks to the Dunstan Foundation for inviting me to speak in Adelaide, which led me to rethink the impact of the Dunstan premiership. Colleagues at La Trobe were often remarkably kind and helpful: special thanks to Gavin McLean, who helped me through my computer incompetence. And kindness and support also came from Anthony's former colleagues at La Trobe's Australian Research Centre in Sex, Health and Society.

There are also some longstanding friends overseas who have been with me through the year, but especially when I made a quick trip to Los Angeles, shortly after Anthony's death: special thanks to Sofia Gruskin, Jeff O'Malley, Neville Hoad, Alistair McCartney and Tim Miller, Vernon Rosario and Hilly Hicks, and Tony Valenzuela. Back in Melbourne, there was remarkable and ongoing support from Andrea Goldsmith, Chris Healey, the Langer family, Anne Mitchell, Danny Vadasz, Ben Keith and Simon Westcott, Judith Brett, Sandy Gifford, Vivian Lin, Bill O'Loughlin, Christos Tsiolkas, Robyn Eckersley and Peter Christoff, and Stephanie Trigg and Paul James.

Special thanks go to both Anthony's and my families, especially Julie, Nick, Rafael and Vivien, who were always there when things got really tough.

NOTES

Introduction

1 See Clive Moore, *Sunshine and Rainbows: The Development of Gay and Lesbian Culture in Queensland*, UQP, St Lucia, 2001, pp. 183–187.

2 See Leonie Rowan & Jan McNamee, *Voices of a Margin: Speaking for Yourself*, Central Queensland University Press, Rockhampton, 1995; see also Kate Ames, 'Regional Radio and Representations of Homosexuality', in Catriona Elder & Keith Moore (eds), *New Voices, New Visions: Challenging Australian Identities and Legacies*, Cambridge Scholars Publishing, Newcastle upon Tyne, 2012, pp. 261–76.

3 Lindsay Murdoch, 'Restaurant Insult Shocks Gay Author', *The Age*, 18 March 2011; 'Gay Slur Casts a Shadow on Us All', *The Age*, 21 March 2011.

4 Barry Humphries, 'A Shudder of Revulsion', *Time*, 17 December 1990.

5 See David Malouf, 'Made in England: Australia's British Inheritance', *Quarterly Essay* 12, 2003; Hilary McPhee, *Other People's Words: The Rise and Fall of An Accidental Publisher*, Picador, Sydney, 2001.

6 See Carolyn d'Cruz & Mark Pendleton (eds), *After Homosexual: The Legacies of Gay Liberation*, UWA Publishing, Perth, 2013.

7 Raymond Williams, *Culture and Materialism: Selected Essays* 2nd edn, Verso, London/New York, 2005 [1980], pp. 40–2.

8 Martin Hoffman, *The Gay World: Male Homosexuality and the Social Creation of Evil*, Basic Books, New York, 1968.

9 See, for example, Martin Duberman, *Stonewall*, Dutton, New York, 1993.

10 Edmund White, *The Beautiful Room is Empty*, Vintage, New York, 1988, p. 184.

11 Peter Robinson, *The Changing World of Gay Men*, Palgrave Macmillan, Basingstoke, 2008 (especially conclusion).

12 Tim Miller, 'Jumpstart', in Jim Elledge & David Groff (eds), *Who's Yer Daddy: Gay Writers Celebrate their Mentors and Forerunners*, Terrace Books, Madison, 2012, p. 236.

13 Dennis Altman, *The Comfort of Men*, Heinemann, Melbourne, 1993, p. 247.

PART ONE

What Has Changed? What Remains the Same?

1 Note added in 1915; see Sigmund Freud, 'The Sexual Aberrations', in *Freud on Sexuality* (volume 7), Pelican Freud Library, Harmondsworth, 1977, p. 56.

2 See The Kinsey Institute, 'Prevalence of Homosexuality', www.kinseyinstitute.org

3 Rudi Bleys, *The Geography of Perversion: Male-To-Male Sexual Behavior outside the West and the Ethnographic Imagination, 1750–1918*, Cassell, London, 1996, pp. 266–7; see also Robert Aldrich, *Colonialism and Homosexuality*, Routledge, London & New York, 2003.

4 Neville Hoad, *African Intimacies: Race, Homosexuality, and Globalization*, University of Minnesota Press, Minneapolis, 2007.

5 Donald Horne, *Time of Hope*, Angus & Robertson, Sydney, 1980, p. 4. Donald's book had some parallels to my own *Rehearsals for Change*, published the same year by Fontana/Collins.

6 Raewyn Connell, 'Ours Is in Color: The New Left of the Sixties, Forty Years On', *Overland*, 12 November 2008.

7 Julie Stephens, *Anti-Disciplinary Protest: Sixties Radicalism and Postmodernism*, Cambridge University Press, Cambridge, 1998.

8 Dennis Altman, 'Bazza McKenzie', *Nation Review*, 11 November 1972 [reprinted in Dennis Altman, *Coming Out in the Seventies*, Wild & Woolley, Sydney, 1979.]

9 Aaron Shurin, 'Full Spectrum', in Rebecca Solnit (ed.), *Infinite City*, University California Press, Berkeley, 2010, p. 45. For an insight into the importance of drag in Australian theatrical life, see Reg Livermore et al, *Drag Show*, Currency Press, Sydney, 1977.

10 Anne Summers, 'How the Sixties Changed Us Forever', *Good Weekend*, 11 April 1986; 'Sisters Out of Step', *Independent Monthly*, July 1980.

11 John D'Emilio, 'Capitalism and Gay Identity', in John D'Emilio, *Making Trouble: Essays on Gay History, Politics, and the University*, Routledge, New York & London, 1992, p. 7.

12 See, for example, George Chauncey, *Gay New York*, Basic Books, New York, 1994; Julie Abraham, *Metropolitan Lovers*, University of Minnesota, Minneapolis, 2009.

13 Witi Ihimaera, *Nights in the Gardens of Spain*, Secker & Warburg, Auckland, 1995, p. 69.

14 Robert Dessaix, 'Introduction', in Robert Dessaix (ed.), *Australian Gay and Lesbian Writing*, Oxford University Press, Melbourne, 1993, p. 17.

15 Barbara Vine, *The Chimney Sweeper's Boy*, Viking, London, 1998, p. 412.

16 Graeme Blundell, *King: The Life and Comedy of Graham Kennedy*, Pan Macmillan, Sydney, 2003.

17 Alan Hollinghurst, *The Swimming Pool Library*, Vintage, New York, 1989, p. 140. In similar vein, Jonathan Kemp explores changes over the past century in his novel *London Triptych* (Myriad, Brighton, 2010).

18 Garry Wotherspoon, *City of the Plain*, Hale & Iremonger, Sydney, 1991.

19 Robert Brain, *Friends and Lovers*, Hart Davis, London, 1976, p. 72.

20 Geoffrey Bolton, *Oxford History of Australia 1942–88*, Oxford University Press, Melbourne, 1990, p. 207.

21 Russell Ward, *The Australian Legend*, Oxford University Press, Melbourne, 1988 [1955], pp. 99–100.

22 Frank Bongiorno, *The Sex Lives of Australians: A History*, Black Inc., Melbourne, 2012, pp. 30–7.

23 John Rickard, *Australia: A Cultural History*, Longman, London & New York, 1988, p. 178.

24 Quoted by Nicole Moore in *The Censor's Library: Uncovering the Lost History of Australia's Banned Books*, University of Queensland Press, St Lucia, 2012, p. 231.

25 Michael Browne, 'From the Trenches', *Outrage*, September 1989, p. 12.

26 For an overview, see Suzanna Walters, *All the Rage: The Story of Gay Visibility in America*, University of Chicago Press, Chicago, 2001.

27 See Dennis Altman, 'Reading Agatha Christie', *Inside Story*, 5 January 2009 (http://inside.org.au).

28 Dennis Altman, *Gore Vidal's America*, Polity Press, Cambridge, 2005, pp. 131–3.

29 Jill Johnston, *Lesbian Nation*, Simon & Schuster, New York, 1973, p. 155.

30 Charlotte Wolff, *Bisexuality*, Quartet, London, 1977, p. 109.

31 Gayle Rubin, 'The Traffic in Women', in Rayna R Reiter (ed.), *Toward an Anthropology of Women*, Monthly Review Press, New York, 1975, p. 159.

32 Judith Butler, 'Against Proper Objects', *Differences*, vol. 6, no. 2–3, 1994, pp. 1–26; Donna J. Haraway, *Modest_Witness@Second_Millennium.FemaleMan©_Meets_OncoMouseTM: Feminism and Technoscience*, Routledge, New York & London, 1997.

33 Gayle Rubin with Judith Butler, 'Sexual Traffic', *Differences*, vol. 6, no. 2–3, 1994, pp. 62–99.

34 Judith Butler, *Undoing Gender*, Routledge, New York, 2004, p. 213.

35 David Stevens, *The Sum of Us*, Fireside Theatre, Garden City, 1990, p. 64.

36 Kath Weston, 'The Moveable Feast of Economy and Biology' (unpublished paper).

37 'Study Looks at Impacts of Being Gay in School', *Star Observer*, 14 September 2012, p. 9.

38 Tom Boellstorff, 'But Do Not Identify as Gay', *Cultural Anthropology*, vol. 26, no. 2, pp. 287–312.

39 Keith Boykin, *Beyond the Down Low*, Perseus, New York, 2006.

40 Gregorio Millett et al., 'Focusing "Down Low": Bisexual Black Men, HIV Risk and Heterosexual Transmission', *Journal of the National Medical Association*, vol. 97, no. 7 (suppl.), 2005, pp. 52S–59S.

41 Garrett Prestage, 'The Term "MSM" Demeans Us All', occasional paper, Kirby Institute, Sydney, 2011.

42 David Valentine, *Imagining Transgender: an Ethnography of a Category*, Duke University Press, Durham, 2007; Stephen Whittle, *Respect and Equality Transsexual and Transgender Rights*, Cavendish, London, 2002.

43 Steven Epstein, 'Gay Politics, Ethnic Identity: The Limits of Social Constructionism', *Socialist Review*, vol. 93, no. 4, 1987, pp. 9–54.

44 Jeffrey Weeks, *Invented Moralities: Sexual Values in an Age of Uncertainty*, Polity Press, London and New York, 1995.

45 See David Marr, *Patrick White: A Life*, Random House, Sydney, 1991, pp. 582–5.

46 Patrick White, *Flaws in the Glass*, Viking, New York, 1981, p. 154.

47 Robert Brookey, *Reinventing the Male Homosexual: The Rhetoric and Power of the Gay Gene*, Indiana University Press, Bloomington, 2002.

48 Kenneth Walker, *The Physiology of Sex*, Penguin Books, 1940, p. 130.

49 Joshua Tabak & Vivian Zaykas, 'The Science of "gaydar"', *The New York Times*, 1 June 2012.

50 Sunnivie Brydum, 'New Theory: Sexual Orientation Determined by Brain Hemisphere Dominance', *The Advocate*, 6 August 2012.

51 Jeffrey Weeks, *The Languages of Sexuality* (s.v. 'Essentialism'), Routledge, Abingdon & New York, 2011, p. 45. This is a very valuable source for many contemporary debates on sexuality.

52 Valerie Monchi, 'Former British Chief Rabbi Endorses Genetic Means to Stop Homosexuality', *Jewish News Archive*, 23 July 1993.

53 Lucas Grindley, 'Cynthia Nixon: Being Bisexual "Is Not a Choice"', *The Advocate*, 30 January 2012.

54 Kare O'Riordan, 'The Life of the Gay Gene: From Hypothetical Genetic Marker to Social Reality', *The Journal of Sex Research*, vol. 49, no. 4, 2012, pp. 362–71.

55 Dean Hamer, *The Science of Desire: The Search for the Gay Gene and the Biology of Behavior*, Simon & Schuster, New York, 1994.

56 Teresa de Lauretis, *The Practice of Love: Lesbian Sexuality and Perverse Desire*, Indiana University Press, Bloomington, 1994, p. xix.

57 John Irving & Edmund White in discussion, *OUT Magazine*, June/July 2012, p. 66.

58 Bertram J Cohler, *Writing Desire: Sixty Years of Gay Autobiography*, University of Wisconsin Press, Madison, 2007, p. 225.

59 See, for example, Anthony d'Augelli et al., 'Predicting the Suicide Attempts of

Lesbian, Gay and Bisexual Youth', *Suicide and Life Threatening Behavior*, vol. 35, no. 6, 2005, pp. 646–60; Rob Cover, *Queer Youth Suicide, Culture and Identity*, Ashgate, 2012.

60 Ritch C Savin-Williams, *The New Gay Teenager*, Harvard University Press, Cambridge (MA), 2005, p. x.

61 Lynne Hillier et al., *Writing Themselves in 3: The Third National Study on the Sexual Health and Wellbeing of Same Sex Attracted and Gender Questioning Young People*, La Trobe University, Melbourne, 2010.

62 George Weinberg, *Society and the Healthy Homosexual*, St Martin's Press, New York, 1972, p. 4.

63 Stevi Jackson, 'Gender, Sexuality and Heterosexuality: the Complexity (and Limits of) Heteronormativity', *Feminist Theory*, vol. 7, 2006, pp. 105–121.

64 Tom Boellstorff, 'The Emergence of Political Homophobia in Indonesia: Masculinity and National Belonging', *Ethnos*, vol. 69, 2004, p. 471.

65 Garry Wotherspoon, *City of the Plain*, Hale & Iremonger, Sydney, 1991, p. 113.

66 Ashley Currier, 'Political Homophobia in Postcolonial Namibia', *Gender & Society*, vol. 24, 2010, p. 125; see also Suzanne LaFont, 'Not Quite Redemption Song', in David A B Murray (ed.), *Homophobias: Lust and Loathing Across Time and Space*, Duke University Press, Durham, 2009; Barry Adam, 'Theorizing Homophobia', *Sexualities*, vol. 1, 1998, pp. 387–404.

67 Martin Duberman, *Waiting to Land*, New Press, New York, 2009, p. 45.

68 Daniel Mendelsohn, *The Elusive Embrace*, Knopf, New York, 1999, p. 194.

69 Frank Browning, 'Sex, Pride and Desire', *HGLR*, Spring 1998.

70 See Sally Munt, *Queer Attachments: The Cultural Politics of Shame*, Ashgate, Aldershot, 2007; David M Halperin & Valerie Traub, *Gay Shame*, Chicago University Press, Chicago, 2009.

71 Rupert Smith, *Man's World*, Arcadia Books, London, 2010, p. 87.

72 Eleanor Hogan, *Alice Springs*, NewSouth Books, Coogee, 2012, pp. 149–151.

73 Clive Moore gives a history of Brisbane's beats in *Sunshine and Rainbows*, UQP, St Lucia, 2011, pp. 69–71,153–155.

74 Wayne Brekhus, *Peacocks, Chameleons, Centaurs: Gay Suburbia and the Grammar of Social Identity*, University of Chicago Press, Chicago, 2003.

75 See, for example, Jasbir Puar, *Terrorist Assemblages*, Duke University Press, Durham, 2007.

76 Julie Abraham, *Metropolitan Lovers: The Homosexuality of Cities*, University of Minnesota Press, Minneapolis, 2009, p. 299.

77 Richard Elkins & Dave King, *The Transgender Phenomenon*, Sage Publications, London, 2006, pp. 117–119.

78 See www.impcourt.org for more details.

79 Roberta Foster, 'The Bois of King Vic', in Yorick Smaal & Graham Willett (eds), *Out Here: Gay and Lesbian Perspectives VI*, Monash University Publishing, Melbourne, 2011, pp. 156–167.

80 Doug Pollard, 'Do You Still Want Drag with That?' *The Star*, 4 March 2010.
81 Jez Pez, 'Dude', *ALSO Directory 2011*, Melbourne, 2011, p. 122
82 Josephine Emery, *The Real Possibility of Joy*, Pier 9, Sydney, 2009.
83 Kim Westwood, *The Courier's New Bicycle*, Harper Voyager, Sydney, 2011, p. 199.
84 William Leonard et al., *Coming Forward: The Underreporting of Heterosexist Violence and Same Sex Partner Abuse in Victoria*, Monograph Number 69, The Australian Research Centre in Sex, Health and Society, La Trobe University, 2008.

The World that Made Gay Liberation

1 I fictionalised some of these early experiences in my only novel, *The Comfort of Men* (Heinemann, Melbourne, 1993).
2 D J West, *Homosexuality: Its Nature and Causes*, Penguin, New York, 1960, pp. 220, 261.
3 Ann Aldrich, *We Walk Alone*, The Feminist Press, New York, 2006 [1955], p. 24.
4 See John Donald Gustav-Wrathall, *Take the Young Stranger by the Hand: Same-Sex Relations and the YMCA*, Chicago University Press, Chicago, 1998, pp. 180–182; for the role of San Francisco in the life of one gay man, see Justin Spring, *Secret Historian: The Life and Times of Samuel Steward*, Farrar, Straus and Giroux, New York, 2010.
5 Michael Kirby, *A Private Life*, Allen & Unwin, Crows Nest, 2011.
6 Adam Carr, 'The Wowser's Last Stand', *Outrage*, June 1997.
7 'Riposte' [to Ray Taylor's review], *Pol Magazine*, no. 7, June 1969.
8 Rafael de la Dehesa, *Queering the Public Sphere in Mexico and Brazil*, Duke University Press, Durham, 2011, pp. 17–18.
9 Clive Faro with Garry Wotherspoon, *Street Seen: A History of Oxford Street*, Melbourne University Press, Melbourne, 2000.
10 Neal Drinnan, *Glove Puppet*, Penguin, Melbourne, 1998, p. 53.
11 See Don Teal, *The Gay Militants*, Stein & Day, New York, 1971, pp. 267–9.
12 This interview was published in the Toronto journal *Body Politics* (no. 13, 1974); thanks to Scott de Groot for finding this for me.
13 Freud, *Civilisation and Its Discontents* (Penguin Freud Library, vol. 12), Penguin, London, 1985, p. 294.
14 Vernon Rosario, 'Rise and Fall of the Medical Model', *HGLR*, Fall 1999.
15 Martha Shelley, personal communication with the author, August 2012.
16 I have written of some of these events in *Homosexual: Oppression & Liberation*, UQP, St Lucia, 1971, (pp. 135–136).
17 See Lillian Faderman & Stuart Timmons, *Gay L.A.: A History of Sexual Outlaws, Power Politics and Lipstick Lesbians*, University of California Press, Berkeley, 2001.
18 Richard Florida, *The Rise of the Creative Class: and How It's Transforming Work, Leisure, Community and Everyday Life*, Basic Books, New York, 2002, p. 257.
19 Erick Alvarez, *Muscle Boys: Gay Gym Culture*, Routledge, London & New York, 2008.

20 John Edwards, 'Working Class Camp', *The Nation*, 25 July 1970.

21 Noel Tovey, *Little Black Bastard: A Story of Survival*, Hodder, Sydney, 2004, p. 109.

PART TWO

The 1970s: New Affirmations

1 Tim Reeves, 'The 1972 Debate on Male Homosexuality in South Australia', in R Aldrich (ed.), *Gay Perspectives II*, Department of Economic History, University of Sydney, 1994.

2 Jill Roe, 'Coming Up for Air', *Nation*, 22 July 1972, p. 22.

3 Dino Hodge, 'The Okayness of Gayness', in Smaal & Willett (eds), *Out Here*, Monash University Publishing, Melbourne, 2011, pp. 37–55.

4 Denise Thompson, *Flaws in the Social Fabric: Homosexuals and Society in Sydney*, Allen & Unwin, Crows Nest, 1985; Graham Willett, *Living Out Loud: A History of Gay and Lesbian Activism in Australia*, Allen & Unwin, Crows Nest, 2000; Robert Reynolds, *From Camp to Queer: Remaking the Australian Homosexual*, Melbourne University Press, Melbourne, 2002.

5 David Marr, 'Political Enemy: The Making of Tony Abbott', *Quarterly Essay* 47, 2012.

6 Albert Field, quoted in George Megalogenis, *The Australian Moment*, Viking, Melbourne, 2012, p. 76.

7 Dennis Altman, 'Human Beings Can Be Much More than We Have Allowed Ourselves to Be', in Sally Warhaft (ed.), *Well May We Say: The Speeches that Made Australia*, Black Inc., Melbourne, 2004, pp. 261–7.

8 Quoted in Sean Scalmer, *Dissent Events: Protest and the Media in Australia*, University of New South Wales Press, Coogee, 2001, p. 77.

9 Quoted in Marilyn Lake, *Getting Equal: The History of Australian Feminism*, Allen & Unwin, Crows Nest, 1999, p. 221.

10 Dennis Altman, *The Homosexualization of America, The Americanization of the Homosexual*, St Martin's Press, New York, 1982, p. 217.

11 Peter Thompson, *Bob Brown of the Franklin River*, Allen & Unwin, Crows Nest, 1984, pp. 43–7, 151–53.

12 Frank Moorhouse, 'Beyond Stigma', *Griffith Review*, no. 33, Spring 2011, p. 103.

13 Kerryn Goldsworthy, 'The Pink Shorts' (Chapter 8 in her book *Adelaide*, NewSouth Books, Sydney, 2011).

14 Neal Blewett, 'Don Dunstan and the Social Democratic Moment in Australian History', in Robert Foster & Paul Sendziuk (eds), *Turning Points: Chapters in South Australian History*, Wakefield Press, Kent Town, 2012.

15 Alexandra Chasin, *Selling Out: The Gay and Lesbian Movement Goes to Market*, St Martin's Press, New York, 2000, p. xvii. Compare the discussion in Alice Echols,

Hot Stuff: Disco and the Remaking of American Culture, W W Norton, New York, 2010, especially pp. 52–5.

16 Liz Ross, 'From Homosexuals at Work to Union Pride', in Graham Willett, Wayne Murdoch & Daniel Marshall (eds), *Secret Histories of Queer Melbourne*, ALGA, Melbourne, 2011, pp. 143–146.

17 *The Weekend Australian*, 4–5 March 1978.

18 Jacky Archer, 'Homosexual Candidate Assured of Gay Vote', *The Australian*, 3 March 1983.

19 Richard Wherrett (ed.), *Mardi Gras: From Lock Up to Frock Up*, Viking, Melbourne, 1999.

20 Peter Spearitt & Jim Davidson, 'City Images', in Jim Davidson (ed.), *The Sydney–Melbourne Book*, Allen & Unwin, Crows Nest, 1986, p. 230.

21 Marian Maddox, *God Under Howard: The Rise of the Religious Right in Australian Politics*, Allen & Unwin, Crows Nest, 2005, pp. 42–48.

22 Graham Willett, *Living Out Loud*, Allen & Unwin, Crows Nest, 2000, Chapter 11.

23 Graham Willett, *Living Out Loud*, Allen & Unwin, Crows Nest, 2000, pp. 209–11.

24 See the exchange of letters in *Outrage*, no. 10, February 1984, p. 3.

25 Michael Hurley, 'Aspects of Gay and Lesbian Life in Seventies Melbourne', in 'Queen City of the South: Gay and Lesbian Melbourne', *The La Trobe Journal*, no. 87, May 2011, pp. 44–59.

26 See Dennis Altman, 'Introduction: Scenes from Provincial Life' (introduction to Sumner Locke Elliott's *Fairyland*, Text Publishing, Melbourne, 2013).

27 Neil Miller, *Out in the World: Gay and Lesbian Love from Buenos Aires to Bangkok*, Random House, New York, 1993, p. 360.

28 William Yang, *Friends of Dorothy*, Macmillan Australia, Sydney, 1997.

29 Quoted in Dennis Altman, 'Gay Theatre: Not Much of It, and What There Is, Not Very Gay', *Meanjin*, vol. 43, no. 1, Autumn 1984, p. 171.

30 Robert Dessaix makes this point in his introduction to *Australian Gay and Lesbian Writing: An Anthology*, Oxford University Press, Melbourne, 1993.

Back in the US of A

1 Tristan Garcia, *Hate: A Romance: A Novel*, Faber & Faber, London, 2010, p. 25

2 Olivier Michel, 'Herve Claude: les ours et les cons', *Tetu*, no. 161, p. 32.

3 See, for example, Richard Parker, *Bodies, Pleasures and Passions: Sexual Culture in Contemporary Brazil*, Beacon Press, Boston, 1991; James N. Green, *Beyond Carnival: Male Homosexuality in Twentieth-Century Brazil*, University of Chicago Press, Chicago, 1999; Rafael de la Dehesa, *Queering the Public Sphere in Mexico and Brazil: Sexual Rights Movements in Emerging Democracies*, Duke University Press, Durham, 2010.

4 Dennis Altman, 'Down Rio Way', *Christopher Street*, April 1980, pp. 12–15.

5 Jairo Ordonez, 'In Bogotá, Freedom Is in the Ghetto', *Gay & Lesbian Review Worldwide*, vol. 17, no. 4, July–August 2010, p. 18.

6 John D'Emilio, 'Capitalism and Gay Identity', pp. 3–16.

7 Dennis Altman, 'The Gay Movement Ten Years Later', *The Nation*, 13 November 1982, p. 496.

8 Ryan Gierach, *Images of America: West Hollywood*, Arcadia Publishing, Charleston, 2003.

9 For a discussion of lesbians in West Hollywood, see Moira Kenney, *Mapping Gay L.A.*, Temple University Press, Philadelphia, especially Chapter 2.

10 Ned Polsky, *Hustlers, Beats and Others*, Pelican Books, New York, 1971 [1967], pp. 87–8.

11 See Black AIDS Institute, *Back of the Line: the State of AIDS Among Black Gay Men in America 2012*, Black AIDS Institute, Los Angeles, 2012.

12 For the origin of the Gay Games, see Tom Waddell & Dick Schaap, *Gay Olympian: The Life and Death of Dr. Tom Waddell*, Knopf, New York, 1996; Caroline Symons, *The Gay Games: A History*, Routledge, London & New York, 2012.

13 Aditya Bondyopadhay, posting on A/P Rainbow, 3 November 2002 (ap-rainbow@yahoogroups.com).

14 See Audrey Yue, 'Same-sex Migration in Australia', *GLQ*, vol. 14, no. 2–3, 2008, pp. 239–62.

15 Martha Nussbaum, 'The Softness of Reason', *New Republic*, 13 & 20 July 1992.

Where Were the Women?

1 Rosemary Pringle, 'Absolute Sex?: Unpacking the Sexuality/Gender Relationship', in R W Connell & G W Dowsett, *Rethinking Sex: Social Theory and Sexuality Research*, Melbourne University Press, Melbourne, 1992, p. 83.

2 Carroll Smith-Rosenberg, 'The Female World of Love and Ritual: Relations between Women in Nineteenth-Century America', *Signs*, vol. 1, no. 1, Autumn 1975, pp. 1–25.

3 Graham Willett, 'An Intimate Friendship', in Willett, Murdoch & Marshall (eds), *Secret Histories of Queer Melbourne*, p. 68.

4 Both books were edited by Len Richmond and Gary Noguera, and published by Ramparts Press (Palo Alto).

5 See Anne Coombs, *Sex and Anarchy: The Life and Death of the Sydney Push*, Viking, Melbourne, 1996, pp. 273–275.

6 Henry Rubin, *Self-Made Men*, Nashville, Vanderbilt University Press, 2003, especially pp. 65–75. Karla Jay takes a rather different view: see her *Tales of the Lavender Menace*, Basic Books, New York, 2000, p. 141.

7 Hester Eisenstein, *Gender Shock: Practicing Feminism on Two Continents*, Beacon Press, Boston, 1991.

8 Jean Taylor, *Brazen Hussies: A Herstory of Radical Activism in the Women's Liberation Movement in Victoria, 1970–1979*, Dyke Books Inc., Melbourne, 2009.

9 Quoted in Rosemary Auchmuty, 'The Truth about Sex', in Peter Spearritt & David Walker, *Australian Popular Culture*, Allen & Unwin, Crows Nest, 1979, p. 187.

10 For an Australian example of this debate, see Reynolds, *From Camp to Queer*, Melbourne University Publishing, 2002, pp. 165–167.

11 Elaine Noble, 'Freedom to Discriminate', in the program of the Second Annual Human Rights Campaign Fund Dinner, New York, 1983, p. 31.

12 Simone de Beauvoir, *The Second Sex* (translated by Constance Borde & Sheila Malovamy-Chevallier), Vintage, New York, 2011, pp. 356–8.

13 Kimberley O'Sullivan, 'Dangerous Desire: Lesbianism as Sex or Politics', in Jill Julius Matthews (ed.), *Sex in Public: Australian Sexual Cultures*, Allen & Unwin, Crows Nest, 1997. An early Australian contribution to the 'sex wars' was Susan Ardill & Nora Neumark, 'Putting Sex Back into Lesbianism', *Gay Information*, no. 11, Spring 1982, pp. 4–11.

14 Carole Vance (ed.), *Pleasure and Danger: Exploring Female Sexuality*, Routledge, Boston, 1984.

15 Jill Julius Matthews, 'The Present Moment in Sexual Politics', in Connell & Dowsett, *Rethinking Sex*, Temple University Press, Philadelphia, 1993, pp. 126–127.

16 Deborah Dempsey, 'Beyond Choice: Exploring the Australian Lesbian and Gay "Baby Boom"', thesis submitted to La Trobe University, May 2006, p. 5.

17 Kath Weston, *Families We Choose: Lesbians, Gays, Kinship*, Columbia University Press, New York, 1991; Louise Wakeling & Margaret Bradstock (eds), *Beyond Blood: Writings on the Lesbian and Gay Family*, BlackWattle Press, Sydney, 1995.

18 Margaret Bradstock, 'Old Woman, Old Woman, Who Lives in a Shoe', in Wakeling & Bradstock (eds), *Beyond Blood*, BlackWattle Press, Sydney, 1995, pp. 34–9.

The 1980s: HIV/AIDS and Working inside the System

1 Jonathan Engel, *The Epidemic: A Global History of AIDS*, HarperCollins, New York, 2006; Peter Piot, *No Time to Lose*, W W Norton, New York, 2012.

2 In Adam Mars-Jones & Edmund White, *The Darker Proof: Stories from a Crisis*, Faber & Faber, London, 1987; David Leavitt, 'Saturn Street', in *Arkansas: Three Novellas*, New York, Houghton Mifflin Harcourt, 1997.

3 Evan Whitton, 'AIDS!: The Media, Paranoia and the Wrath of God', *Sydney Morning Herald*, 17 August 1985.

4 Paul Sendziuk, *Learning to Trust: Australian Responses to AIDS*, University of New South Wales Press, Coogee, 2003.

5 Quoted in Garry Wotherspoon, *City of the Plain*, Hale & Iremonger, Sydney, 1991, p. 223.

6 Letter to *The Australian*, 21 March 1987.

7 Willett, *Living Out Loud*, Allen & Unwin, Crows Nest, 2000, pp. 230–31.

8 Michael Hurley, 'Then and Now: Gay Men and HIV', Monograph Number 46, The Australian Research Centre in Sex, Health and Society, La Trobe University, 2003, p. 18.

9 The Hon. Dr Neal Blewett, 'AIDS in Australia: The Primitive Years: Reflections on Australia's Policy Response to the AIDS epidemic', Commissioned Paper Series 2003/07, Australian Health Policy Institute, The University of Sydney, 2003, p. 19.

10 Letter to the author from Lex Watson, 1 March 1985.

11 Much of those early years has been captured in a website established for the thirtieth anniversary of the VAC.

12 'The Politics of AIDS: Wilson Tuckey's Address', *National AIDS Bulletin*, September 1988, p. 45.

13 Miranda Morris, *The Pink Triangle*, University of New South Wales Press, Coogee, 1995, p. 21.

14 Mathew Jones, 'Life, Love and the Tasmanian Revolution', *Outrage*, July 1997, p. 74.

15 See Neal Blewett, *A Cabinet Diary*, Wakefield Press, Adelaide, 1999, pp. 162–164, 267–70.

16 Dennis Altman et al., 'Men Who Have Sex with Men: Stigma and Discrimination', *The Lancet*, vol. 380, July 2012, pp. 439–45.

17 Michael Connors, 'Acting Up', in Graham Willett (ed.), *Thinking Down Under: Australian Politics, Society and Culture in Transition*, Wissenschaftlicher Verlag, Trier, 2007, p. 53.

18 On artistic responses more generally, see Ted Gott (ed.), *Don't Leave Me this Way: Art in the Age of AIDS*, National Gallery of Australia, Canberra, 1994.

19 Other memoirs and books by PWAs include Eric Michaels, *Unbecoming*, Empress, Sydney, 1990; John Foster, *Take Me to Paris, Johnny*, Minerva, Port Melbourne, 1993; Peter Blazey, *Screw Loose*, Picador, Sydney, 1997; Robert M. Ariss, *Against Death: The Practice of Living With Aids*, Gordon & Breach, New York, 1997; David Menadue, *Positive: Living with HIV/AIDS*, Allen & Unwin, Crows Nest, 2002.

20 Douglas Crimp, 'Mourning and Militancy', *October*, no. 51, Winter 1989, p. 16.

21 Michael Schiavi, *Celluloid Activist: The Life and Times of Vito Russo*, University of Wisconsin Press, Madison, 2011.

22 There is an extensive American literature of the sexual abandonment of this time; see Edmund White, *The Farewell Symphony*, Knopf, New York, 1997; Samuel Delaney, *Through the Valley of the Nest of Spiders*, Magnus, New York, 2012. There is far less in Australia, but one example is Nigel Triffitt's *Cheap Thrills: A Novel*, Outlaw Press, Melbourne, 1994.

23 Dennis Altman, 'Report from the Sexual Trenches', *Outrage*, September 1985, pp. 16–17.

The Queer Moment and Reborn Radicalism?

1 Steven Seidman (ed.), *Queer Theory/Sociology*, Blackwell, Oxford, 1996, p. 13. For an Australian view of the excitement of queer theory, see Dean Kiley, 'Notes

Towards a Queer Coalitionism', in the proceedings of *Health in Difference 2*, Melbourne, 1998.

2 Virginia Woolf, *Orlando: A Biography*, Vintage, New York, 2004 [1928], p. 88.

3 Henry Abelove, Michèle Aina Barale & David Halperin, *The Lesbian and Gay Studies Reader*, Routledge, New York, 1993.

4 Gary Dowsett, *Practicing Desire: Homosexual Sex in the Era of AIDS*, Stanford University Press, Palo Alto, 1996, pp. 1–4.

5 Janet Halley & Andrew Parker, 'After Sex?: On Writing since Queer Theory', *South Atlantic Quarterly*, vol. 196, no. 3, Summer 2007.

The Emergence of the 'Global Gay'

1 There is a growing literature on contemporary Japanese homosexuality; see, for example, Mark McClelland, *Queer Japan from the Pacific War to the Internet Age*, Rowman & Littlefield Publishers, Lanham, 2005; Katsuhilo Suganuma, *Contact Moments: The Politics of Intercultural Desire in Japanese Male-Queer Cultures*, Hong Kong University Press, Hong Kong, 2012.

2 Rafael de la Dehesa and Arianya Mukberjea, 'Building Capacities and Producing Citizens: the Biopolitics of HIV Prevention in Brazil', *Contemporary Politics*, Routledge, London, vol. 18, no. 2, 2012, pp 186–99.

3 Much of the English-language work on these changes seems to have been written though literary studies. For a more political overview, see Albert Ferrarons, *Rosa Sobre Negro: Breve historia de la homosexualidad en la Espana del siglo XX*, Barcelona, Egales, 2010.

4 Deborah Amory, 'Mashoga, Mabasha, and Magai: "Homosexuality" on the East African Coast', in Stephen Murray & Will Rosco (eds), *Boy-Wives and Female Husbands: Studies in African Homosexualities*, St Martin's Press, New York, 1998. Afsaneh Najmabadi, 'Transing and Transpassing Across Sex-Gender Walls in Iran', *Women's Studies Quarterly*, vol. 36, no. 3, 2008, pp. 23–42.

5 Tanaz Eshaghian, *Be Like Others* [documentary film], Forties B LLC, 2008.

6 See Dino Hodge, *Did You Meet Any Malagas?*, Little Gem Publications, Darwin, 1993.

7 Dr M Stevens, 'A North Queensland Perspective', *National AIDS Bulletin*, vol. 3, no. 3, April 1989, p. 19.

8 Richard Parker et al., 'Global Transformations and Intimate Relations in the 21st Century', *Annual Review of Sex Research*, vol. 15, 2004, pp. 362–97.

9 Sonia Correa & Richard Parker, 'Sexuality, Human Rights and Demographic Thinking', *Sexuality Research and Social Policy*, vol. 1, no. 1, pp. 15–38.

10 Ara Wilson, 'Lesbian Visibility and Sexual Rights at Beijing', *Signs*, Autumn 1996, pp. 214–17.

11 Haneen Maikey, 'Signposts from Al Qaws', posted on www.bekhoos.com, 27 May 2012.

PART THREE

Reconnecting with My Tribe
1 Anthony Smith et al., *Mapping Gay Men's Communities*, Monograph Number 73, The Australian Research Centre in Sex, Health and Society, La Trobe University, 2009.

Normalisation and the Glass Ceiling
1 Shirleene Robinson, 'Introduction', in Shirleene Robinson (ed.), *Homophobia: An Australian History*, The Federation Press, Sydney, 2008, p. 2.
2 Nadia Salemme, 'Open the Closet', *mX*, 3 May 2012.
3 Alan Wolfe, *One Nation, After All: What Americans Really Think About God, Country, Family, Racism, Welfare, Immigration, Homosexuality, Work, The Right, The Left and Each Other*, Viking, New York, 1998, p. 72.
4 See Jane Mayer, 'Bully Pulpit', *New Yorker*, 18 June 2012, pp. 56–65.
5 Randeep Ramesh, 'Report on Fairness Cites Gains, but Race Is Still the Main Issue', *The Guardian Weekly*, 15 October 2010, p. 13.
6 Lucy Tobin, 'Nothing to Be Hung Up About', *The Guardian Weekly*, 14 January 2011, p. 37.
7 Chris Rissel et al., 'Attitudes Towards Sex in a Representative Sample of Adults', *Australia and New Zealand Journal of Public Health*, vol. 27, no. 2, 2003, p. 119.
8 Michael Flood & Clive Hamilton, 'Mapping Homophobia in Australia', in Robinson, *Homophobia*, 2008.
9 Pew Research Centre, 'Most Say Homosexuality Should Be Accepted by Society', press release, 13 May 2011.
10 Christopher Pearson, 'Beneath a Tough Exterior Tony Has a Caring Nature that Is Definitely not Homophobic', *The Weekend Australian*, 15–16 September 2012.
11 Peter Craven, 'The Homophobic Horror Show of the Slipper Affair', *The Drum*, 8 August 2012.
12 Josh Gordon, 'The Liberal MP for Frankston', *The Age*, 12 October 2012.
13 See E J Graff, 'The Afterlife of Gabriel Arana's Ex-Gay Life', *The American Prospect*, 25 April 2012.
14 Benjamin Law, *Gaysia: Adventures in the Queer East*, Black Inc., Melbourne, 2012, pp. 157–182.
15 Lyn Hillier et al *Writing Themselves in 3*.
16 Rachel Aviv, 'Netherland', *New Yorker*, 10 December 2012, p. 62; Gillian A. Dunne, Shirley Prendergast & David Telford, 'Young, Gay, Homeless and Invisible: A Growing Population?' *Culture, Health & Sexuality*, vol. 4, no. 1, 2002, pp. 103–115.
17 Peter Dankmeijer & Marinus Schouten, *What Do We Do with the Sissies? Homophobia, Gender, Stereotypes and Emancipation Strategies among Young and LGBT People in the Netherlands*, Amsterdam, GALE/EduDivers (see www.nisoproject.eu).

18 Paul Sheehan, 'Gay Hate: The Shameful Crime Wave', *The Sydney Morning Herald*, 4 March 2013.

19 William Leonard et al., *Private Lives 2: The Second National Survey of the Health and Wellbeing of GLBT Australians*, Monograph Series Number 86, The Australian Research Centre in Sex, Health and Society, La Trobe University, 2012.

20 Michael Bachelard, *Behind the Exclusive Brethren*, Scribe Publications, Brunswick, 2008, p. 68.

21 Tiffany Jones, 'Why Queensland Schools are Failing Gay Students', *The Conversation*, 25 February 2013.

22 Laurie Berg & Jenni Millbank, 'Constructing the Personal Narratives of Lesbian, Gay and Bisexual Asylum Claimants', *Journal of Refugee Studies*, vol. 22, no. 2, 2009, pp. 195–223.

23 David Marr, 'Labor's Anti-discrimination Legislation is Bigots' Charter', *The Age*, 14 January 2013.

24 Robert Simms, 'Licence to Kill?', *The Drum*, 22 August 2012.

25 Daniella Miletic, 'Gay Men Haunted by Old Convictions', *The Sydney Morning Herald*, 7 January 2013.

26 Garry Wotherspoon, *City of the Plain*, Hale & Iremonger, Sydney, 1991, p. 113.

27 Colm Tóibín, 'A Man of No Mind', *The London Review of Books*, 13 September 2012, p. 16.

28 A rather different view of generational shifts is found in Jeffrey Grierson & Anthony Smith, 'In from the Outer: Generational Differences in Coming Out and Gay Identity Formation', *Journal of Homosexuality*, vol. 50, no. 1, 2005, pp. 53–70.

29 Matthew Mitcham, *Twists and Turns*, HarperCollins, Sydney, 2012, pp. 65, 105.

30 Nicola Smith & Mary Laing, 'Working Outside the (Hetero) Norm', *Sexualities*, vol. 15, no 5/6, 2012, pp. 517–20.

31 Grant O'Sullivan, 'Internalised Homophobia: Our Cultural Cringe?', *Star Observer*, 27 April 2012, p. 19.

32 Howard Jacobson, *The Finkler Question*, Bloomsbury, London, 2010, p. 242.

33 Raymond Gill, 'A Voter Plays his Part for Change', *The Age*, 4 May 2010.

34 See, for example, Kane Race, *Pleasure Consuming Medicine*, Duke University Press, Durham, 2009, pp. 121–128.

35 Benjamin Law, *The Family Law*, Black Inc., Melbourne, 2010, pp. 201–05.

36 Lisa Cohen, *All We Know: Three Lives*, Farrar, Strauss & Giroux, New York, 2012 (quoted in Terry Castle, 'You Better Not Tell Me You Forgot', *The London Review of Books*, 27 September 2012).

37 Deb Dempsey, 'Surrogacy, Gay Male Couples and the Significance of Biogenetic Paternity', *New Genetics and Society*, vol. 32, no. 1, 2013, pp. 37–53.

38 Barbara Miller, 'From Here to Maternity', *Good Weekend*, 22 December 2012.

39 Jaime Hovey, 'Introduction: Queer Change Agents', in Kevin Barnhurst (ed.), *Media/Queered: Visibility and its Discontents*, Peter Lang, New York, 2007, pp. 162–163.

40 Emmanuel Yekutiel, personal communication with the author, February 2012.

41 Paul Schwartzman, 'End of the Story for Gay-oriented Bookshop: Lambda Rising to Close within Weeks; Owner Proud of Impact', *The Washington Post*, 8 December 2009.

42 Christos Tsiolkas, *Loaded*, Vintage, Sydney, 1995, p. 92.

43 Min Fuh The (ed.), *A-Men*, Sydney, ACON, 2012. See also Gilbert Caluya, 'The {Gay} Scene of Racism', *Australian Critical Race & Whiteness Studies*, e-journal 2, 2006.

44 Robert Reynolds, *What Happened to Gay Life?*, NewSouth Books, Coogee, 2007, p. 194.

45 Andrew Burry, 'Review of *What Happened to Gay Life?*', *HIV Australia*, vol. 7, no. 1, 2009, p. 36.

46 Paola Totaro, 'Top Diplomat Bows Out Ruing "Crude Debate"', *The Weekend Australian*, 24–25 November 2012.

47 Sarah Schulman, *Ties That Bind: Familial Homophobia and Its Consequences*, The New Press, New York, 2009.

48 Jesse Graham & Sarah Estes, 'Political Instincts', *New Scientist*, 3 November 2012, p. 42.

Global Inequalities

1 See, for example, Joseph A. Massad, *Desiring Arabs*, University of Chicago Press, Chicago, 2008.

2 Mark Gevisser, 'The Ultimate Defiance', *The Guardian*, 14 May 2011.

3 *Call Me Kuchu: A Film by Katherine Fairfax Wright & Malika Zouhali-Worral*, HD Cam, 2012.

4 Lusita Lopez Torregrosa, 'A Harbinger of Civil Rights to Come?' *The New York Times*, 28 July 2010.

5 Aleardo Zanghellini, 'Neither Homophobic nor (Hetero)sexually Pure: Contextualizing Islam's Objections to Same-Sex Sexuality', in Samar Habib (ed.), *Islam and Homosexuality* (vol. 2), Preager, Santa Barbara, 2010, p. 270.

6 Ian Buruma, 'Parade's End', *New Yorker*, 7 December 2009, pp. 36–41.

7 Aeyal Gross, 'After a Global Tour, Pinkwashing Comes Home', *Haaretz*, 11 January 2013.

8 Meredith Weiss & Michael Bosia, *Global Homophobia: States, Movements and the Politics of Oppression*, University of Illinois Press, Champaign, 2013.

9 Stanley Cohen, *Folk Devils and Moral Panics: The Creation of the Mods and Rockers*, Paladin, St Albans, 1973, p. 9.

10 David K Johnson, *The Lavender Scare: The Cold War Persecution of Gays and Lesbians in the Federal Government*, University of Chicago Press, Chicago, 2004.

11 See Chapter 8 in Dennis Altman, *Global Sex*, University of Chicago Press, Chicago, 2001.

12 On fundamentalist Christian attitudes, see Thomas J Linneman, 'Homophobia and Hostility: Christian Conservative Reactions to the Political and Cultural

Progress of Lesbians and Gay Men', *Sexuality Research & Social Policy*, vol. 1, no. 2, 2004, pp. 56–76.

13 Naomi Lindt, ' By Ancient Ruins, a Gay Haven in Cambodia', *The New York Times*, 16 March 2010.

14 Alexis Okeowo, 'Out in Africa', *New Yorker*, 24 & 31 December 2012, pp. 64–70.

15 Richard S Bangoura, coordinator of the NGO Afrique Arc-en-Ciel, to the Global Forum on MSM and HIV, 28 August 2012 (see www.msmgf.org).

16 'Samoa Fa'afafine Association (SFA) Oppose Same-Sex Marriage', *Pacific EyeWitness*, 11 August 2012 (see http://pacificeyewitness.com/2012/08/11/samoa-faafafine-association-sfa-say-no-to-same-sex-marriage).

Sex, Love and Same-sex Marriage

1 Transcript of interview, *Australian Agenda*, Sky News, 20 March 2011.

2 Troy Bramston, *Looking for the Light on the Hill*, Scribe Publications, Brunswick, 2011, p. 10.

3 Jonathan D Katz & David C Ward, *Hide/Seek: Difference and Desire in American Portraiture*, Smithsonian Books, Washington DC, 2010, pp. 192–193.

4 Elaine Woo, 'Richard Adams Dies at 65', *Los Angeles Times*, 22 December 2012.

5 George Chauncey, *Why Marriage? The History Shaping Today's Debate Over Gay Equality*, Basic Books, New York, 2004.

6 Luke Gahan, 'The Ins and Outs of Marriage (and Divorce)', in Victor Marsh (ed.), *Speak Now: Australian Perspectives on Same-Sex Marriage*, Clouds of Magellan, Melbourne, 2011.

7 Mark Lilla, 'The Beck of Revelation', *The New York Review of Books*, 9 December 2010, p. 18.

8 Emily Nussbaum, 'Small Wonders', *New Yorker*, 24 & 31 December 2012, p. 140.

9 Deborah Dempsey, 'More Like a Donor or More Like a Father? Gay Men's Concepts of Relatedness to Children', *Sexualities*, vol. 15, no. 2, March 2012, pp. 156–174.

10 Ryan Heath, 'Love in a Cold Climate', *Griffith Review*, no. 29, 2010.

11 See Ryan Conrad (ed.), *Against Equality: Queer Critiques of Gay Marriage*, Against Equality Publishing Collective, Lewiston, 2010.

12 As Judith Stacey argues in *Unhitched: Love, Marriage, and Family Values from West Hollywood to Western China*, New York & London, New York University Press, 2011, pp. 198–204.

13 Judith Butler, 'Is Kinship Always Heterosexual?', *differences*, vol. 13, no. 1, 2002, pp. 14–44.

14 Timothy Hildebrandt, 'Same-Sex Marriage in China? The Strategic Promulgation of a Progressive Policy and its Impact on LGBT Activism', *Review of International Studies*, vol. 37, no. 3, July 2011, pp. 1313–1333.

15 David Cole, 'Getting Nearer and Nearer', *The New York Review of Books*, 10 January 2013, pp. 27–9.

Coda: the End of the Homosexual?

1 As Anna Pertierra notes in a review of three recent books: 'Unlucky in Love', *Inside Story*, October/November 2012, p. 17.
2 Geordie Williamson, *The Burning Library: Our Great Novelists Lost and Found*, Text, Melbourne, 2012.
3 Germaine Greer, 'Her Twist in the Knickers', *The Saturday Age*, 15 September 2012.
4 Eddie Cockrell, 'Let's Talk About Sex', *The Weekend Australian Review*, 14 April 2012, p. 14.
5 Dan Slater, 'A Million First Dates', *The Atlantic*, January/February 2013, pp. 41–6.
6 On the Melbourne 'SlutWalk', see Karen Pickering, 'What SlutWalk Means to Me', 27 August 2012 (see www.slutwalkmelbourne.com).
7 See Hanna Rosin, 'Boys on the Side', *The Atlantic*, September 2012, pp. 55–9.
8 Dan Martin, 'The Lady Gaga Backlash Begins', *The Guardian*, 20 April 2011 (see www.guardian.co.uk).
9 David Halperin, *How to be Gay*, Belknap Press, Cambridge, 2012, p. 10.
10 Shannon Gilreath, *The End of Straight Supremacy: Realizing Gay Liberation*, Cambridge University Press, Cambridge, 2011 (see also my review in *The Gay & Lesbian Review Worldwide*, March–April 2012, pp. 30–1.
11 Daniel Harris, *The Rise and Fall of Gay Culture*, Hyperion Books, New York, 1997, p. 270.
12 Suzanna D. Walters, 'The Kids Are All Right but the Lesbians Aren't', *Sexualities*, vol. 15, no. 8, 2012, p. 919.
13 'Germaine Greer "Glitter Bombed" by Queer Avengers', *The New Zealand Herald*, 15 March 2012.
14 Raewyn Connell, 'Two Cans of Paint: A Transsexual Life Story, with Reflections on Gender Change and History', *Sexualities*, vol. 13, no. 1, February 2010, p. 18.
15 Patrick Caifia, *Sex Changes: Transgender Politics*, Cleis Press, San Francisco, 2003.
16 Raewyn Connnell, 'Transsexual Women and Feminist Thought', *Signs*, vol. 37, no. 4, 2012, p. 874.
17 Jesse Matheson, 'Generations of Love', *Star Observer*, 12 October 2012, p. 16.
18 John D'Emilio, 'Foreword', in St Sukie de la Croix, *Chicago Whispers: A History of LGBT Chicago before Stonewall*, University of Wisconsin Press, Madison, 2012.

INDEX